TURNSTILE IMMIGRATION
Multiculturalism, Social Order &
Social Justice in Canada

For Matthew, my hero.

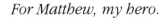

"Turnstile: a post with arms pivoted on the top set in a passageway so that persons can pass through only on foot one by one."
—Webster's Ninth Collegiate Dictionary

TURNSTILE IMMIGRATION

Multiculturalism, Social Order & Social Justice in Canada

Lorne Foster

THOMPSON EDUCATIONAL PUBLISHING, INC.
Toronto

Copyright © 1998
Thompson Educational Publishing, Inc.
14 Ripley Avenue, Suite 104
Toronto, Ontario, Canada M6S 3N9
Tel (416) 766–2763 / Fax (416) 766–0398
email: thompson@canadabooks.ingenia.com

We acknowledge the financial support of the Government of Canada through the Book Publishing Industry Development Program for our publishing activities.

Canadian Cataloguing in Publication Data

Foster, Lorne
    Turnstile immigration

Includes bibliographical references and index.
ISBN 1-55077-097-7

1. Canada - Emigration and immigration - Government policy. 2. Canada - Emigration and immigration - Social aspects. 3. Multiculturalism - Canada. I. Title.

JV7225.F67 1998   325.71   C98-930598-8

Copyedited by Elizabeth Phinney.

Printed and bound in Canada on acid-free paper.
1 2 3 4   04 03 02 01 00 99 98

Contents

Preface

This book is written from my perspective as an urban sociologist, a former immigration officer and a person of immigrant stock. In terms of the analysis presented, this means that the scope of my appraisal is tempered by a kind of intimate commiseration. I am in support of a vigorous immigration system and I believe that, at its best, Canada's immigration system should be a means for strengthening the social order and promoting social justice. Yet, as I will endeavour to show, this is not always the case. Instead, at crucial junctures the principles of social order and social justice not only contradict and conflict with one another, but they do so in such a way as to render Canada's immigration system virtually inept.

A classic illustration of this breakdown occurs right at the nation's turnstiles. Prior to entry into the country, a legal immigrant would find the accent on a version of social order. All categories of potential residents are expected to apply abroad and are subject to exacting "admissibility" criteria, ostensibly designed to assess their ability to adapt to Canadian life and to settle successfully, as well as ensuring that criminal elements and undesirables are kept out of the country. After entry, however, the accent is on social justice as it relates to nondiscriminatory treatment and the protection of individual rights. All persons unlawfully residing in the country, including hardened criminals as well as run-of-the-mill illegal aliens, can be assessed on the basis of "humanitarian and compassionate" criteria for the purpose of waiving the original visa entry requirements. Of course, the paradox, as every frontline officer knows, is that Canada's immigration system makes it very difficult for ordinary people to meet the standards required to immigrate legally into the country; but, if someone were to get into the country illegally, it can be as difficult to remove them once they are here. As a result, the present system can end up discouraging many law-abiding people from applying for immigration while encouraging many law breakers to do so, while at the same time curtailing the effectiveness of immigration officers to act (as a corrective) in either direction.

At the top of the immigration system in Canada sits an enormous bureaucracy that is responsible for both elucidating the public interest and providing advice on public policy. So, for the most part, the general public are the beneficiaries of immigration policy initiatives that they do not fully understand and over which they have no real influence or control. Consequently, informed public debate regarding Canada's immigration policy is virtually nonexistent, and the resulting vacuum is rather easily filled in daily life with prejudices that subvert a commitment to basic values such as a belief in multiculturalism. In this connection, calls for a moratorium on immigration have become a recursive theme and rallying cry in many sectors of society and political life.

Canada is a multicultural society, a kaleidoscope of ethnicity, a variegated composition of many peoples, whose distinctive cultures have given colour and texture to the whole. Further, visible minorities are expected to triple in the next twenty years to 7.1 million, or one in five Canadians and one in four school children. Blacks will become the second largest group with nearly 1.3 million people, up from 540,000 in 1991. South Asians, who numbered 543,000 in 1991, will fall to third place with 1.2 million. West Asians and Arabs will be the fastest growing minority group, increasing by 217 percent to 1 million in 2016 from 315,000 in 1991 (Statistics Canada, "Projections of Visible Minority Population Groups: Canada, Provinces and Regions 1991-2016," Catalogue 1-54XPE, February 27, 1996). But, ironically, as the ethnic mix is moving from one that is overwhelmingly European in origin to one that includes substantial minorities from outside Europe, there seems to be growing public disorientation and public exhaustion with Canada's multicultural experiment.

In this climate of uncertainty and bureaucratic control of immigration knowledge, tensions and insecurities abound. Immigration is coming to be perceived by many Canadians as a threat, or potential threat, to their turf, sensibilities and lifestyles. And to address or contain the negative public sentiments and dubious racial attitudes that it unwittingly inspires, the bureaucracy has continually raised the stakes in the immigration business by introducing progressively sophisticated system designs in areas of visa restrictions, entry and exit controls and active recruitment of select immigrants. The result is that Canada is a society of immigrants but one that is continually raising the ante for new immigrants—a multicultural society increasingly wary of multiculturalism (Lipset, 1989; White and Samuels, 1991; Henry et al., 1995).

My own interest in immigration policy seriously began several years ago on the frontline doing "grunt" work—first as a case presenting officer (CPO) and later as a program specialist (Pro Spec) in the Hearings and Appeals Division. I was aware that, like other frontline officers, my commitment to public service was being tested virtually every day and was undergoing a strange metamorphosis. I was becoming acutely aware of ignorance, abuse and bureaucratic mismanagement everywhere, often of biblical proportions. And I began to question my ability to make a difference on the frontline. In addition, as a visible minority, I felt strangely uncomfortable with the interpersonal dynamics of the system. Since the so-called "developing world" or Third World contains many of the primary source countries for Canadian immigration at present—and visible minorities make up a large portion of the clientele—I began to feel caught in an awkward position between a commitment to an occupational role and a commitment to my race and ethnicity which, of course, exacerbated my uneasiness.

I began collecting data and assuming the role of a participant-observer in order to come to terms with my place in the system. I forced myself to review data, events and situations with a view to finding and understanding the basic "principles" on which the immigration system worked. Slowly, the answer became clearer to me: order and justice are not alternate requirements depending upon the situation, or the program, or the part of the system you're talking about; but rather they are reciprocal concepts. In this respect, the themes that dominate official thinking today—like entry and exit controls, visa restrictions, optimum intake levels, and active recruitment of immigrants with "the right stuff"—are not the answer to our immigration woes. The problem lies in the process and not in the immigrants themselves. It is now the sum total of my observations from the frontlines and the sidelines that order is only good when it is just, and justice is only complete when it is orderly. Yet, Canada's immigration system today is rudderless, and a dynamic balance of order and justice does not exist.

Now, anyone who engages in a discussion or writes a book about immigration would like to have what he or she has to say about the topic to be authoritative. And anyone who reads a book judges it on the basis of the authority the person and the work is perceived to have. We are bombarded with information about every conceivable topic with conflicting opinions from all sides, and we tend to define a person's authority in the same way we define people themselves, categorically. We resort to social categories to sum up anonymous strangers and the status of occurrences in our everyday life. In this respect, if someone who writes a book about immigration is a social scientist, we might expect that person to bring a certain trained eye to the topic before we have even read a word. If someone were a frontline immigration officer, we might expect a certain insight or wisdom that comes from doing this work. And if someone were of immigrant stock, we might expect a certain sensitivity to the topic. All of these social categories may present authoritative criteria and possibilities that sanction the interest of an individual to engage the topic of immigration for a relevant audience.

Of course, my examples here are not random. I am a trained social scientist, a former senior immigration officer and a descendent of escaped African slaves who found their way to Canada. Hence, I possess the ingredients for the authority often granted in the public arena: a trained eye, the wisdom that comes from doing, and sensitivity to the topic. In these terms, I may even be something of an ideal writer. Many academics can write rigorously about immigration, but they may have never even been in an immigration office. Many immigration officers have first-hand experience of what goes on in the trenches but may not have the inclination or the ability to formulate it adequately. And many citizens of immigrant stock may have a sensitivity to issues surrounding immigration in Canada, but they may not have a trained eye or an intimate knowledge of the field. Since I am all the above, I would, of course, like to be seen as brimming with uncontested authority and have the world hang on my every word.

In actuality, though, social categories are both important and unimportant. They are important insofar as they can serve as an invitation to the reader to engage or pique an initial curiosity. But the fact that I am what I am ultimately does not confer authoritative status since this only comes from my actual interpretation. Real authority only comes from the contribution to a dialogue that this book may achieve. Only by advancing the public debate about immigration in Canada can a substantive influence be conferred.

In the end, the particularity of my analysis is embedded in my own experiences. At the same time, there is an serious ambition on my part not to be too preoccupied with what I am personally and to have this ambition translated to others. So, I do not want to deny my particulars, but I do want to substantiate my analysis. The broad, or what I call three-dimensional, task here is to move the subject of immigration in Canada beyond the opposing requirements of a simple "order or justice" question—that is, for instance, beyond the competition between interest groups who are on the right or left of the political spectrum and beyond the machinations of the bureaucratic elite to commandeer public policy. I want to try to reach a level of understanding that genuinely engages any and all sides and captures the intricacies of the immigration business.

There are also a number of other specific things I hope to accomplish. For one, I will try to provide a fresh look at the system so fellow Canadians will be able to understand what has been going on in recent years. But I caution that this book is not primarily data or case-study driven, and those looking for the "inside scoop" or the "dirty laundry" found in newspapers and popular magazines will be disappointed. I use data, events, situations and other anecdotal material as occasions for analysis. So, I review the material and conduct of the various actors with a view towards revealing the possible roots of our immigration problems. For example, I speak in some detail about the work and thought processes of frontline immigration officers in the trenches, but they are not a self-contained topic. My purpose is to connect the concerns on the frontline to the guiding principles of Canadian immigration in order to initiate a better understanding of both. The same is true of all the issues addressed. In addition, I hope to stimulate a serious public dialogue on a variety of issues affecting our present and future—such as designer immigration; queue-jumping and quasi-residency; asylum shopping and family class "echo"; the Convention Refugee Determination System and the Humanitarian and Compassionate Review System—all with an eye towards shedding some light on the immigration system and its impact on Canadian society.

Finally, the ultimate goal of this book is to contribute to public dialogue, as well as encourage it. I wish to plant the seed of a firm conviction that I hold about immigration; namely, that we need to maintain a dynamic balance between social order and social justice. In light of this conviction, throughout the probe of *Turnstile Immigration*, I will advance my own solutions. These may be summarized as follows:

1. Rather than being the sole province of an expert bureaucratic elite, mechanisms should be created to ensure an informed public debate and participation at all levels of public policy developments, thus actively promoting a coherent and open society.

2. Rather than a defensive system design based on elaborate visa-entry-control strategies, a modern immigration program should

be designed around aggressive human resources and human capital strategies, maximizing the opportunities of newcomers.

3. Rather than being based on short-term labour market needs, immigration should be part of a broad-based social planning and population policy, mobilizing the creative energy of Canadian society as a whole.

4. Rather than focusing on short-term occupational demands, criteria for entry should favour immigrants who have transferable skills and who are work flexible and adaptable to change, which is the key to nation building in a new globalized world.

5. Rather than centre on the selection and recruitment process to attract preferred newcomers to help build Canadian society, the immigration program should centre on a pro-active settlement process, ensuing long-term achievement and the continued contributions of all immigrants.

The pages that follow elaborate on these themes.

Introduction

The immigration system asks society's question: Who is best suited to join our regime? The answer to this question, of course, is that Canadian society wants to invite people who are in accord with its fundamental principles. It wants to draw people who are both industrious and compassionate, people who can create a life of progress and equality and people who can help build a nation of abundance and generosity. In short, Canadian society is animated by the principles of "social order" and "social justice," and our society prefers new recruits who can build on these principles. The responsibility of immigration policy is to be consistent with these guiding axioms of the nation.

It is my contention that Canada has a problem converting its principles from theory into practice. Since the guiding principles remain largely unspecified, the current immigration system tends to take on a life of its own, independent of those who attend it, those who use it, or those whom it effects, and things go on without an effective measure of public comprehension or control. To a degree, immigration in Canada has become a bureaucratic codification system that has little to do with democratic principles and a lot to do with finding a way into or out of the country through a labyrinth of exacting passageways and an unfathomable maze of red tape. I call this halting procession of humanity "turnstile immigration"—where select persons gain entry to the promised land only on foot, one by one.

New World Order

Turnstile immigration is in part a guarded reaction to the external phenomenon of global migration. For the last twenty years, hordes of migrants from around the world, and of every description, have been compelled or enticed to flee their homelands. They have come from distant lands with very different cultures, languages and habits—from India, Sri Lanka, Hong Kong, Vietnam, Cambodia, Ethiopia, Ghana, Afghanistan, Iran, Lebanon, Colombia, Chile, Argentina, Haiti, Uganda, El Salvador, Guatemala, Turkey and Bulgaria. The developing countries were far more affected by the worldwide economic decline in the 1970s and 1980s than were their wealthier global neighbours in the West. Their bursting populations, burgeoning deficits and chronic unemployment launched a massive movement of people in search of opportunities for a better life. In terms of modern sensibilities, these migrants have come to be defined as economic refugees, and it is estimated by the Worldwatch Institute that 60 to 70 million are on the move around the world right now, fleeing all manner of desolation, despair and poverty. Add to these the estimated 20 to 25 million exiles collected under the official United Nations' designation of Convention refugees, fleeing from actual persecution and possible demise, and we have a composite picture of the age of global migration. In a world where the population numbers are growing at an annual rate of 1.7 percent, or more than 95 million, and the total world population will likely exceed 6 billion by the end of the century, Canada is now, and by all "population pressure" indicators will remain, a country of first asylum for the clamouring hordes.

The growing complexity of population movements throughout the world is part of what has been called the new world order (NWO) that is benchmarked by the collapse of the Soviet Union and the communist economic system (Galbraith, 1991; Fukuyama, 1991; Richmond 1994). In this new world order, as economic interdependence encourages transnational movements of capital and tends towards what has been called a borderless world (Ohmae, 1990), socio-political pressures tend to pull in the opposite direction. So, while capital moves relatively freely and easily across international borders today in search of opportunities, people do not. Typically, developed countries and less-developed countries alike have gone into a defensive mode in an attempt to restrain the torrential flow of unwanted and unsolicited migrants. In fact, in some countries, violent protests and attacks on foreigners are becoming more and more common. In others, voting rights and citizenship are denied, even to long-term residents, unless they are of the same ethnic origin as the majority group (that is, unless they are made of "the right stuff"). Immigration is not a subject of de-regulation around the globe; if anything, it tends to be re-regulated in attempts to firmly establish territorial integrity and national sovereignty and, oftentimes, cultural purity.

The result of restrictive immigration measures around the world is a greater propensity to migrate, illegally if necessary. So, the numbers of documented and undocumented migrants are on the rise (Appleyard, 1991). In addition, the subject of immigration tends to formalize the cognitive boundaries and intense conflicts (based on mediations of ethnicity, race, religion, nationality and so on) that still exist in the context of a borderless, worldwide market economy. And it is in this respect that the term "ethnic cleansing" has entered our vocabulary (although "pogrom," "genocide," and "extermination" would be more apt descriptions), when talking about not only the former Yugoslavia and Rwanda but also about other parts of the world where indigenous populations and ethnic minorities are oppressed (Richmond, 1994: XV). The upshot is, to the extent that the new world order globalizes the economy, too often it seems also to tribalize impulses and unleash profound insecurities.

The movement towards increasing regulatory constraints on the flow of unwanted immigration to Canada is clearly reflected in the 1998 report by the Immigration Legislative Advisory Group. The overall focus of this most recent official report, entitled *Not Just Numbers: A Canadian Framework for Future Immigration*, endorses the establishment of formal in-take limits for all immigration categories; the intensification of economic-based criteria for the selection and admissibility of immigrants; and the legislation of bureaucratic control over the refugee issue. The aim of the three-person panel—comprising two ex-bureaucrats and a chair from Quebec (and no visible minorities)—is to cut down immigration levels by instituting a professionally mediated, iron-clad immigration quota system. The panel's restrictive recommendations have once again, and inevitably, brought the race issue to the forefront, since those most disadvantaged in terms of admissibility are from non-white Third World countries.

The panel recommends, for instance, the overhaul of the autonomous, quasi-judicial refugee determination system in order to bring it under the aegis of a "protection agency," consisting of a cadre of career civil servant protection officers assigned to determine protection claims both abroad and in Canada, and appeal officers who would review decisions on in-Canada (in-land) protection claims. The panel stipulates that "Canada should take a position of leadership in generating international protection-oriented responses to refugee crises." However, by reformulating the refugee issue as a protection issue, the report changes the traditional Canadian position from a compassion-oriented, "community-based" response to international refugee crises; to a service provider-oriented or "system professional" response.

Many of the panel's other recommendations are a matter of common sense within the context of an economic-nexus and frame of reference for immigration, such as allowing family members of foreign workers to work in Canada, and allowing foreign workers to apply for immigration from within Canada. However, the panel also advocates the establishment of both targets and ceilings for visa issuance for each immigration category, and the Immigration Act should prohibit the department from issuing more visas in a given year than the announced ceilings. The report further suggests that potential immigrants who are forty-five or over should be disqualified from coming to Canada under any category.

In addition to other proposals, the panel recommends that immigrants pay for their own language training, a point that captured media attention as well as the ire of many ethnic communities. It proposes that the government collect a tuition fee reflecting the costs of basic language training in Canada from all sponsored Family Class immigrants who are six years of age or older and have not achieved a basic knowledge of English or French as measured by standardized tests. If one is bringing a child who is not proficient in one of the official languages, a fee will be payable as well. This new call for increasingly bureaucratized and restrictive immigration measures will further retard the arrival of immigrants, especially from not-so-rich countries (Legislative Review Advisory Group, *Not Just Numbers: A Canadian Framework for Future Immigration*, Ministry of Public Works and Government Services Canada, January 1998).

The inclination on the part of Canada's citizen democracy to extend its avowed generosity and compassion, and offer of safe haven to others around the world, has been challenged in the last two decades by the exponential growth of global migration; and the temptation now is to close the flood-gates, so to speak, and to put in state-of-the-art pay-turnstiles. In other words, there is a huge imbalance between international emigration pressures on the outside and domestic immigration needs in Canada that places a heavy burden on the forces of order and a heavy tax on the forces of justice.

There has simultaneously been a preoccupation with the advanced technology and science of "admission and control" procedures. Infrared surveillance devices, magnetic-strip documentation, telephonic fingerprinting, computer databanks, x-ray security at airports, electronic filing systems and automated mail-in centres all serve, in a rather emphatic attempt, to regulate the flow of economic migrants and refugees from Africa, Asia, the Caribbean, and Latin America. In addition, our highest principles of nation building have been reduced by a bureaucratic elite to minute and technical calculations of Can-

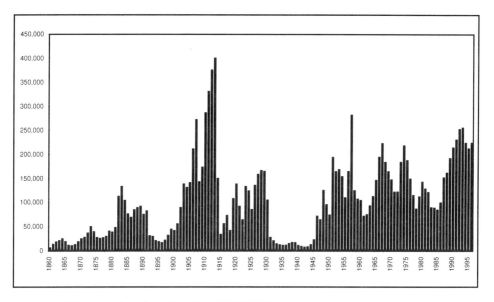

Canadian Immigration Trends, 1860-1996
Source: Adapted from "Facts and Figures 1996," Information Management and Technologies Branch and Strategic Policy, Planning and Research Branch of Citizenship and Immigration Canada.

ada's population size, rate of growth and demographic structure, measured against labour market needs and population goals in order to arrive at an "operative plan." And to keep "the other" at bay psychologically as well as physically, he or she has become a potential legal or illegal alien, whose eventual admission as an authorized person or repudiation as an undesirable is determined by his or her ability to negotiate the pay-as-you-play turnstile technology.

Turnstile immigration is related to some internal dynamics as well. For instance, it is significant that Canada is a place where the land is relatively large and the population is relatively small. Its land mass is roughly as big as China (excluding Taiwan). Its population, however, is about one-tenth that of the United States. According to a study by McGill professor Morton Weinfeld, if only 10 percent of Canada's land were settled at the density of Holland, we would have 400 million people living here (*The Toronto Star*, January 15, 1998). As a result of these and other facts, Canada belongs both to the large and to the small nations of the world—and to neither. The eminent Canadian sociologist Kaspar Naegele (1965: 511) early on identified these disparities as "aspects of Canada's marginality." This marginality is now reflected in an immigration policy that can at times think big and reach out to people and at other times think small and pull back. The rest of the time it tends to do neither.

Are we a large nation responsible to others or are we a small nation who can barely take care of itself? This is the internal and abiding question that has plagued the Canadian mind for at least the last twenty years, and it remains historically unresolved. Canada's marginality challenges its liberal democratic ethos and heightens the order-justice problem in public policy development. That is, it raises fundamental issues in the collective psyche of the nation regarding the extent of our responsibilities as a large nation to those less fortunate than ourselves; but it also raises our concerns as a small nation regarding how much we can actually contribute to the well-being of others. For example, Canada's marginality as a nation has led to deep-seated insecurities about the productivity potentials and limits of the nation, and these insecurities have led to a lingering and widespread ambivalence among the general population about immigration, especially noticeable in times of recession or economic slump. Therefore, public support for immigration has traditionally gone up or down with swings of the economy. At any given time, the pollsters who canvass public opinion now find that 45 to 85 percent of the population favour cuts in immigration intake. Furthermore, from time to time, the same number are nonplussed by any immigration at all. Being on the borderline between bigness and smallness in an age of global migration creates a palpable sense of foreboding among the masses: Why are all these people coming to Canada? How did they all get in anyway? Aren't these immigrants a drain on the economy? Did they come here to collect welfare and not to work? Did they come here to take our jobs?

Suffice it to say, Canadian society has not as yet been able to come to terms with the phenomenon of global migration or to grasp the country's marginality in a way that could affirm a shared purpose or stimulate its people to greatness. At the best of times, the public is equivocal about immigration; at the worst, it is downright skittish. Instead, there tends to be a widespread sense of a divided purpose, disunity and discord. What is commonly discerned is the potential incompatibility of our noble instincts in relation to our pragmatic interests: Can we continue to help people from foreign countries and build a strong economy and society at the same time? Why do we have to bring outsiders here anyway, as opposed to helping them in their own native land? And, last but not least: If we continue to try to subsidize the world, will we mortgage our children's future?

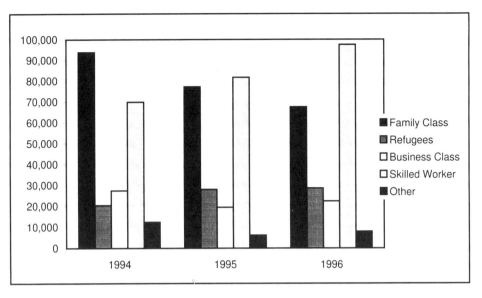

Immigration by Admission Class, 1994, 1995 and 1996
Source: Adapted from "Facts and Figures 1996," Information Management and Technologies Branch and Strategic Policy, Planning and Research Branch of Citizenship and Immigration Canada.

Today, approximately half of Canada's current population growth comes from immigration, a pattern that is strikingly different from most advanced countries—including the United States—which derive more of their growth from births (Beaujot, 1991). The birth rate first fell below the level needed to replace the population in Canada in 1974 and has fallen further since. And, according to Statistics Canada's medium-growth forecasts (where fertility stays the same, immigration rests at about 250,000 a year, and life expectancy improves somewhat), the natural increase (without immigration) will stop in about 2030. In other words, the number of deaths will then begin to outstrip the number of births, and the Canadian people would begin, as it were, to die out (Statistics Canada, "Population Projections for Canada, Provinces and Territories, 1993–2016," Catalogue 19152, 1996).

So immigration continues to play an important role in Canadian nation building. Yet, we struggle with our own uniqueness—with both the vastness of our land mass and the insignificance of our population. We want Canada to be a large nation, and we want it to act like a large nation on the forefront and cutting edge of world

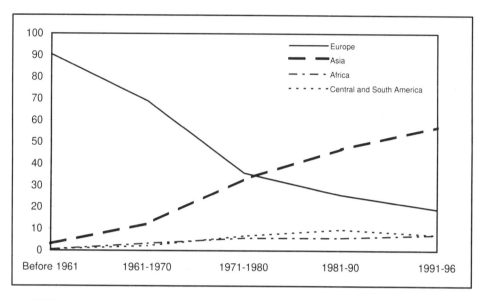

Shifting Origins: Source of Canadian Immigration, 1996 (%)
Source: Adapted from "Facts and Figures 1996," Information Management and Technologies Branch and Strategic Policy, Planning and Research Branch of Citizenship and Immigration Canada.

history, but we fear we are only a small and ineffectual nation, and by striving for too much we may actually cause harm to ourselves and others. This is the juncture of what I regard as our national role conflict—where our national interest can be, and often is, in a contest with our moral itinerary.

When we speak of the social order of society, we are referring to a condition of society characterized by fluent social relationships and a relative lack of conflict. Here, social order depends upon the successful interrelation and coordination between individuals, individuals and groups, and between social institutions. Social justice, on the other hand, refers to the predominance of open and equalitarian social relationships, guided by the values of liberty, equality and the rule of law. The principle of social order relates to values of industry and productivity and finds a practical expression in Canada's national economic objectives. The principle of social justice, however, relates to the values of fairmindedness and compassion and finds expression in Canada's progressive social and humanitarian objectives in relation to family reunification and safe sanctuary for the displaced and persecuted from all parts of the world. Only a dynamic balance of these principles can create a constructive unity of our national and moral agenda.

Still, at present, some groups in Canada favour more order and some favour more justice. Some want society to be a prosperous association before anything else, while others see the strength of society as residing not in its degree of industrial productivity, but rather in its degree of compassion. Therefore, some argue forcefully that immigration should be used to fortify society's division of labour, while other arguments are just as intense in support of Canadian largesse and humanitarian efforts around the world. Some want more restrictive measures imposed on people arriving in Canada claiming to be refugees. Others want the government to allow refugees and displaced persons to enter unhampered so they can state their case. Some want more wealthy immigrants who can invest in Canada and create jobs for unemployed Canadians. Others want only educated or skilled immigrants.

Meanwhile, in the middle of this whirlpool, it is ostensibly the administrative task of those who tallow the nation's turnstiles—the senior suits in Ottawa—to calibrate these forces and thereby channel Canada's national and moral impulses into positive courses of action. As I hope to show, the contemporary immigration system is, however, often reduced to a state of inconsistency and incoherence where there is neither order nor justice. The system is bogged down in a perpetual quagmire of frontlogs and backlogs that threaten total collapse. It is, at the same time, overrun by unwieldy torrents of refugees, displaced persons and other humanitarian status claims at the front end and plagued by inordinate numbers of people with rejected claims at the backend who go underground. In the meantime, operating costs, as well as the financial burden on the existing health and welfare system of the country, continue to be dangerously high. The repercussions of all of this are clear. Today, immigration is a field of public policy that is rife with dilemmas and is now a major area of contention in our society, threatening the commitment to ethnic diversity and the promise of multiculturalism.

Ordinary citizens usually express their concern about immigration by focusing on the level of immigration and how it affects their jobs and their family's future. Here, negative economics is linked to a fear of the other. So, whether favourably disposed to immigration or inclined against it, the public want the flow curtailed when it is perceived to have negative economic consequences. In this respect, the general public tend to treat the integrity of the immigration system as a "volume issue." For their part, however, those who actually staff the turnstiles do not usually perceive the volume or level of immigration as a problem in and of itself. They do not see the situation in exactly the same way as the average Canadian citizen, who might want immigration to be adjusted according to unemployment levels or job shortages. Indeed, I would venture to say that as a group, immigration officers tend to be the happiest when the entry requirements are relaxed; i.e., when they can let people enter rather than turn them away. As a rule, frontliners would like to make it easier for law-abiding people to get into Canada, but they would also like to make it easier to get the law breakers out. They favour an open-door policy, if you will, where the door swings both ways.

This is the frontline version of turnstile justice. Typically, frontliners tend to favour lowering the admission requirements and accelerating the removal process as a method of restoring sanity to the system. Ironically, then, their proximity to the scene actually recommends the reverse of the present situation at the nation's borders, where social order is accentuated prior to entry and social justice is accentuated thereafter. They would prefer, instead, that justice be the standard of entrance and order be the rule of residence—that is, liberal admission requirements and steadfast settlement guidelines. In this regard, frontline immigration officers usually see the integrity of Canada's immigration system as a "method issue."

Meanwhile, the senior officials in Ottawa, who are actually in charge of making immigration policy and effecting their own will, tend to be more narrowly focused on improving administrative techniques in order to guarantee faster service and smoother program delivery. Here, volume is something of a non-issue. Despite public concerns and apprehensions, for instance, it has already been officially decided that annual intake levels have to be maintained at approximately 1 percent of the total population in order to preserve the efficacy of the system. Any other intake views or lay theories circulating in the public domain are treated as something of a nuisance. Similarly, despite the growing frontline malaise, the senior management in Ottawa is also self-satisfied with its current backroom methods of determining immigration policy. In virtually every Speech from the Throne in recent years, successive governments have continually emphasized a renewed commitment to the creation of an immigration system that is more "manageable and efficient." Today, the official thinking is that, if the system is streamlined to its maximum, the volume and method problems, which are of so much concern today for the masses in society and workers in the trenches, will be mitigated because immigration will be both cost effective and expeditious. Here the integrity of the immigration system is treated as a technical and administrative issue.

Volume levels, methods of intake, administrative techniques, and other like considerations are all real concerns, to be sure, and are all worthy of discussion. But the solution to Canada's immigration problems is not simply a matter of adjusting the right level or volume of human flow, or adapting the precise method of intake, or instituting the proper administrative technique; it requires calibrating our own axioms of nation building in a way that affords the opportunity for newcomers to become all that they can be and for our society to be more than what it was before. Any level of intake or technique of administration will be a problem for Canada, and will be a problem for Canada's future, if immigrants are unable to contribute effectively to the host society and society is unable to enhance effectively the lives of its newcomers. The paramount task of our immigration system is to advance both the individual newcomer and society and, at the same time, to make both better.

In the end, this book is an indictment of Canada's current immigration program. Turnstile immigration is a disparaging term, signifying the crucial difference between the search for a codified society and the search for an exemplary one. And, in this regard, the underlying thesis of this book is rather straightforward: to restore sanity to Canada's immigration system, the field of immigration must ultimately, and perhaps continuously, realign its principles such that it is conducive to both the implementation and the expression of democratic values.

1

Notes from the Front

There is no doubt that being on the frontline in the immigration business affects one's view of the human panorama. The first time I realized the full gravity of this situation was in a case involving the deportation of a young man from India, who broke down in front of me and begged me not to send him back to New Delhi. He was dripping with fear. He was so distraught that he went limp and collapsed.

The New Delhi Shuffle

I was stunned and dumbfounded by his response. The first thing I surmised was that New Delhi must be some kind of hell-hole to elicit this type of reaction. At one point the young man, who was being detained in Toronto's Don Jail on an immigration hold, pleaded with me to leave him in "The Don"—as if, as an alternative to the plane ride, I, or other immigration authorities, could just leave him in jail for the rest of his life and save the price of the ticket back to India for the Canadian taxpayers. This young man would rather have spent the rest of his life in a Canadian jail than live in New Delhi.

The fact that he preferred the Don Jail was really astounding. As a an immigration officer, I had been to a number of jails—Toronto East and West Detention Centres, Mimico, even Collins Bay. Compared to the Don Jail, the others are almost vacation resorts. Prisoners in the Don are crammed in, stacked up and dispirited. They have to compete with rats and cockroaches for sleeping space. The place is a health hazard. In 1990, the place was so jam packed, and presented such a security risk, that this guards went on strike. This is the place that the young man from New Delhi was willing to spend the rest of his life.

Only later did it occur to me that it's probably not that New Delhi is so bad, but rather that, for this young man, Canada is the promised land. Outside the walls of the Don Jail lies his paradise, his forbidden fruit. Inside the Don Jail, in the exercise court, he could at least smell the sweet fragrance of Canada. In the Don Jail he could at least dream about window shopping on Yonge Street, and maybe stopping at an outdoor cafe for a hot creamy cappuccino or a cold beer. In the Don Jail, he could almost taste the heavenly fruit of Canada. But in New Delhi the dream becomes a pipedream—indistinct, amorphous and ephemeral; the promised land becomes a wasteland and a no-man's land.

Imagine Canada as the promised land. It is sometimes difficult for those who have been born and bred in this country to understand that for many "outlanders" Canada is like a heaven on earth. It is a place one can choose to stand or lie or sit. We complain about useless politicians, traumatizing taxes, the lack of an identity and the seemingly endless search for a viable federalism. Outsiders, on the other hand, see something akin to the garden of Eden. Viewed from the outside Canada epitomizes possibility, a prolific and golden place untainted by old poisons. For the clamouring horde, this is more than mere metaphor. The world still has more mud huts than two-bedroom condos. And sticks and rocks serve the "mud tribes" as major home appliances. Clearly, outsiders often don't see anything to complain about, and they would give anything to join one of the "electric tribes."

Canada, like most affluent societies, has become a country of first asylum for hundreds of thousands of people throughout the world. Many are economic migrants, seeking a better life outside their homeland. Many are refugees fleeing persecution in their country of origin. Large-scale migration may also be sparked by events such as conflict in the Middle East, famine in North Africa and geo-political revision in Eastern Europe. Migration and its possibilities can excite the utmost determination in the human mind. So much so that would-be migrants will swim across the shark-and-gunboat-infested straits between the southern shores of Canton and Hong Kong, will cross the English Channel on a stormy winter's night in a rowing boat, and will come across our own southern borders concealed in tire wells, lengths of tubing and oil drums. Some will even attempt a death-defying shimmy, hand-over-hand, along the undergirders of Canada-U.S. bridge crossings, hoping to land softly in a safe haven.

The young man from India, whom I encountered at the Don Jail, had come into contact with the Immigration Commission two years prior as a refugee claimant, following a clandestine landing on the shore of Nova Scotia. He claimed he was persecuted for his political views in his native country. When it was clear to him that his claim was going sour at his refugee hearing and immigration officials were not convinced, he took evasive manoeuvres and went underground into the netherworld of busted dreams.

The New Delhi Shuffle consisted of the following: he moved out from his residence without informing immigration officials, obtained a false social insurance card, and began gainful, albeit, illegal employment in a small hamlet outside the big city. The negative decision in his case was rendered in absentia. However, since he was nowhere to be found, he could not be informed or removed from the country.

As routinely happens in the case of "undergrounders," a nationwide warrant was issued for his arrest for failing to abide by immigration requirements, and his file went back to the records department to collect dust until such time as the young man resurfaced. Again, as routinely happens in the case of undergrounders, a minor traffic violation lead to his demise. He was not aware that if he used a driver's license in his own name the computer in the police cruiser would light up like a Christmas tree ornament. He was subsequently detained and put on immigration hold in the Don Jail, pending the completion of his case. Of course, his original precarious position was further complicated because he was now the subject of new and additional immigration allegations that he wilfully eluded an immigration inquiry—Section 27(2)(f)—which is itself a deportable offense.

In the new inquiry the "person concerned" or "PC"—as the immigration bureaucracy so quaintly defines its captives—claimed that two years ago he had forgotten what day he was told to return to the immigration office, so he didn't bother. Now, he swore, he was willing to cooperate with immigration authorities, and he only wanted the opportunity to prove that he belonged in Canada. ("Too late! You're going home! Send me back some good curry recipes when you get the chance!") At this point he was informed of the only outstanding question to be answered: In what fashion are you going to leave this country?

This news, when it finally sank in, was the cause of the emotional breakdown of which I spoke earlier. Of course, as a senior immigration officer, knowing he was not willing to accept his situation, it was my job to ensure he remained in detention, without the possibility of a bond for release, until his removal arrangements were complete. Furthermore, his detention had to be reviewed every week, which meant having him transported from the Don Jail to the immigration office shackled and cuffed, an indignity reserved for illegals with happy feet as well as your basic criminal types. Since there was a chance he would attempt to run away while in the immigration office as well, he was shackled as he was trudged to and from the detention area and the boardroom for detention reviews. His legal string played itself out in a matter of a few months.

The person concerned was escorted from Canada one frosty morning via Air India with the following itinerary: Toronto, New York, London, Bombay and Delhi. He currently resides in a ramshackle hut in the Patel Nagar slum, behind the Faridabad Goodyear Tire Factory on the outskirts of New Delhi.

Little Tribes and Big Tribes

To my knowledge, when I began working for the Canadian Immigration Commission in 1988, I was the only African-Canadian senior immigration officer in the Toronto area. There were, of course, people of African descent and other visible minorities in various capacities throughout the organization and its satellites, some who had prestigious government appoints on Immigration Appeals Boards and Refugee Boards, and so on. But black was not a prevalent colour in the trenches and on the business side of the nation's turnstiles.

Since Canada has become a country of first asylum in the age of global migration, what I had in common with the vast majority of the Commission's clientele was that they were also visible minorities. Because of this, I was an officer in demand. "Clients" from visible minority groups tended to presume an immediate sympathizer, anticipating a certain commiseration with their problems. Justified or not, they were much more comfortable dealing with me than with other officers.

I was continuously approached by people in the streets who recognized my face from the immigration office. People even approached me in restaurants and bars, asking questions about their cases or those of their relatives. People approached me on the subway on numerous occasions. People looked up my number in the phone book and contacted me at home. They contacted people who knew me in order to request an introduction. Often, when in attendance at the immigration office, individuals would seek me out, anticipating a confidante and fellow-traveller. The word was out, the jungle drums were thumping, and I was beseeched by the glazed and mahogany masses for whom Canada is not simply a heterogeneous and upscaled lifestyle but an entirely new sense of possibilities.

I was once approached on the subway by a man from Sri Lanka, who was so persistent about obtaining information regarding his refugee case that I actually felt threatened. It occurred to me that the man was desperate and could lose composure if I didn't tell him what he wanted to hear. I got off the subway before my intended stop. The man followed me off the subway and continued his unrelenting queries. No social sanction or breach of public etiquette registers with a person whose existence and entire prospects for life and future are threatened.

Now, much has been written about the Canadian mosaic to emphasize the cultural diversity of our population (see, for example, McLeod, 1983; Mitges, 1987; Reitz & Breton, 1994). The fact of the matter is, however, the walls of race and colour tower in our consciousness and continue to confer special meaning and relevance. The large contingent of Third World immigration today can rouse alarm and resentment among the dominant white majority in Canada, and is a major source of social divide and alienation. Hence, visible minorities often took liberties with me that they would not take with other officers. They expected me to be different, to understand their problems and to have sympathy for their plight. Furthermore, they would become belligerent and challenge me when I was perceived as not living up to their expectations.

This was, of course, noted by other officers, who offered advice on occasion. The consensus was that I should be particularly vigilant about maintaining a distance from clients, precisely because it always arose as an issue. Some officers were solemn about taking me aside, warning of the dangers of becoming too familiar with clients and the potential for exploitation or compromise. Others often used jokes and sarcasm in an attempt to "bring me into line." They sometimes referred to me as "The Brother" in reference to the black man's burden of togetherness and sense of bondedness in oppression which, in modern times, has been fashioned into a kind of ésprit de corps.

The point of maintaining a healthy "social distance" from clients may have been well taken, but I believed the general strategy that most white officers employed for achieving distance was wrong for me and would have had distressing results. Most officers assumed a Sergeant Joe Friday posture—"Just the facts, ma'am"—and projected a dispassionate and bland demeanour. Their body language said, "I am not here to be engaging, so our encounter and any subsequent dealings will be all business, all matter of fact and devoid of any sloppy emotional sentiment."

I believed it was impossible for me to sustain this strategy of projecting an aloof and indifferent persona. My doing so was interpreted as antagonistic and insulting and would often induce animosity. My common bond as a visible minority was expected, and I had to be very careful how I interacted with others. I felt it was necessary not to act remote and disinterested and, therefore, risk being perceived by visible minorities as an "uppity nigger" or an "imitation honky."

I employed two different strategies in public encounters, inside and outside of the work context. Most often I would attempt to respond to a genuine question or concern as fully as possible without compromising neutrality, a kind of "resource person" approach. On other occasions, depending on the person's need and the complexity of their situation, I would refer individuals to a professional advocate, a lawyer or consultant that I felt was particularly knowledgeable in their area of interest.

I eventually refused to equate remoteness with professionalism, and I believe this was a constant source of consternation for other officers. Ironically, the less remote I was on the job, the more remote I became from my profession. Whereas visible minorities expected me to be one of them, to identify with the group "visible minority," immigration officers expected me to be one of them, to identify with the rank of enforcement and control professional, "the frontliner."

I am a person of colour *and* I had a job to do on the frontline—an interminable dilemma. It's interesting, however, that for both sides of the equation there is no dilemma. To people of African descent, the brotherhood of oppression is stronger than any alliance or club or union or occupation that can be imagined. And it is unconscionable to think otherwise. It's like religion—once you've come to know the true god, everything else is blasphemy. And life here in the diaspora is like a holy war, where the end can justify the means. There is often a taken-for-granted understanding among people of African descent that North American society has always been a rigged contest; so, any favour, advantage, or prerogative they can muster is simply a kind of historical reparation—that is, affirmative actions and special initiatives are justified when placed in the historical context of roughly four centuries of slavery and oppression on this continent.

To seasoned immigration officers the matter is almost equally as clear: you either do the job of enforcement and control or you get out. There is no alternative or in-between. For the frontliner, the big tribe always has precedent over little tribes; there is no priority for the African North American Brotherhood (ANAB) or any other kind of brotherhood. There are only the "good guys" and the "bad guys." You do your damnedest to get the good guys in and get the bad guys out.

Today, the frontline immigration officer presupposes that individual newcomers and society are linked through an interweave of rights and responsibilities, protections and observances. In this regard, Canadian immigration *is* colour blind. In conjunction with the 1976 Immigration Act, which was purged of all racial references, ordinary frontline officers do not as a matter of practice distinguish between black and white. The system is applicable to all equally. All have individual rights as human beings and responsibilities to the whole, or to the host, society in equal measure.

On the other hand, for people of African descent this concept of "universality" or the equal distribution of rights is conceived to be restrictive and ahistorical insofar as it falsely presumes a level playing-field in a game where some pale people have had a running start for centuries; therefore, to invoke it now is just another way of ensuring a continuous disadvantage. In some sense, then, the fact that the Canadian immigration system is now colour blind is interpreted by many people of colour as just a new attempt at entrenching the status quo ante.

Frontline immigration officers generally and genuinely believe that everyone who has queued up deserves a chance to come to Canada, and the bad guys are those who have had their chance but have failed through some folly of their own. For the dutiful officer, more than one chance to come to Canada constitutes a violation of the queue and is a mis-allocation of immigration and other resources. This is the good-guy-bad-guy equation on the frontline that is based on a version of affirmation and responsibility and guides immigration officers' conduct beyond explicit rules.

For the most part, the custodial "feeling" or desire of the frontline immigration officer is to wrestle the bad guy to the ground right at the nation's turnstiles, take him for a spin and send him home. It is only a feeling of custodianship, mind you, and not a job description or policy initiative. This is the implicit feeling that united the frontline as a group. Despite all the fine print and officialese, seasoned frontline immigration officers are really only concerned with one thing—rooting out the bad guys; everything else is bureaucratic minutiae and "small potatoes" and not really worth worrying about.

The official job description, of course, is about good guys, bad guys *and* small potatoes alike—indeed, mostly about small potatoes. Hence, the immigration business has been aptly described as a "paper storm," where multi-tracked documents, forms, transmittals, printouts, reports, memorandum and dispatches of all descriptions fall from the sky on people's heads like confetti at a ticker-tape parade. Yet, while bureaucratic minutiae carries the day in the immigration business, it doesn't exhaust frontline morality; it does not change the fact that in the deep recesses of their group consciousness, frontliners are serious about presiding over screening and recruitment into the "big tribe."

I often learned this the hard way, as the following incident shows.

The Buffalo Blunder

On one memorable occasion, I was temporarily ostracized for arranging the transportation of a young African-American woman to this psychiatric hospital near her parents home in Buffalo, New York. I had attended the Ontario Psychiatric Hospital on Queen Street in Toronto on behalf of the Minister of Immigration in regard to this young lady, who had been caught shoplifting music cassettes. The police had arrested her and put her in the Toronto West Detention Centre for Women pending a criminal court trial, where it was discovered through a routine medical examination that she was on medication for schizophrenia. The physician on staff at the jail had then shipped her directly to the mental hospital for full examination and treatment. By the time I arrived at the hospital, this woman was either willingly or unwillingly off her medication and literally bouncing off the walls.

At that particular point, there was little doubt in my mind that this young Nubian princess would be the subject of my deportation submissions, following, perhaps, an exorcism. From an immigration standpoint, it was not only important to direct her removal from Canada, but also to be able to monitor and control her future intentions towards our country. Since she was clearly incompetent and unable to appreciate the nature of the proceedings at the time, though, the matter was adjourned in order to arrange suitable counsel for her at the Minister's expense. I also informed her attending psychiatrist that if he could not "mellow out" the person concerned, or put her in a straitjacket or something, the inquiry would have to be conducted in her absence, and I would direct a couple of burly escort officers to drive her to the Peace Bridge, Niagara, in the back of an armoured, caged Oldsmobile 88 after I had deported her.

However, upon my return to the hospital the following week, through the miracle of modern medicine, the young Buffalo native was in complete control of her senses and demonstrated such temperance and equanimity that I could hardly believe it was the same person. My position on the matter changed. It was clear she was a foreign national who had committed a criminal offence and was, therefore, in violation of the Canadian Immigration Act. It was also clear she could probably be shown to be medically inadmissible to Canada, given her psychiatric condition. But I asked myself what good it would do anyone to deport the young lady for circumstances resulting from a medical condition that seemed to be completely manageable. In my estimation, she wasn't a criminal; she was sick, and her sickness could be treated. In the end, I agreed to allow her to attend a psychiatrist to arrange a transfer from the medical facility in Toronto to a similar one in the United States in order to ensure her continuous and uninterrupted treatment. In addition, the psychiatrist convinced me to allow him to arrange hospital transportation to the American border, where she was to be met by American hospital attendants and taken into their care.

Of course, I was in for some trouble. This was completely un-precedented on the frontlines of the immigration business. It was inconceivable to many of my colleagues that I would just let a "wacko" go scot free with the possibility of her coming back to be "crazy" all over Canada again, anytime she pleased. How could I just relinquish the control of our borders for a "nut case"? Several officers, who were otherwise normally restrained, started to go a bit crazy themselves. I am sure they were visualizing a bureaucratic body-slam—plotting the revocation of *my* citizenship and my eventual deportation back to the motherland—"Send me back some good yam recipes. You're going home, Kunta Kinte! The only question now is in what manner are you going to leave the country?"

There was nothing frivolous about the substance of the complaint. Unless I had just rewritten the Immigration Act, criminal and medical inadmissions were still on the books. From a frontline standpoint, the young woman from Buffalo had had her chance to be admitted to Canada but had failed in her responsibility to her host, so she was a bona fide "bad guy." There was no explanation that could have justified my actions, and none was asked for. The only possible variable that could be imagined by my colleagues as intruding into the decision-making process here was that of "colour" (and, of course, "sex" is all wrapped up in this variable, too, as the Martinique psychiatrist Franz Fanon proved; Fanon, 1967, 1968): "What, did the young sister promise to give you a little action on the side, stud? What, are you running for office in the NAACP? What is this 'black thing'?" I was the subject of derision and ridicule for several days. "Where is this Foster character? I want to meet this quintessential exponent of negritude and pan-Africanism; the man who would be king and saviour of all of black America and the diaspora!"

Of course, derision and ridicule can have a status beyond mere reproach, or mere raillery. It's my firm contention that this royal bureaucratic jeer, as it were, was, and is, connected to an important and enduring issue that is actually deeper than the issues of colour or sex, although these are its concrete manifestations. It is more than just the question of whose side are you on or what tribe you belong to. The broader underlying question is one regarding the dispensation of social order and social justice in the immigration business in Canada. Which comes first, the industrial efficiency or the human-heartedness of our society? What is the proper coordination of the orderly and the just?

When all is said and done, for the typical frontline immigration officer, order is a prerequisite for justice. The notion is: There is no true justice without social order. "Wackos" need a strong dose of the orderly. And what made my transgression so grievous in the mind of the typical frontliner is that I was supposed to be aware of this. I was supposed to be "in the know." I was supposed to have seen it all in the trenches and not be churned by vagaries. I was a frontliner. I was one of them. I belonged to the "inside dopesters." I was not supposed to be apathetic, or simply negative, like the average "Joe Canadian Public." I was not supposed to be some obtuse political patronage appointment, collecting big bucks, listening to immigration sob stories from behind an oversized podium in a quasi-judicial boardroom. And I was not supposed to be abstract like the big-time bureaucrat in Ottawa, who may never even have seen normal processing, let alone a wacko. I was supposed to know that you do not fiddle around with wackos and nut cases. You dispense a little social order (also known as "rough justice" or "turnstile justice"). You put them in a headlock, spin them around on the turnstile for awhile, and get them out of here on the next available flight, train or bus, whichever comes first. You remove the bad guys forthwith, in order to preserve more time to process the good guys. It is that simple. Order and justice in a nutshell. The bad guys get order and the good guys get justice.

The question is: What was I doing? How could an immigration officer who had seen "The New Delhi Shuffle" make "The Buffalo Blunder?" How could I allow a young African-American woman to come and go as she pleased without regard to entry and exit control vis-à-vis her possible medical and criminal inadmissibility? How could

I affirm her rights and protect her as an individual and not insist on her demonstration of responsibility to her host?

I must admit, at the time I wasn't thinking of the situation as a "black" thing. I did not consciously think, or say to myself, "I'm going to show sympathy towards the young woman from Buffalo because she belongs to the African North American Brotherhood just like me." But, the fact is I didn't have to think of it. Something just kicked in like a cultural imperative, mitigating against frontline consciousness and altering the order-justice complex.

In the black perspective, "blackness" is in and of itself historically worthy of favour. Therefore, when all is said and done, social justice is spontaneously embraced as a prerequisite for any worthwhile social order. The bottom line for visible minorities is this: There is no true order without justice. In this respect, if the frontline perspective subscribes to an "orderly justice," then the black perspective implores a "just order."

If anything, at the time of the incident I was thinking it wasn't a "black" thing at all. At the time, awash in the illusion of a disembodied moment, I thought my actions were based on right and wrong, not colour. But, of course, my version of right and wrong is not independent of my own experiences; and my experience, in large part at least, is as a person of colour. It is a reality that leaked into the frontline reality of the immigration business and contaminated the format. It is as if some cultural imprint in the deeper recesses of my being guided my conduct like an involuntary reflex and landed me smack dab in the middle of the war of the worlds—the world of "doing" and the world of "being."

I had, in effect, announced to my immigration colleagues that while I am one of (and with) them, I am also a person of colour. While I am aware of frontline reality, I can and will exercise veto power, in at least some instances on the grounds of my particulars, and that my "black" thing takes priority sometimes. In this regard, I automatically, and more or less unconsciously, felt an essential connection, an abiding and unspoken covenant with the young woman from Buffalo, not as "There but for the grace of God go I," but rather "There go I." Not as merely kindred spirits, but, in some sense, as standing together in the same spirit, embodying varying degrees of strength and vulnerability.

This is the "black" thing to be sure. Call it "Afrocentrism"; call it a common humanity in the microcosm. When I thought she was simply crazy, I took it personally, as a personal embarrassment, and an affront to sensibilities of all people of colour who might like to go crazy themselves but, instead, hang in to fight the good fight another day. When I thought she was merely sick, I took it as equally personal and took it upon myself to assure her continued treatment and protection in the face of my statutory duties.

Role Conflict and the Equilibrium of Society

The immigration officer in me says, "Surely, there is no justice without order." And the minority background in me says, "Surely, there is no order without justice." In the end, they comprise clashing sets of norms and values. Immigration officers are commonly pledged to a version of turnstile justice because of a frontline appreciation of the need for orderly conduct in society. At the same time, minority shareholders in Canada tend to be advocates of benign order in society, because fair and equitable conduct is intimately experienced as an interactional imperative.

In sociological terms, this interminable dilemma is known as role conflict—where the behavioural expectations associated with one role are inconsistent with the behaviour expectations associated with an-other concurrent role. Role conflict arises, then, when a person occu-pies two or more roles that place contradictory expectations or demands on him or her. Furthermore, when there is a failure, per-ceived or actual, in terms of the expectations of role fulfilment, it represents not only a breakdown of the normative aspects of social order, but a breakdown of the moral order as well. Thus, it has been suggested that role conflict is a source of deviance that is inherent in the structure of society itself (Erikson, 1966).

Canadian society is marked by its rich differentiation and develops along a multiplicity of lines, including those of race and ethnicity, vocation, kinship, religion, region, age and sex, to name but a few. These lines, of course, often intersect in our daily lives. Individually we are always the representatives of several components and groups of society. In our encounters, our individuality is a compound of idiosyncrasy, membership and representativeness. "The actor in this sense is a composite bundle of statuses and roles" (Parsons, 1957: 26). Sociologically speaking, we are all status-role bundles, compris-ing a multiplicity of castes and stations. Yet, our composite lives are not always fluid. Our role in one group can violate our role in another. So it is not surprising, in a complex society, that the relevant structures and meaning complexes of our group memberships may not only intersect, but collide head on.

What is surprising, perhaps, is that in our complex society there is no common stock of knowledge or standard mechanisms for conflict resolution. We cannot call on proven recipes to find an equilibrium or comfort level for our everyday life blunders. Society is not always a self-correcting or self-regulating system. So, it does not spontaneously adjust itself, like a home-heating unit with an automatic thermostat. It can host "conflicts of interest" in social life, so to speak, but it does not necessarily resolve them. Individuals can be, and often are, subject to the jurisdiction of clashing sets of norms and values, without recourse to societal devices of control and stability.

In this regard, almost all sociologists agree that role conflict results in psychological tension and moral turmoil, and some have suggested that such conflicts increase the probability of suicide (Gibbs and Martin, 1964). Suicide, of course, is an extreme resolution. The more common ways of obviating conflict are avoidance (of an established social role) or capitulation (to an established social role). For instance, one way to obviate the tension that being a visible minority may create in regard to holding a particular kind of occupation is to avoid such occupational roles altogether. This would explain why blacks and, perhaps, other visible minorities are more reluctant than whites to go into occupations like immigration and law enforcement. From a visible minority standpoint, some occupations can be viewed as instruments of oppression or agencies of the status quo majority. An alternate solution, of course, would be to do just the reverse—minimize the visible minority or ethnic role in one's life. By concentrating on individual career aspirations and social mobility, minorities can attempt to become part of the mainstream and to integrate *de facto* into the dominate majority of society, as it were. There is still another alternative, however; role conflict can be a call to adventure—the consummate challenge being to redefine the social roles and so change the expectations associated with them.

The working knowledge of the frontline immigration officer in me conflicts with my visceral knowledge of the black world, and to choose one perspective is to violate the other. To adopt the role and sensibilities of a visible minority is, in some sense, to be absent from the role of the immigration officer, even though a formal resignation may not be tendered. And, of course, the reverse is also true. These life-positions are non-negotiable, diametrically opposed and irreparably contradictory. This is an example of one of the ways in which the adventure can begin. A blunder—apparently the merest chance, the fortuitous exposure to this and that, the random and existential circumstances of birth and place, biology and biography—drew me into a relationship with forces that are not easily understood or easily reconcilable, yet afforded me the opportunity of a lifetime.

This hypothesis has some formidable precedents. Sigmund Freud (1963), for instance, held that blunders are not the merest chance but rather the result of suppressed desires and conflicts. They are ripples on the surface of life, produced by unsuspected springs. And these may be very deep—as deep as the soul itself. Furthermore, as Joseph Campbell (1973: 51) acknowledged sometime later, something creative can come from a blunder: "The blunder may amount to the opening of a destiny." Precisely at the moment of a blunder lies the opportunity of a lifetime—where the familiar life horizons are to be outgrown and the time for the passing of a prodigious threshold is at hand. Both Freud and Campbell realized that only when the individual becomes unhinged from the confines of social roles is there possibility for real movement. The multiple realities that cause role conflicts, and the disintegrated integration of the self in modern life, call for a new resolution and synthesis that transcends former perspectives and leads to a higher unity and form of integration.

My blunder, which I call the "Buffalo Blunder," is a blunder not by chance but rather the result of suppressed desires and latent hostilities. In the final analysis, it is the role of the immigration officer within me to know that justice has limits. Social justice is not only about the rights and privileges of the individual, it is also about the duties, obligations and responsibilities of the individual towards the host society. This is the frontline immigration officer's rule of affirmation and responsibility: only those who are responsible to society should be affirmed by it. Meanwhile, it is critical to the person of colour within me, and to the sensibilities of the disaffected and ethnic minorities everywhere, to know that society's social order has a conscience. Order is not only about fluid relationships and the smooth functioning of our systems and institutions, it is also about the search for community and the need to respect honest differences along the way. This is the ethnic-mosaic rule of recognition and embrace—with society as well as with the individual, there is a strength and dignity in the acceptance and embrace of other.

It is as a result of the conflict of these roles that I have come to believe that justice has limits and order has responsibilities, and a just order embraces a common humanity. The chapters that follow develop this theme.

2

Turnstile Bureaucrats: The Frontline Immigration Officer

rontline immigration officers staff the turnstiles of the nation. They work in the trenches as ordinary "grunts" with an extraordinary view of the passageways to Canada. The problem with immigration, at least from the vantage of the typical frontliner, is that in reality it is too difficult to get the good guys in and even harder to get the bad guys out. In addition, frontliners often feel overwhelmed by the enormity of immigration's bureaucracy, which faces them like an abstract force and authority, a thing out of control, a thing represented by the "senior suits" in Ottawa who really don't have a clue as to what is going on. Furthermore, frontliners are the flak-catchers for lawyers and consultants who know how to "shake the bureaucratic tree" and the various elected officials who wish they knew how to. While they often feel overwhelmed by it all, frontliners also believe their everyday work life and life's work is not abstract or superficial; they believe they work in the trenches where the action is and attempt to provide custodianship for the nation by wrestling the bad guys to the ground (in the face of opposition from lawyers, consultants, and assorted politicians and bureaucrats in Ottawa). Thus, for frontline immigration officers, the paramount reality of immigration takes place in the spirited relationships they develop in the trenches.

The Frontline Versus the Hardline in Immigration

Since this is a country of immigrants, most Canadians have had a personal encounter of some form or another with a negative, rule-obsessed immigration officer, who lacks interactional skills as well as a sense of tact and decorum, and who may seem to engage on occasion in gestapo-like tactics. This phenomenon is so renowned that, in the parliamentary debate on the Immigration Act, Bill C–86, several elected officials used their allotted debating time to lament what they described as "the bad apples of the immigration barrel" that always seem to be strategically located—answering the phones in local offices in their constituencies and at visa offices and embassies abroad. The common complaint was that arrogant immigration workers routinely stated that they didn't care if they were speaking to a Minister of Parliament or God of the Universe, their position was non-negotiable on this or that matter, and the conversation was immediately terminated. Some of the parliamentarians went so far as to call for a new provision in the Immigration Act either to increase their own discretion and influence or to subdue the discretionary powers of immigration officers.

When the general public, or the parliamentarians that serve them, speak of the terrible experiences they have had with immigration, they are usually referring to contact they have had with an immigration officer who perverts the good-guy-bad-guy equation. In everyday life they fit well within the confines of the general definition of "the hardnose bureaucrat." But, within immigration itself, these officers are often known as "hardliners" (those who have hardened over time).

There is a difference between a frontliner and a hardliner. Hardline immigration officers simply react badly to the human quagmire of immigration. For frontline immigration officers it is good guys in and bad guys out; but for hardline immigration officers it is as if everybody is a bad guy. Hardliners are a breed of turnstile terrorists who see barbarians at the gate. And when immigration officers start seeing barbarians at the gate, they can, themselves, become barbarians.

Of course, because of the nature of the work, the transition from a frontline view to a hardline view is an ever-present threat. A reporter for *The Globe and Mail* newspaper in Toronto catalogued for posterity the following tension-filled remarks of an examination officer on a busy day at Pearson International Airport:

> One inspector expressed his frustration to this reporter more vehemently. Dealing with a Ghanaian refugee claimant who said he had destroyed his passport and had no documents of any kind, the inspector said it was ridiculous that inspectors cannot search people.

> "How do I know he doesn't have his passport or his ticket or his boarding pass or identification in his pocket?" he asked. "We're not allowed to look. What kind of an immigration system do we have? This whole thing is a sham, and nobody gives a damn."

> An Immigration Department manager, who was accompanying the reporter, cautioned the inspector to moderate his comments. "Why should I?" he said. "People should know what a waste of time this is. Anybody gets into Canada. We are not allowed to do anything. People should know what is going on" (*The Globe and Mail*, Oct. 27, 1988).

Often, because of their general frustration with the system and a feeling of powerlessness to do anything about it, immigration workers become hardliners and take out their frustrations on all outsiders. In this event, they tend to regard clients, parliamentarians and other outsiders as objects rather than subjects, as an interminable nuisance rather than as the very purpose of the system. They are often rude, suspicious, cynical, accusatory and prosecutory. Furthermore, there is a marked tendency to evaluate the subjects of the immigration system in terms of varying degrees and categories of deceit, fraud, duplicity and abuse. And, as they see the matter, it is their job to rectify the situation.

Most frontline officers feel a profound sense of frustration and powerlessness from time to time, but they do not take the hardline; they generally attempt to accentuate the positive. Of course, this is little comfort for anyone who has had to deal with a bona fide hardline immigration officer. It only takes one hardliner to ruin a family's life or alter its course forever through misplaced hostility. Still, in the immigration business there is an analytical difference between the frontline and the hardline, in the same way that there is an analytical difference between aspiring towards the good and merely seeking to avert the bad. Hardliners are strictly one-dimensional thinkers; they think you can preserve the good by eliminating the bad. Here, bad is the rule and good is the exception. Good is merely an aberrant expression of the bad. So, rather than accentuating the positive, hardliners tend to expend themselves and all their energies trying to rectify the negative.

However, the vast majority of frontliners genuinely believe the immigration law is aimed at the good, and the continual crises in which the country finds itself arise out of the failure to apply it. In this respect, most immigration officers are two-dimensional thinkers: they think "The Act" represents the highest potential of Canadian society in regard to its order and justice, and they see themselves as attending the reciprocal relationship between the people and the system of immigration—the rights and the responsibilities of immigration—in equal measure. Accordingly, they speak about their commitment at times, almost reverently, in terms of "Upholding the Act," "Observing their Statutory Responsibility" and ensuring "Procedural Fairness."

Nevertheless, ordinary immigration officers, across the board, often feel as if they have to *become* the instrument of order and justice in the system, which is not without its own risks of excess. As with the examination officer quoted above—"This whole thing is a sham, and nobody gives a damn"—the lack of real power can lead to the desire to exercise excessive situational power. Here, the frontline goal can become one of mediating order and justice in the system to the strict letter of the law, beyond the machinations of all outsiders and even the senior bureaucrats in Ottawa, if at all possible.

For instance, frontline immigration workers have gone so far as to engage in covert fundraising efforts aimed against their own employer:

> Frustrated frontline Toronto immigration workers have begun a covert drive to help Metro Police raise funds to sue their employer.
>
> Metro Police have launched a suit against the federal immigration department for not deporting two illegal immigrants charged in the killings of Const. Todd Baylis and Georgina "ViVi" Leimonis.
>
> Immigration workers involved in the fundraising effort refused to be identified, fearing they'd be fired from their jobs (*The Toronto Sun*, Sept. 4, 1994).

Participating in covert efforts to undermine their employer is a indication of how frontliners often feel—that they are, in fact, the Canadian border. That is, they commonly assume, at least psychologically, an awesome charge of safeguarding the nation from external trespass and internal mismanagement. This grand aspiration, however, is where the potential snare of hardnosed, intellectual rigidity and emotional bankruptcy lies. The grievous criminal acts perpetrated by some illegal aliens, such as murder and rape, can easily be interpreted as "every alien is a potential murderer and rapist." Or, more specifically, since the illegal immigrants charged in the brutal killings of Police Constable Todd Baylis and Georgina "ViVi" Leimonis (mentioned in the news item) happened to be Jamaicans, the hardnosed solution to cracking down on these heinous killers is to tighten the border restrictions on Jamaican immigration. By taking on the momentous psychological role as the custodians of the nation, frontliners always risk becoming hardliners—de-personalizing and de-humanizing others on the spot. Here, rather than focusing on the prosecution of a group of law breakers and criminals, they can actually generalize and thus criminalize entire groups.

The Subject-Object Split

Further complications are caused by the nature of the work itself. Immigration officers wrestle the subjectivity of the people they encounter with the objective designations of classes, categories and procedures which stand opposed to any human particularities. On the frontline, people are "PC's" (person's concerned) and their needs and aspirations are the stuff of programs and streams. As a result, the individuals who are the subjects of immigration are typed or typified, transformed into objects or calculable events for purposes of manage-ability and control, and referred to with object-like or objectifying procedural language about "cases," "action on a case," and "case termination" as a matter of routine. Individuals are typified and then objectified—creating a tension between the subjective and the objec-tive bases of the immigration system.

Hardline immigration officers go a step farther. For them, there is no tension between subjects and objects in immigration. Individuals are typified and then objectified and then reified—that is, they come to be treated as "thing-like"; therefore, their humanness is distorted. When individuals are reified, they are implicitly viewed by hardliners as alien beings or entities migrating to Canada in the same way that amoebas move towards the sunlight for sensual gratification. These officers always look for a hidden negative agenda—the short-comings of people and the pitfalls of procedure. And the negative possibilities always seems to override anything that could be conceived to be positive.

No amount of "client service training," which is regularly con-ducted within the immigration commission to sensitize staff to the people they serve, has had any appreciable effect in transforming the subject-object split of hardline or negative immigration officers. When client-newcomers are perceived to represent varying degrees of self-indulgence, deceit, fraud, duplicity and abuse, service training is interpreted as merely a naïve waste of time and energy, concocted by some mush-brained, high-power bureaucrat in Ottawa. Here, hardlin-ers perceive that the immigration officer's function is not to give good service or to serve the greater good; it becomes one of making sure the global "riff-raff" doesn't contaminate the authentic character of Canadian society.

Social Rights and Individual Responsibilities

There is another distinction that may help illuminate frontline atti-tudes in the immigration business revolving around the issue of social rights versus individual responsibilities. When we speak of social rights, we are referring to the claims on the social system by all members of society to a basic standard of living and to equal oppor-tunities for education, health, and so forth. The emergence of social rights' claims in the twentieth century accompanied the advent of universal adult suffrage and the phenomenon of widespread partici-pation in the political system. This development of social rights and entitlements in the political sphere has meant a very slow but gradual erosion of privilege in other spheres as well, which may be viewed as part of the process of secularization that the classical social scientists identified early on as a distinguishing feature of advanced industrial society (Durkheim, 1947; Weber 1958; Simmel, 1978). Sectors of society and culture are removed from the domination of religious institutions and symbols, as well as the princely or elite classes. Coincident with this secularization and the development of social rights in Canada, governments have sponsored activities ranging from educational to medical and health insurance, and the growth of the "welfare state" has absorbed many of the functions that used to be performed by the church and other private charitable organizations.

This has not been an easy transition. In most developed societies around the world, there is ambivalence and disagreement about how far social rights should extend in society. For some, general welfare measures are viewed as a safety net indispensable to the truly advanced society; for others, they are seen as ultimately bringing about human and social decay. And the matter is even more ambivalent and complex when it comes to immigration, and the possibility of recognized entitlements for those who are not yet even citizens, only potential members or temporary residents of society. Doubts still rage everywhere regarding foreign nationals having any rights, claims or entitlements in society at all.

However, to the extent that "universality" is advocated and exists in Canada's immigration system, it is an extension of the concept of social rights as it relates to the tenets of liberal democracy and the welfare state. Here, in accordance to the 1976 Act, immigration policy is translated into tangible admission regulations and practices that prohibit discrimination based on grounds of race, nationality or ethnic origin, colour, religion or sex; protect the civil rights of all those who would set foot on Canadian soil; and ensure that every individual is afforded the full protection of the Charter of Rights and Freedoms and due process of the law.

The extension of social rights in the field of immigration is perceived as both a blessing and a curse by typical immigration officers. To their way of thinking, it is precisely the extension of social rights and the growth of the welfare state that has made Canada into a country of international acclaim and recognition, on the one hand, and a potential dupe, on the other. So, while frontliners are typically committed to the liberal democratic ethos (insofar as it is embodied in the Immigration Act that they attend), this commitment is tempered by the conviction that there is an inordinate number of people in the world who want to take a free ride on Canada's social democratic highway.

This classic "chain" letter detailing arrival instructions was found in the luggage of an Sri Lankan national en route to Canada:

> When you arrive in Canada they will ask you on what name you travelled. Who sent you here? Tell them the following: You had been in India only for a month. Your friends paid money to a travel agent and they only helped you to go to Canada. If they ask you the agency name or address just give them an imaginary name. These are routine questions, no problem. The agent only brought you to Bombay and boarded the aircraft. If they ask you on what name did you travel, tell them you were frightened, so you did not take any notice. ... do not tell the authorities anything other than what I have told you in writing. As soon as you arrive at the Canadian airport, at the counter tell them "I need political asylum." Then they will give you immigration forms. Immigration, with the help of an interpreter, will do the enquiries. At that time tell them lies as if they are true. *You must tell them lies in such a way that they must be able to believe you. Do not be frightened. Everyone who comes here, they come like you. They tell the same thing and they are all here, so this is not happening only to you but to everybody.* Do not tell them you stayed in India for a long period. Do not tell them you were a member of a terrorist organization. Tell immigration, house and everything is destroyed, so, in order to save my life, I came via India here only. Parents stay in relatives' house. Even tell them brothers and sisters not there. Brothers and sisters in Sri Lanka; only parents are there. Tell them the army arrested you 2–3 times and harassed you. They will ask you the time and month. Just give them some date. They will ask you which month, what date you were arrested, so just be prepared with specific dates. At the end only parents came to the camp and after arguing and screaming the army let us go. Army did not feed us, they really beat us. When the officer asks you this tell them as if you are telling them a real sad story which has happened" (Immigration Intelligence Division Bulletin No. 89–04, from the Visa Section of the Canadian Embassy in Colombo).

It is often difficult for even seasoned immigration officers to distinguish "the real sad story which has happened" from "the real sad-story which didn't happen," and it becomes more difficult all the time when there are informal correspondence courses for bogus refugee claimants around the world.

Of course, Sri Lanka, like all other countries in the developing world, symbolizes the queue between today and tomorrow. In this age of global migration—when millions of people from around the sphere are in flight from desolation, despair, poverty, persecution and death—immigration officers know that Sri Lanka, China, India, Jamaica, and so on, are the primary source countries of Canadian immigration. They also know that this age of global migration can generate global appetites or a burning desire for a better life, which many people around the globe will do anything to fulfil.

In this regard, an Immigration Act that is based on enlightened colour blindness, if you will, is not immune to slipping into just plain old blindness. The difference for the frontliner can be clarified subtly. Plain old blindness means the equal distribution of rights and privileges. Enlightened colour blindness means the equal distribution of rights and responsibilities. In this respect, the typical frontliner doesn't separate social rights from social responsibilities in his or her thinking. And nowhere in the everyday world of immigration is this more apparent than in the area of immigration investigations.

Immigration investigators specialize in the dirtiest of the dirty work—tracking down illegals and charging them under applicable sections of the Immigration Act. They have their own units; they work day and night; they carry badges; they wear flak-vests and jackets; and they are perhaps the frontliners who are the most truly engaged in the practical tasks of enforcement and control. Yet, they are not hardnosed, per se, but they are hardboiled; they have a protective interaction shield that is referred to in the business as being "tough skinned." These are the officers (and the image) to which people refer when they say, "Immigration is coming to get you." It is their existence (hardboiledness) that raises the liberal democratic question often posed in the media about the profession of the immigration officer—in an age of global migration, are the heightened senses of the craft too acutely attuned to "Sri Lankans," to "Chinese," to "Sikhs" and other "visible minorities" and to "Third-Worlders," such that their very thoughts or daydreams violate the necessary idea of a common humanity? On the other hand, they also represent the clearest, albeit inverted, reflection of the typical immigration officer's version of true egalitarianism. Their motto is, "We go after everybody regardless of race, creed or colour."

The following Bulletin No. 89–01 from the Immigration Intelligence Division from the Visa Section of the Canadian embassy in Islamabad details the discovery of a Pakistani smuggling ring producing fraudulent Canadian travel documents:

> Acting on a tip from an airline employee stating that two Iranian nationals carrying fraudulent Canadian travel documents would try to board Pakistan International Airline (PIA) flight 723 (Islamabad-Toronto) that same evening after allegedly bribing a Federal Investigation Agency (FIA) agent responsible for checking passports of departing passengers boarding that flight, as well as a counter clerk, the FIA arrested the suspected Iranians in the airport parking lot.

The documents—Canadian refugee documents—were similar to some other ones reported previously. Two other persons have been arrested in connection with the case.

Through questioning it has been determined that a smuggling ring is currently producing blank Canadian travel documents in Karachi using a colour photocopier. The blanks are then sold to various smugglers or forgers across Pakistan, and perhaps abroad.

Chinese syndicate operations likewise seem to follow a set pattern as suggested by Immigration Intelligence Division Bulletin No. 89–01 from the U.S. State Department:

Chinese aliens enter Singapore via a third country usually Nepal.

In Singapore they receive their photo-substituted passport and are introduced to their "escort" who coaches them and teaches them English.

They check in at Singapore's Changi Airport with their PRC (Peoples Republic of China) passport and a ticket to Hong Kong or some other location.

After passing through immigration an accomplice provides them with a ticket to join a tour group in the USA or Canada.

From the airport itself they mail their PRC passports to a contact in Singapore and then board the flight with the altered passports.

The aliens and their escorts split from the tour group in the USA or Canada and head for New York or Toronto.

The following Bulletin No. 89–01 from the Immigration Intelligence Division outlines the document fraud tendencies in Jamaica:

Document fraud is endemic in Jamaica today but it is not a new phenomenon. It is also similar to that of any country with a large population seeking economic opportunity outside its borders.

False document vending is big business in Jamaica today and almost any documents, from passports to bank books, can be purchased. Other scams are also used to facilitate the operations of the smuggling industry such as "fly now, pay later" plans, development of close contacts with government officials, entry without inspection, USA Farm Labour Program abuses, the different stamps and seals needed, arranged marriages and ship's crew visas, to name a few.

Among the documents found available in Jamaica are British and Canadian photo-subbed documents.

What distinguishes the Jamaican document industry is its close link to organized crime groups in the USA. Even officials at the highest levels of the Jamaican government have acknowledged those links among alien smuggling, document vending and narcotics trafficking.

It is believed that there are about 6 to 8 organized gangs dominating the industry employing more than 80 individuals in Jamaica today. It also has been noticed that the industry's ranks are being swelled by naturalized American citizens and Jamaican legal permanent resident aliens.

So far there has been few successful prosecutions and although some document vendors have been arrested and jailed, other gang members are able to quickly reopen the business.

Life at the front today is not about being ethnically top-heavy or heavy-handed, and it is not about left and right, although these issues are intimately interwoven into the fabric of everyday life; it is really about the frontliner's version of the good guys and the bad guys. So, while frontliners may have nothing against Sri Lankans or Jamaicans or any ethnic or cultural group *per se*, for whom Canada is now a country of first asylum, they have everything against the workings and manipulation of the system. Within the order-justice equation, the immigration officer represents a conscious attempt to order the consciousness of other and make it receptive to the justice that is offered. Their deep and abiding commitment is a crusade to make the system as a whole work in the face of those who would work the system. Sri Lankan Tamils (like the Liberation Tigers, who choose to import terrorism) and Jamaican Posses (like The Black Rose, whose chosen calling is to import narcotics and firearms) are the ones who bear most fully on the consciousness of frontline immigration officers.

Frontline immigration is hardly alone in the conviction that our democracy requires an intellectual tough skin in order to be preserved and sustained. These same sentiments have been echoed at the highest levels of jurisprudence. The Federal Court of Canada—in *Orantes v. Canada (Minister of Employment and Immigration)*, fed. T.D., Doc. No. 90-T–602, March 13, 1990—was of the opinion, for instance, that maintaining the fabric of Canada's social order has primacy over "the asserted entries by aliens no matter how sympathetic the immigration case":

> If parliamentary democracy is to survive in Canada, parliament must make choices about which foreigners, if any, may be legally admitted for permanent residence and not become helpless in the face of asserted entries by aliens no matter how sympathetic their cases. It takes a certain degree of intellectual toughness to support the principles of democracy in the face of various individuals who seek migration into Canada against the will of the democratically elected representatives of the people. If the Charter is interpreted in such a manner as to obviate the will of parliament in a matter such as this, it is the sort of frustration which would ultimately destroy national government by amputating the lawful means of governance.

In the *Orantes* case, an immigration officer refused to grant a humanitarian and compassionate exemption to the law and allow a foreign national permission to be processed as a landed resident of Canada because the individual was a person described in subsection 19(1)(b) of the Immigration Act. That is, there were reasonable grounds to believe the individual would be unwilling or unable to support himself and those persons who were dependent on him for care and support.

The commitment to the democratic ethos is tempered on the frontline by the conviction that the very good of democracy could spell its own demise if and when the rights of individual newcomers become an end in themselves, rather than a means to an end. Thus, the ultimate challenge for every immigration officer is to remain true to the frontline version of the order-justice equation. For them, there are crucial problems to be negotiated every day related to what I have called the "subject-object split" and "social rights versus individual responsibilities," and these can be digressive or hardening. And every day, many officers have been known to become digressive and hard.

Frontline Immigration and the Blasé Attitude

Of course, the public has its own views on the situation. Many people tend to think of the immigration officer as just doing a job—a bureaucratic, do-nothing, government job at that. Bureaucrats, it is said, are like cockroaches in that they have no redeeming earthly value, and, like the cockroach, they are almost impossible to exterminate. The most indoctrinated are supposed to be rich in caution, clever, curiously cool, with neat desks, inconspicuous clothes and inoffensive haircuts. They pass their days poring over the minutiae of fat dossiers in relative anonymity. The universal joke is that they never look out of their office windows before lunch because then they'd have nothing to do in the afternoon. Rightly or wrongly, it is a commonly held supposition that government bureaucrats squander public funds and do not do any real work. This becomes a common stock of knowledge in everyday life and speaks volumes in regard to the taken-for-granted understanding that they belong to a general class of de-erotized minds—merely paper shuffling automatons dealing in human flesh with a contemptuous attitude and a generous annuity.

In the classical analysis of *The Metropolis and Mental Life*, Georg Simmel maintained, "There is perhaps no psychic phenomenon which has been so unconditionally reserved to the metropolis as has the blasé attitude" (1950: 413). His usage was a descriptive lampoon of sorts, signifying that the bureaucratic schemata of big city life can numb the mind, and the mind, of course, is a terrible thing to waste. Today, however, with the ever-increasing bureaucratization of life attendant to the intensification of urbanism, Simmel's original character description seems to have expanded into a full-blown social psychology. Bureaucratic government jobs have become even more odious in the public mind as something in the order of "the blasé attitude with a strong dose of indolence, a smidgen of misanthropy, and daydreams of a big fat pension at the end of the road." What we have here is what W.I. Thomas (1980) called the creation of a spontaneous and public definition. In the public mind, or in the public "definition of the situation," as Thomas would say, the government bureaucrat is a generic type or universal concept for the rule-obsessed automaton, locked into a world that resembles a huge paper factory with a negative purpose. Of course, in regard to immigration officers specifically, this prevailing public imagery can go even further to suggest a rule-obsessed automaton with his face buried in the public trough, on the one hand, or a rule-obsessed automaton handsomely paid for inflicting more misery on the mounting masses of miserable global migrants, on the other.

The following is a rather typical view of the nature of immigration work: "Some people have all the luck. All you have to do is 'whack a few wetbacks' (punish illegal immigrants) and they pay you for it!" The impression (and perhaps the venting of a latent hostility at the same time) is that the pay and benefits for performing a necessary service for the community are relatively lucrative and that it is nearly impossible to be fired from such a position. This pedestrian idea is that being an immigration officer is akin to winning a lottery and never having to really work again the rest of your life.

Individuals may also say things such as "How many poor people did you kick out of the country today?"—meaning the job of being an immigration officer is inherently ruthless and mean-spirited. The implication is clear—no amount of financial remuneration could possibly justify the inhumanity of man towards man, or woman towards woman, that is built into this job description. Here, there is no sense of necessity, let alone intrinsic worth or dignity, connected to the work of a frontline immigration officer; and there is no sense that an individual could truly be committed to such a vocation, let alone take pride in the profession. For the typical conservative, who wants less immigration, the frontline immigration officer is a lazy sloth who doesn't do anything; otherwise, he would get rid of all the "illegal aliens" who infest and debase our society. The typical liberal who wants more immigration sees the frontline immigration officer as a stony cretin ("bou-bou-macoutes" as the French would say), who is hell-bent on banishing "potential fellows" and ignoring human travail.

The conservative normally conceives of the frontline immigration officer as liberal (meaning: namby-pamby, milquetoast, spineless). The liberal, on the other hand, normally conceives of the frontline immigration officer as a conservative (meaning: bigoted, intolerant, narrow-minded). The conservative wants the frontliner to be more of the liberal definition of the immigration officer, and the liberal wants the frontliner to be more of the conservative definition.

For their part, seasoned immigration officers have their own twist on Simmel's urban blasé. For instance, having learned over time that the topic of immigration evokes extremely strong reactions, the test of audience approval, far more than the test of truth, influences their own social comment. So, while the lay public may be fervidly committed to liberal or conservative opinions on immigration issues, professional immigration officers tend to see such opinions only as useful devices to assuage their detractors.

In this respect, for veteran officers, liberalism and conservativism are often merely invoked for public consumption; they are stances that a professional in the field can adopt to try to gain acceptance and mitigate public criticism. And, of course, since they are not fervidly committed to a conventional political persuasion dedicated to a version—pro or con, increase or decrease, open or closed—frontline officers always risk evoking public criticism when they speak about immigration issues: "I don't care if I'm speaking to a Minister of Parliament or God of the Universe, the case is closed!"

In some sense, the consummate expression of the immigration officer's blasé attitude is this ability to articulate and confirm the audience's own beliefs about immigration: "Yes we need more immigrants in Canada and, as an immigration officer, I am happiest at my job when restrictions are relaxed!" and "Yes we need to protect our precious borders against illegal migration by investing more resources and technology into entry and exit controls!" At the same time, because they don't really have a strong allegiance to any constituency, they may, on occasion, react with some disdain towards both the right and the left—"Yes I am happiest at my job when the good people get in and the bad people get the hell out!"

All of this fits well with the Simmelian concept of urban blasé, but the matter goes even further.

Frontline Immigration and Conventional Wisdom

John Kenneth Galbraith (1958: 5) once noted that "in the interpretation of all social life, there is a persistent and never-ending competition between what is right and what is merely acceptable." He coined the term "conventional wisdom" (1958: 5–38). In Galbraith's usage, conventional wisdom refers to the ideas which are esteemed at any time for their acceptability. He also alluded to the fact that conventional wisdom is the democratic version of speaking the holy: "In some measure, the articulation of the conventional wisdom is a religious rite. It is an act of affirmation like reading aloud from the Scriptures or going to church" (1958: 8). Conventional wisdom is produced by generating an unquestioned orientation to the acceptable rather than the truth. In the context of our political democracy, says Galbraith, *liberals* and *conservatives* are both implicated.

> The conventional wisdom is not the property of any political group. On a great many modern social issues, as we shall see in the course of this essay, the consensus is exceedingly broad. Nothing much divides those who are liberals by common political designation from those who are conservatives. The test of what is acceptable is much the same for both. On some questions, however, ideas must be accommodated to the political preferences of the particular audience. The tendency to make this adjustment, either deliberately or more often unconsciously, is not greatly different for different political groups. The conservative is led by disposition, not pecuniary self-interest, to adhere to the familiar and established. These underlie his test of acceptability. But the liberal brings moral fervour and passion, even a sense of righteousness, to the ideas with which he is most familiar. While the ideas he cherishes are different from those of the conservative, he will be no less emphatic in making familiarity a test of acceptability. Deviation in the form of originality is condemned as faithlessness or backsliding. A "good" liberal or a "tried-and-true" liberal or a "true blue" liberal is one who is adequately predictable. This means that he forswears any serious striving towards originality (1958: 7).

The general public can be seen as committed to a kind of Galbraithean liberal (approval) and conservative (disapproval) conventional wisdom with regard to immigration. The immigration officer can be seen as often using this for strategic advantage. They can, for example, talk up accelerated growth and increased levels of immigration as a positive factor or negative factor for the country's advancement. They can do surface-level media talk (like an opinion piece in the newspaper or success-and-abuse anecdotes), and hold an audience with some titillating human interest story. They can schmooze lawyers and consultants and politicians acting as advocates for people with immigration problems. But it is rare for a veteran frontline officer to actually buy into liberal ("yes" to immigration) or conservative ("no" to immigration) conventional wisdom. Consequently, on occasion, because of this lack of a political commitment, pacifying the politicians or schmoozing the advisors can turn into hardline sarcasm and even ridicule.

For the most part, however, in order to avoid public controversy of what is now a highly contentious topic, seasoned frontline officers, in public encounters, usually aim for a view of the world of immigration that is more agreeable or otherwise conforms to the tastes of their particular audience at hand. For example, in the presence of lay people, knowing that audiences applaud what they like best, officers tend to lean towards a criterion of acceptability. They may appear to embrace liberalism, or they may appear to embrace conservativism, depending upon what the audience most wants to hear. With varying degrees of skill and alacrity, they can argue accelerated growth and increased levels of immigration or decelerated growth and decreased levels of immigration; they can argue the general propositions of an open-door or closed-door policy; or they can present admission-oriented arguments or population and border-control arguments—at the drop of a hat.

The veteran officer learns the importance of mollifying any audience of laymen to avoid a social quagmire. One on one, this may mean letting the outsider take the lead, feeling them out for their political persuasion and then supplementing his or her conversation. In public or social encounters outside of the immigration office setting, for instance, immigration frontliners often present a non-threatening and non-disputatious posture by engaging in anecdotal conversation or relating interesting little historical or neutral titbits of information (for example, "Did you know that there used to be a 'head tax' on Chinese immigrants? Did you know that a Barbadian was once turned down as an immigrant because of 'climate'? Did you know that we processed over 500 million visitors in the last decade? Did you know that our beloved Canada received the prestigious Nansen Medal from the United Nations High Commissioner for Refugees in 1988? Did you know that Canada was cited by the United States State Department in 1994 for the best refugee record in the civilized world?").

In the "persistent and never-ending competition between what is right and what is merely acceptable," as Galbraith would say, right only occasionally finds a way to the surface. The true commitment of the frontline is rarely exposed in public because officers are usually busily engaged in the construction of an effective persona or "presentation of self" for relevant audiences (Goffman, 1959). The impulse to placate the public is so strong that the typical immigration officer rarely takes the time to bask in the glory of recognized achievements. So, even international accolades and medals of honour are not actually held in esteem as sources of pride on the frontlines in the same way that workers in other industries may prize distinguished service awards—though they may be presented as such. Rather, they are more often used as situational devices in conducting everyday tasks.

A positive international standing, such as Canada currently enjoys, can cushion situational conflicts between frontline workers and clients that result from such things as excessively long processing delays or allegations of discrimination and fascist behaviour (levied against all officers some of the time and some officers all of the time). In addition, such accolades and honours often ease the conscience of officers in regard to minor transgressions of public propriety, ranging from incivility and impersonalization to illegal search and seizures (for example, confiscating foreign passports and travel documents).

While veteran frontliners know how to perform the liberal and conservative melodramas of "moral fervour" and "pecuniary self-interest" (Galbraith, 1958: 7) and how to emulate political persuasions dedicated to propositions of pros or cons, increase or decrease, and so on, they also deeply believe that the antagonism between liberal and conservative public opinion is not meaningful in the everyday life of the immigration business. Therefore, when they speak in liberal and conservative terms to assuage an audience, they still more or less consciously believe that the complexities and subtleties of the issues preclude the possibility of a conventional "political" analysis. Reality in the trenches is thought to be too complex for the dispositions on the right or on the left. This conviction emanates from a shared belief that knowledge is "dirty work," and only they do the dirty work required to have knowledge. So, living and working in the "muck-and-mire," of immigration is perceived as a rite of passage. In this regard, the public are merely abstract because they never get their hands dirty. Meanwhile, the big-time bureaucrats in Ottawa not only don't get their hands dirty, they can get in the way of those who do.

In the same way that black people may believe that others really can't know what it is to be black, or women may believe men can't know what it is to be a woman, frontline immigration officers tend to believe in their heart-of-hearts that others really can't know anything about immigration. They are inclined to believe that you really can't know what is going on, or make an informed judgement, unless you are on the frontline. They tend to see themselves as having the "inside scoop" on immigration. So, while they may often attempt to appease the conventional wisdom, the truth is that frontline immigration officers have their own brand of conventional wisdom, which is quite different from the liberal and conservative brands and tends to edit reality from their intimate experiences at the front, wrestling the bad guys. The frontline is where the action is, and to know immigration is to know what goes on in the trenches. Of course, this relates to the first major problem of immigration in Canada today—there are people who make immigration policy without ever having to be on the frontline, where the action is.

Frontline Immigration and Insider Knowledge

In sociological terms, "insider knowledge" (Becker, 1963) is tacit or taken-for-granted understandings shared by the members of a particular group. Being on the frontline means having access to insider knowledge about the immigration business that others don't have. Part of the knowledge of the inside is that there are bureaucrats and there are bureaucrats—those who work on the frontlines and those who work behind the lines, or behind the scenes. There are bureaucrats on the frontlines, and senior bureaucrats or "superbureaucrats" (Campbell and Szablowski, 1979) behind the local scenes and off the human stage in Ottawa. The ones who work on the frontline execute immigration policy. The ones who work behind the scenes in Ottawa make immigration policy. The problem here, from the perspective of the frontline officer, is that policy is made in a vacuum, unaffected by the wisdom of being on the front line.

Frontline immigration officers believe they know things that other people don't know, even the people in Ottawa at the Policy Division. They do not profess knowledge of "the big picture" or "the whole picture" or "the international picture." They are not necessarily "scholastic" about immigration matters and may not know about macroeconomic modelling or longitudinal studies, but they always feel they have a sense of the "living" picture—"the nuts and bolts, the low-down, the real-skinny." And to the typical frontliner's way of thinking, the real-life picture of immigration is only gleaned from experience on the ground.

For instance, one thing that frontliners know perhaps better than anyone else is that liberal democracy has incited a significant global migratory phenomenon—not democracy as a sophisticated political philosophy articulated in university research departments or mapped out by the senior departmental bureaucrats, but rather democracy as it is exemplified and embodied on television. The biggest boon to immigration in North America is the syndication of television programming and has little or nothing to do with, for example, the complex global-planning levels of big-time policy bureaucrats. Television dramatizes democracy and whets global appetites. In this respect, syndicated television is the universal technology of the immigration business, not "the point system" or "the occupations list" (derived from the National Occupational Classifications System maintained by Human Resources Development Canada). Television is the common denominator of everyday life from Sri Lanka to Tibet. It both propagates liberal democracy and ties us all together around the globe in a mundane commonality of wants and desires. Moreover, since individual wants and desires around the globe are now substantially the same, it is also more or less implicitly understood by seasoned immigration officers that many individuals from around the globe will often do anything to try to achieve them.

This understanding is tacit, implicitly shared among frontline insiders, seldom explicitly declared to outsiders, and usually anecdotal in nature and expression. For instance, when frontline immigration officers are in a crowd of people on a bus or a subway, they can't help sizing up pedestrian strangers with electric speed, building a "case profile" in their mind's eye. From my experience, this is a typical mass transit internal conversation for an immigration officer:

(Prologue) ... That one over there looks like he might have come to Canada on a false Sri Lankan passport. The old Sri Lankan passport scam. They sell like hotcakes all over the world to everybody, it seems, except Sri Lankans. Or he could have arrived on a counterfeit Canadian Refugee Travel Document. He probably got one right here in Canada before the RCMP shut down the printer in Montreal in June 1988. I'd like to ask him a few questions through a Commission interpreter. Check his bona fides:

Question: "What's the capital of Sri Lanka—administrative and commercial?" (If he doesn't say Sri Jayewardenapura, Kotte and Colombo, he's detained.)

Question: "What are the principal languages?" (He had better say Singhalese, Tamil, and English or he's detained.)

Question: "What's the currency of Sri Lanka?" (He had better say rupees and cents or he's detained.)

Question: "What's the national anthem?" (He had better say Sri Lanka Maa Thaa or he's detained.)

Question: "What's the first line of the anthem?" (He had better say Namo Maa Thaa or he's detained.)

Question: "What's the major airport?" (He had better say Katunayke International or he's detained.)

Question: "When is the Sinhala and Hindu New Year?" (He had better say the 12th and 13th of April or he's detained.)

Question: "What's the famous landmark in the capital city?" (He had better say Galle Face Green, Boc Tower and Vihara Maha Devi Park or he's detained.)

Question: "When is independence day?" (He had better say February 4th or he's detained.)

Question: "What national holiday is celebrated on May 22nd?" (He had better say Republic Day or he's detained.)

Last Question: "What's the most popular television show?" (He had better say Dynasty and Falconcrest or he's detained.)

(Prologue) ... That one over there looks like he might be one of the Chinese Red Guard—"The Red Circle Boys" involved in drugs and alien smuggling. How many of the Red Circle Boys have claimed refugee status on the basis that they were students in Tiananmen Square? God only knows. Or he could be one of the Chinese nationals who came to Canada using a counterfeit Hong Kong I.D. card. Ya! After all, the cards are so sophisticated and deceptive that when they are used with a good-quality, photo-substituted Hong Kong (British) passport, they can easily pass through the Primary Inspection Line (PIL) or Immigration Secondary. In the past, Canadian Ports of Entry (POE) partly relied on Hong Kong I.D. cards to verify bona fide Hong Kong residency. I'd like to check out his documentation:

Question: "Does the print on the Biodata (photo) side of your Hong Kong I.D. card appear to float above the surface of the inner paper core?" (If so, you're detained.)

Question: "Does a strong oblique light cause the lettering on your I.D. card to leave a shadow on the paper's surface?" (If so, you're detained.)

Question: "Does the print quality show feathered edges, breaks in letters and smudging of fine details—such as the date of birth?" (If so, you're detained.)

Question: "Is there an extra layer of lamination visible between the outer two layers enclosing the paper core—which would indicate doctoring of the genuine inner paper core beneath the outer lamina?" (If so, you're detained.)

Question: "Is there any visible evidence of erasure of the original entries on the paper core?" (If so, you're detained.)

Question: "Is there a detectable third layer of lamination bearing photo and biodata sandwiched between the outer clear lamina and the inner paper core?" (If so, you're detained.)

Last Question: "What's the most popular television show in Hong Kong?" (He had better say Dynasty and Falconcrest or he's detained.)

(Prologue) ... That one over there, minus ceremonial garb, probably claims to be a Patit Sikh (a lapsed member of the Sikh religion, who has ceased to observe the outward marks of Khalsa orthodoxy). [After the storming of the Sikh Golden Temple in Amritsar in 1978 by the Indian police during the Vaisakhi Festival, Denmark experienced a rush of Sikh asylum seekers. In order to tighten its borders, and speed up the refugee determination process, Denmark instituted a new aliens act, which effectively eliminated spontaneous refugee arrivals. Denmark no longer recognizes Sikhs as legitimate refugees from India under its refugee determination system. As a preemptory strategy to counteract removal to India, Sikh asylum seekers headed for the safe haven of Canada, many as stowaways on ocean liners and other chartered vehicles. Off-shore, they unload into dinghies and wash ashore. Unlike Denmark, the success rate for Sikh refugee claimants in Canada was as high as ninety percent and is only now declining slowly. Consequently, even East Indians in Canada who are not Sikhs have claimed an abiding commitment to the religious doctrine.] I'd like to ask this guy a few questions through a Commission interpreter. Check out his bona fides:

Question: "Who is the founder of the Sikhism?" (He had better say Guru Nanak, born in 1469, or he's detained.)

Question: "What's the Sikh holy book?" (He had better say Adi Granth, the 'Original Book' of Sikh scriptures first compiled in 1604, or he's detained.)

Question: "What is Khalsa?" (He had better say the 'Company of the Pure,' the military order of orthodox Sikhs instituted by Guru Gobind Singh, or he's detained.)

Question: "When is the Baisakhi festival?" (He had better say April the 13th, celebrating the birth of Kalsa, or he's detained.)

Question: "What is Khalistan?" (He had better say the 'Land of the Khalsa,' a coinage used to denote the idea of an independent Sikh state, or he's detained.)

Question: "What's the acronym AISSF stand for?" (He had better say The All-India Sikh Students' Federation founded in 1943 as the youth wing of the Akali Dal, or he's detained.)

Question: "What is the Akali Dal?" (He had better say the political party that controls the SGPC and has dominated Sikh affairs for the past 60 years, or he's detained.)

Question: "What does the acronym SGPC stand for?" (He had better say the Shiromani Gurdwara Parbhandhak Committee which controls the major gurdwaras of the Punjab, or he's detained.)

Question: "What is a Gurdwara?" (He had better say a Sikh temple—'door of the Guru,' or he's detained.)

Question: "What is a Granthi?" (He had better say the 'reader' in charge of the scriptures in Gurdwara, or he's detained.)

Question: "What is the Jatha?" (He had better say the original detachment of Sikh guerrilla aries, now applied to a group participating in an Akali demonstration, or he's detained.)

Question: "What is a Kirpan?" (He had better say the sword or dagger worn by orthodox Sikhs, one of the 'Five K's', or he's detained.)

Question: "What is Morcha?" (He had better say the 'entrenchment', the term applied to the mass agitations that are an important part of Akali strategy, or he's detained.)

Question: "What is the Panth? (He had better say the 'path', the term usually used to describe the Sikh community as a whole, or he's detained.)

Question: "What is a Sahajdhari?" (He had better say a Sikh who believes in the Gurus' teachings without observing the Khalsa discipline, or he's detained.)

Question: "What does Sant mean?" (He had better say a title of respect given to Sikh religious leaders, or he's detained.)

Last Question: "What's the most popular television show in the Punjab?" (He had better say Dynasty and Falconcrest or he's detained.)

Every frontline immigration officer worth his salt knows by rote that Dynasty and Falconcrest re-runs are the most effective immigration recruitment films that have been produced in North America to date. Proving that everyday life isn't necessarily a pretty or neat picture that fits nicely into a statistical package, but it is compelling.

Lawyers and Consultants on the Frontline

The frontline immigration officer confronts the immigration lawyer and consultant as an external and coercive force. They have different constitutive accents. Typical immigration lawyers and consultants tend to see typical immigration officers as insensitive, cold-hearted brutes who are swept away by their unique situational power, unable to grasp the big picture of human work; while typical immigration officers tend to see typical lawyers and consultants as abstract idiots, prepared to compromise the well-being of society through their disguised greed. Imagine the following: A lawyer and a senior immigration officer are in the detention area of the Toronto Hearings CIC (Canadian Immigration Commission), and they are locked in an encounter by the presence of a detainee who is cuffed and shackled. The lawyer says to the immigration officer, "What are you people, barbarians?" To which the immigration officer replies: "No. He is the barbarian! But I tell you what. I'll take the jewellery off him if you promise to take him home with you!"

Lawyers and consultants in the immigration business routinely objectify immigration personnel and, so, like immigration workers, also risk distortions of humanity. They routinely impersonalize the impersonalizers, so to speak. Or, as Tom Wolfe (1970) would put it, they "mau-mau the flak catchers"; many will lie, cheat, stonewall, withhold information, run scams and do everything they can think of to disrupt the immigration system because they see "The Commission" as ruled by a cold, unfeeling, invisible hand which is motored by bureaucratic automatons with no concern for the "persons concerned."

Quite apart from the possibilities of personal corruption or greed, this is a violation of the rules and the rule-people, based on a kind of professionalized righteous indignation. It is viewed as a form of justifiable sleaze, usually beginning with the creative interpretation of facts to fit the rules and ending in a version of the reification of the reifiers and the dehumanization of the dehumanizers. Here is an excerpt from a letter written by an immigration lawyer, advising that he will report with his client to immigration authorities if they will overlook the fact that his client is under a deportation order and are willing to regularize his status:

> Dear Sir:
>
> This is an application for a humanitarian and compassionate exemption pursuant to 114(2) of the Immigration Act of 1976, from the visa requirement of subsection 9(1), on behalf of (client's name).
>
> (Client's name) originally arrived in Canada using a false French Passport on 31 October 1987 at Mirabel International Airport in Montreal, where he advised an immigration officer he wished to made a refugee claim....
>
> His refugee claim was subsequently denied and he was the subject of a removal order on 21 January 1991. He failed to report to immigration authorities on his removal date....
>
> Consequently, in order to remain undetected, he sought low-profile employment in Montreal and then Toronto, remaining underground and doing anything to survive. For the last four and one half years, however, he has been employed as a Cheese Maker in Concord, Ontario, where he earns $10.49 per hour and holds a responsible position as Assistant Foreman.
>
> While in Canada, Mr. [Client] has been active in the Toronto Islamic Community and has maintained a good civil record. He speaks nine languages including English, French and German, as well as six African languages. His long residence in Canada has afforded him the opportunity

to increase his proficiency in both official languages of our country, while taking great strides to adapt to and be integrated into society....

Should you be inclined to look favourably on this case, I will report to your office with my client at your earliest convenience....

Immigration lawyers and consultants (qua social activists) have invented justifiable sleaze, in good conscience, on the basis of dealing with immigration personnel not in their status as "people" but rather in their status as extensions of a bureaucratic apparatus. So they often relate to immigration officers as a strange breed of rule-obsessed mutants, turnstile tyrants with twisted souls and snarly attitudes ("What are you people, barbarians?"). Many think they can do anything to immigration officers, say anything, regardless of truth and without compunction or remorse, in order to achieve what is conceived to be a deeper, more humane objective. And what separates sleaze that can be justified from sleaze that cannot is this sense of higher purpose.

One problem that lawyers and consultants have, however, is that it is often difficult to distinguish justifiable sleaze from just plain old sleaziness, and either event can have the same negative consequences. The following news account from *The Toronto Star* serves as an illustration:

> A Toronto lawyer has been found guilty of fraud for telling a visitor from Portugal to lie on an application to get permanent resident status in Canada.... (The lawyer) will be sentenced April 27 for knowingly counselling a client to violate the Immigration Act by advising the woman to claim she had no relatives in Portugal when in fact she did....
>
> The lawyer told them of a special immigration program that allows applications for residency in Canada based on having no remaining relatives in the native country.... (*The Toronto Star,* April 3, 1993).

The court decision referred to above has since been overturned by appeal, partly on the grounds that the lawyer's instructions were not strictly prohibited by the Immigration Act, but it is not an uncommon occurrence.

Justifiable sleaze means that lawyers can manipulate the system for the purpose of achieving a wider good—a positive result for the people they represent. This can be a tricky business, though, because the positive result to which they aspire may be achieved at their own expense when the people they represent conspire with the system. In the immigration business, clients can turn against their counsel out of desperation when things turn sour or when there is a strategic advantage to be gained. Nevertheless, despite the professional hazards and personal risks, lawyers and consultants continue to employ justifiable sleaze as a major interactional tool. Indeed, the immigration system *encourages* them to do so. And, as much as frontline officers hate it, letting lawyers and consultants get away with sleaze mitigates in a way some of the guilt for the low-dosage euphoria frontliners get from muscling the bad guys.

On the other hand, some lawyers and consultants are simply despised or feared because they know how to shake the bureaucratic tree. For instance, some high-profile counsel have more social-class ties with senior bureaucrats in Ottawa (they can be on a first name basis and "do lunch" together) than do the frontline officers. Therefore, they can often cut through the red tape and negotiate with senior management directly. Other talented jurists can shake up the bureaucracy through sophisticated appeal challenges and Charter arguments that can change the direction and course of immigration law.

Consider this 1990 internal immigration memorandum regarding Charter arguments in backlog refugee claims:

> It has been brought to my attention that (counsel's name) is threatening to argue before adjudicators that the long delay in proceedings with backlog cases constitutes a denial of fundamental justice and that these individuals should simply be granted landing.
>
> The purpose of this note is to try to elaborate an argument and present some material to give to CPO (Case Presenting Officer) so that it can be used to formulate a response....
>
> One word should be said about the remedy sought by (counsel's name). The Federal Court of Appeal decided that a panel at an immigration inquiry does have jurisdiction pursuant to section 52(1) of the *Charter* to determine the constitutionality of a law it has the statutory duty to apply *(Gurjinder Kaur* v. *MEI)*. However, the Federal Court of Appeal have stated that the tribunal can only disregard a law it finds inconsistent with the *Charter*. It cannot fashion a remedy pursuant to section 24(1) of the *Charter (MEI* v. *Borowski; Tetreault-Gadoury* v. *MEI)*, these decisions are under appeal). It should be brought to the attention of the adjudicator that the remedy sought by counsel is in the nature of a remedy under section 24(1) of the *Charter.* As you realize, so far the Court is of the opinion that it is not under the jurisdiction of the panel to grant such a remedy.
>
> In summary, I am of the view that even if a claimant could succeed in convincing a court that he had suffered serious psychological stress from the long delay in having his case resolved under the backlog procedures, we would have strong arguments to advance that there has been no denial of fundamental justice.

When a lawyer or consultant can shake the immigration tree through connections or refined legal manoeuvres, it is often easier for a frontline officer to say "yes" than "no." In the immigration bureaucracy, the answer "no" doesn't always mean "no"; it often simply means that you haven't found the right turnstile or passageway yet.

Apart from high connections and legal skills, to shake the tree and grease the turnstiles, ordinary lawyers and consultants can use one of two strategies: they can go over the head of the nay-saying officer or they can use a simultaneous over-and-under manoeuvre.

Straight over-the-head tactics involve requests for a review of negative decisions, following the lines of authority from the bottom to the top of the organization and all places in between—from the frontline through the supervisory level, through the managerial level, through the senior official level, regionally and in Ottawa. A negative decision in regard to an immigration case usually means that counsel needs to send his or her submissions (in original or revised form) up the bureaucratic chain. It also means a possible succession of reports to superiors by immigration officers all the way up the chain, substantiating the original and successive negative decisions.

The over-and-under manoeuvre is more common and slightly more devious than the straight over-the-head tactic. Often, the information presented to an immigration official by lawyers and consultants is already known to them and cannot be made more compelling or compelling enough to warrant a positive decision on a immigration case. This requires that counsel present the matter and the request to several officials at various levels in the organization at the same time, always using third-party references in face-to-face or one-to-one encounters. For example, when speaking to one officer, counsel refers to another official and a prior conversation that was "leaning favourably" towards a positive decision. Or lawyers and consultants can attempt to manipulate a positive decision by reformulating a third-party conversation in ways that may have little semblance to the original conversation—"But so-and-so said this..."; "We were told that if we did this, then The Commission would do this...." The lawyer/consultant game is to keep the immigration ball bouncing, to take the decision out of unfavourable hands, or to make the hands more favourable through the threat of disproportionate work or adverse scrutiny by one's superiors.

In the final analysis, lawyers and consultants are the frontline officer's nemesis in the immigration business. They can induce anxiety in career-conscious grunts by playing on their basic instinct to tow the party line. They can also treat immigration officers as mere instruments of—or impediments to—the system, giving them an ongoing dose of their own "objectifying" medicine.

The Exercise of Discretionary Power by the Bureaucratic Elite

The closest an immigration officer gets to an emotional state on the frontline is not with regard to clients or lawyers or consultants but rather with regard to their relationship to the senior policy and public affairs bureaucrats—"the superbureaucrats."

This was highlighted during the 1991 War in the Gulf, when Mohammed Mashat, the Iraqi Ambassador to the United States, jumped the queue—or rather, he parted the waves of the sea of red tape with such dispatch that he made Moses look like a minor figure. He was able to enter Canada without applying for a visa, buy a house in British Columbia, and obtain landing status in six weeks—this, despite the fact that at the time Canada was formally at war with Iraq. The intrigue was numbing to the Canadian public. People wondered how it was possible for an Iraqi diplomat to be landed in six weeks, when their relatives and acquaintances had spent years seeking admission and landed status to this country, and were still hostage to the immigration bureaucracy.

The public cried foul. *The Toronto Star* reported that,

> while Mohammed Mashat jumped the immigration queue, refugees caught in the Canadian backlog have killed themselves in despair....
>
> And while the former Iraqi envoy to Washington needed a mere 30 days to race through the immigration process here, some 2,300 Kurds who sought refugee status in Canada following attacks by Iraqis in 1988 have not even been interviewed (*The Toronto Star*, May 18, 1991).

Mr. Mashat not only jumped the immigration queue ahead of virtually everyone who applied for residence in Canada up to three years prior to the Gulf War, he jumped the queue ahead of the Kurds, whom his government was reportedly trying to annihilate while he was still a diplomatic official.

The frontline immigration staff, for their part, were embarrassed and demoralized, in part because of the plight of the Kurds and also because they had spent years processing individuals from all around the world—gathering information, maintaining files, interviewing and advising relatives and, above all, counselling patience in the face of all the red tape—assuring everyone that all the security checks, medical checks and personal assessments were necessary to safeguard the community.

The "Iraqi Ambassador Incident" highlights the fact that senior policy bureaucrats are often perceived by the frontline as failures, being both corrupt and immoral. The frustration for frontline officers is that they have no recourse by which to address the failure and corruption of the system, other than protecting themselves with blasé attitudes or by surreptitiously supporting the occasional law suit initiated against the department by some disgruntled member or members of the public.

Unlike some other social systems in our society, there are no appropriate measures to maintain social control in the organization. Frontline officers feel at a loss in the face of mismanagement and bureaucratic bungling. They can't throw the bums out, as they might do as members and citizens in the political system. There is no democratic consensus procedure in place to which one could refer as a form of social sanction and constraint; no elections; no impeachment procedures. Nor can frontline immigration officers defer the matter directly to the usual agencies of social control and national security, like the police or the armed forces, even though the sense and magnitude of their grievance is analogous to that of oppressed peasants towards a cabal of petty dictators. As a result, many frontliners see the bureaucrat elite as no less than a felonious assault against society.

In October 1996, *The Globe and Mail* reported on the indignation of frontline officers towards a new detention policy which "seems to be motivated by a desire within the top echelons of the Immigration Department to pare detention and employment costs and to relieve crowded detention facilities":

> Immigration officers should bend over backward to avoid detaining illegal immigrants and bogus refugees unless they pose an obvious danger to the public or are unlikely to show up at a hearing, according to new policy guidelines that were to be implemented this week.
>
> A draft copy of the guidelines says immigration officers must consider all possible ways to release new arrivals, even if they have criminal records. They also say that having a forged passport is not in itself grounds for detention, nor is a person's lack of credibility at an interview....
>
> (An) officer, who said he would be fired if he revealed his name publicly, said the detention guidelines should really be called release guidelines.
>
> "I feel personally and professionally this is a blatant attempt by management to fetter the actions of immigration officers." Officers are responsible for upholding the Immigration Act, not the whims of immigration managers who may be acting beyond statutory authority, he said.
>
> If managers want to change the responsibilities of immigration officers, he said, they should be proposing amendments to the act that would have to be approved by parliament....

According to internal management electronic mail, immigration managers concede that although the new guidelines are "being called 'a change in interpretation,' they almost change the [Immigration] Act."

The memos anticipate negative reaction by immigration officers and say management will have "to find ways to get staff to buy in...." (*The Globe and Mail*, Oct. 2, 1996).

As there is no effective structural or organizational means for frontliners to register dissatisfaction with the administrative decisions of the bureaucratic elite, the only device for affecting decision making is to lose the file in an attempt to sabotage authority at the ground level. Generally speaking, when someone in Ottawa is considering a favourable decision on a case that frontliners may deem unfavourable, it is a regular occurrence for the case files containing pertinent information for the rendering of the decision to be destroyed in an attempt to preclude a favourable decision. In one instance in 1992, for example, a request was put forward by a Non-Governmental Organization (NGO) to the Office of the Minister, Doug Lewis, for a review of twenty-nine deportees with regard to special relief on humanitarian and compassionate grounds. Of the twenty-nine cases, fifteen case files were reported missing. A new review could only be rendered on fourteen of the twenty-nine requests.

This is a small indication of a larger problem. Frontliners can and do tend to divorce themselves psychologically from any connection to immigration superbureaucrats. Therefore, coherence in and commitment to "the organization" is continually threatened. In a large social system like the Immigration Commission, which employs approximately 30,000 persons, frontline officers do not usually know the policy makers, nor do they really want to know them. The "high office," which ordinarily garners respect in any other modern bureaucracy, only draws contempt. There is a sense that the high-office moguls, those big-time senior suits in Ottawa, are selling the country down the river in a handcart.

For frontliners, the Iraqi Ambassador Incident is the apotheosis of procedural unfairness and differential treatment—a clear case of intrigue and subterfuge at the highest levels, with legislators and top bureaucrats in external affairs and immigration squabbling and pointing fingers at each other. However, the bottom line is this: there was nothing illegal about it. The bureaucrat elite have statutory authority to exercise discretionary powers over and above the substantive law. They are not ruled by the principles of order or justice, per se, but rather by the principle of power.

It is the cornerstone of the Immigration Act that persons apply for and obtain their immigrant visas from outside Canada. Further, the law provides a standard of admissibility applicable to all categories of potential immigrants—the ability to settle and adapt. The law, however, has a parallel counter-reality known in the trade as the "administrative exemption." The parallel belongs to a "special measures" category which is outlined in the IE (Examination and Enforcement) and part of the IS (Selection and Control) Immigration Manuals. This parallel reality is not commonly acknowledged or readily available to the public. IE 9.01 states:

> It is a cornerstone of the Immigration Act that persons apply for and obtain their immigration visas from outside Canada (A9[1]). There may be instances, however, where the requirement to leave Canada to apply for a visa would create undue hardship for the applicant. Therefore, A114(2) enables the Governor-in-Council to facilitate the admission of persons for reasons of public policy or for compassionate or humanitarian considerations. The Governor-in-Council may prescribe regulations to exempt persons from the requirements of A9(1) or from any Immigration Regulation made under 114(1).

The superbureaucrats in Ottawa are lords and masters over the "special measures" category. They can go outside of the law and outside of normal procedure to effect a special measure, as in the case of the Iraqi Ambassador. The ability to enforce the power of the law, or to enforce discretionary powers beyond the law, elevates the decision-making power of the community of senior officials in Ottawa (for example, the Governor-in-Council) to an absolute status.

The special powers extend to policy and programs as well. In November 1994, leaders of the Jamaican community sought and were granted a meeting with Immigration Minister Sergio Marchi to discuss what they viewed as a compassionless and draconian plan to photograph and fingerprint all Jamaicans entering the country on entertainment work visas. (It is believed inside the commission that Jamaican Posses such as The Black Rose, The Strikers, The Jungle Massives and The Bulb Eye Crow control and use many of these visas for illegal alien smuggling operations). It so happened that the senior officials in Ottawa had introduced the special procedures and had also withdrawn the special procedures, deeming the measures unnecessary for enforcement and control purposes. At the meeting, the Immigration Minister told the leaders of the Jamaican community that he knew nothing about the special procedures, and only later did both parties find out that the meeting was unnecessary because the procedures were no longer in force. "The Jamaican Plan" had come and gone before the public or the politicians even knew it had existed.

The individual frontliner has no access to public policy, and the Ottawa policy maker wouldn't be caught dead on the frontline, where the *action* of immigration is. As a result, the lines of communication in the system are severed, and those doing the talking *for* immigration, and in the ear of legislators, have no intimate connection to the topic they are discussing. On this account, the immigration system has become a game of population control, with the superbureaucrats holding the balance of power in the game.

The Frontline Immigration Officers' Good-Guy-Bad-Guy Equation

For the typical frontline immigration officer, the balance (or imbalance) of power in the system can be something that is more than a little disconcerting. Consider, for example, the following internal memorandum (written by a twenty-year veteran) regarding the marriage interview and possible special relief visa exemption for a convicted criminal:

> It is my understanding that we do not do "marriage interviews" on convicted criminals—especially not this type who has SIX criminal convictions from 1981 to 1990. He is 19(1) C [i.e., criminally inadmissible to Canada].
>
> We have a lot of undesirables in this country—he is one of them. I do not want to do a "marriage interview" and couldn't care less if he is married 29 times.
>
> Please advise if you want us to do something other than what we have already done—namely write our memo of November 18, 1989. Also where does it say we should do a "marriage interview"? We already know he is married—we also know he is a crook (Nov. 16, 1990).

This memo, dispatched from Toronto to Ottawa, is perhaps an extreme example of the emotionalism that I have suggested frontliners harbour for the superbureaucrats. However, it is noteworthy for several reasons. Firstly, it is not typical, in the sense that it does not happen every day; but it is typical in terms of the vitriol frontliners may reserve for senior officials in Ottawa. The difference from other internal transmittals is that it clearly exposes an ego on the part of a frontline foot-soldier: "I do not want to do a marriage interview and couldn't care less if he was married 29 times...." The underlying assumption is that if a marriage interview is conducted and the marriage is found to be bona fide, then the frontliner would be providing grounds for a senior official in Ottawa to grant administrative exemption for a criminal he has never met.

Sociologist Max Weber once explained that bureaucracy has an inherent tendency to destroy a person's autonomy and absorb their egos. It is characterized by formalism and it involves subordination, expertise (and hence a rigid division of labour and authority) and obeying rules. Bureaucracy assumes absolute discipline and a high level of predictability. So, it is unusual for frontline immigration officers, in a modern large-scale government bureaucracy, to openly challenge requests, directives, or instructions—or exteriorize interior sensibilities—for a number of bureaucratic reasons, not the least of which is fear of reprisals from superiors. It is as unusual for immigration frontliners to openly challenge senior management as it is for them to openly express their true opinions on the immigration system to lay people. Indeed, such a challenge defies all the subordination and obedience-to-authority tenets of bureaucracy explored by Weber.

Nevertheless, while it is not typical, it is still revealing in the same way that the violation of a rule can bring the rule into clearer focus or in a way that an anomaly can illuminate what is normal. "I do not want to do a marriage interview (*add:* on this criminal type) and couldn't care less if he was married 29 times.... "—this is an internal, internal memorandum, if you will, representative of a kind of "psychic overload," where a pervasive sense of inner indignation has surfaced like a bubble from the depths of a normally composed consciousness.

Finally, and most importantly, there is a directness of perspective here that comes from doing: "I do not want to do a marriage interview (*add:* on this repeat offender, and offensive repeater) and couldn't care less if he was married 29 times.... " This is also an implied moral statement embodying a common, albeit usually tacit, outlook on the bad guy as the one who has had a spin at the turnstile and failed through some dereliction of his own. Frontliners typically want deportees to be deported following the due process of law and not to become the subject of "administrative privileges" or "special relief" in order to stay in the country.

But the fact is that deportees and other illegals can so monopolize the frontline officers' time with administrative reviews, humanitarian and compassionate assessments and other means tests reports to superiors that it is often quite impossible to ensure procedural fairness for cases requiring normal processing. Indeed, there can often be an advantage to those who ignore or violate immigration law. Difficult entry criteria, for instance, can encourage the dishonest and the indolent to violate the law (for example, criminal types, generally, will not submit to a routine security screening for obvious reasons), while honest and hardworking people are often discouraged from even trying to come to Canada. Hence, illegality has become routinized, and some forms of illegality are customary in the Canadian immigration business and have become the established rules of conduct. For instance, many long-term illegals believe that they have the right to remain in Canada even though they are residing in the country illegally. They can get impatient with immigration officials who give them a hard time, especially when they see other illegals in similar situations who are overlooked, reprieved, or exempted from the official immigration regulations. *The Toronto Star* quoted one candid, and anonymous, removals officer who spoke out on the issue, and the problem it creates in the area of job performance:

> Job performance is measured according to how many removals are carried out, and nothing more.
>
> Officers realize that if they spend one month tracking somebody down and removing them, that is one removal. They also know that if they write a letter to an otherwise law-abiding person who is facing deportation and get them to go, that counts as one removal too; but you can do 20 or 30 of those in a month.
>
> The people who are least likely to be a problem to society are the ones most likely to be removed (*The Toronto Star*, June 26, 1994).

Today the circumstances exist whereby it is often the newcomers who are least likely to be a problem to society who are the ones most likely to be removed. It is for this reason that frontliners commonly perceive themselves as the last human link between order and justice. They don't represent clients, like lawyers and consultants, and they don't represent abstract administrative or legislative power, like bureaucrats and politicians. They typically want to see the laws enforced, and they want to ensure fair-mindedness and equity in the system. The catch is that this frontline version of the synthesis requires certain things that do not now exist in the system, such as (1) streamlined immigration procedures without loopholes or notwithstanding clauses activated by a disproportionate access to money and material resources, and (2) the proper allocation of human and financial resources within the system itself.

Immigration as a Machine of Retribution and a Cash Cow

The system as it now stands is nowhere near the kind of machine of retribution to which ordinary frontliners aspire. It is more a "bills-and-skills" machine, based on "cash-nexus thinking," in that it favours those with material resources and marketable skills. Entrepreneurial and investor immigration allows the affluent to buy visas directly. But putting entrepreneurs and investors aside, the overall system design affords those with resources to have a broader access to the system and a fuller range of legal and administrative possibilities. In short, you can buy your way in, and you can also buy your way out of deportation today.

In 1952, the Canadian government established the preference clause in the Immigration Act, formalizing the authority and ongoing practice of limiting or prohibiting the entry of immigrants for reasons of nationality, citizenship, ethnic group, class or geographic area of origin, peculiar customs, habits, modes of life or methods of holding property, unsuitability having regard to climatic, economic, social, industrial, educational, labour or health factors, or probable inability to become readily assimilated. This public policy has been referred to as a "closed policy," since it was inclined towards formalizing a practice that had existed since Confederation of recruiting only designated newcomers from only designated countries. This closed policy resulted in targeted or selective immigration practices, which guaranteed the bulk of newcomers were, and would remain, of European stock.

In 1967, a point system was adopted to allow immigrants to be chosen on the basis of suitability to Canada and the Canadian labour market needs and to mitigate against any discrimination due to religion, race or country of origin. This policy has been termed an "open policy," since the country of origin was not a criterion in immigration-selection process. The unit assessment or point system was formally introduced into immigration regulations and procedures as a means of ensuring that immigration recruitment would be non-discriminatory with respect to sex, colour, race, nationality and religion while still linking the admission decision to domestic labour-market requirements. The open policy, with its point system, resulted in a tangible change in the composition of immigrants with a rise in the flow from non-European, formerly non-preferred, countries.

In 1978, a new Immigration Act was again implemented, which required specific yearly immigration target levels, coupled with a closer scrutiny of the immigrant's potential impact on the labour market. This policy has been termed a "restrictive policy" compared to the 1967 Act. The country of origin was not a criterion, but immigration selection was determined more vigorously on the basis of demographic needs, family reunification, and labour-market considerations. Assessment for each entry class reflected varying degrees of scrutiny for possible labour-market impact. In particular, entry into Canada under the independent class was linked almost solely to labour-market requirements. The restrictive policy of 1978 resulted in the preservation of a certain equality of immigration source countries, but it also marked the beginning of quality controls based on cost-benefits analysis (controlling the kind and quality of immigrants allowed into Canada to ensure that immigration costs did not exceed benefits). One of the quality-control adaptions was the devising of the first occupations list (standard measurements for entry derived from the "Canadian Classification and Dictionary of Occupations").

On February 8, 1986, new criteria and limits for immigration selection came into force. The changes generally consisted of eliminating the "assisted relative" classification as a separate category from skilled immigrants (although immigrants with relatives continue to receive extra points) and placing greater weight on language skills. In order to meet the needs of a contemporary economy, the immigration department recognized that

> there is a clear need to upgrade the methods used to evaluate skilled workers and manage their flow into Canada. The system must adapt itself to a rapidly changing knowledge- and technology-based economy. In such an environment, it is difficult, if not impossible, to predict which specific occupations will be needed in the medium to long term. Therefore, our focus must shift away from selecting individuals on the basis of specific occupation. Instead, we must select individuals who demonstrate qualities that will allow them to adapt to the ever-changing global economy. We need to employ a selection system that rewards desirable qualities that are common across occupations—such as literacy, numeracy and adaptability (*Improving the Selection System for Skilled Workers, Citizenship and Immigration Canada*, November 1995, p.10).

Adapting to "a rapidly changing knowledge- and technology-based economy" does not suggest scrapping altogether such things as occupations lists as antiquated selection devices. Instead, the former classification system, which based its occupational classification list on the very detailed Canadian Dictionary of Occupations, has been replaced by a new National Occupational Classifications System (NOC), which more readily recognizes occupational groupings. The NOC, developed and maintained by Human Resources Development Canada, provides up-to-date classification of occupations in the Canadian labour market and organizes occupations into occupational groups. It is, therefore, still a skills-based selection system, albeit in an acknowledged learning-based world.

On May 15, 1991, during the final days of the Progressive Conservative Party reign, Immigration Minister Bernard Valcourt announced that the department had devised two new lists of occupations to be used in assessing potential independent immigrants' qualifications. The new roster, which remains in force today, contains nine hundred eligible job listings to fill provincial needs. In addition, there is a designated short-list of high demand occupations, which includes cooks, nurses, dental hygienists, electronic engineers, therapists, tool-and-die makers and computer programmers. It was determined that these particular job skills are in short supply in Canada.

It is worthy of note that Mr. Valcourt's announcement came a few month's after his predecessor, Barbara McDougall, closed the general occupation list—except for those with approved job offers—in order to clear a case backlog. The freeze was accomplished by giving no points for a job skill in a specified occupation. Now, it is determined that in order to meet Canada's demographic and labour-market needs, a slight re-adjustment of the selection criteria for independent immigrants is called for. Potential independent immigrants are now to be selected to come to Canada on the basis of a point system, with 70 points needed to qualify for approval. In the general occupations list, jobs are assigned either one, five or ten points. Points allocated to different occupations change over time, based on a labour-force demand assessment. The most highly rated jobs include nurses, therapists, dental hygienists and technicians, cooks, die-setters and blacksmiths. In the designated short-list, a target of the number of immigrants with specific job skills is listed for Newfoundland, Ontario and British Columbia. (Quebec has exclusive control over selection of independent immigrants; Prince Edward Island and Nova Scotia have no designated occupations; and consultations by the federal government with New Brunswick, Manitoba, Saskatchewan and Alberta continue.) According to the list, Newfoundland wants occupational therapists and physiotherapists, and British Columbia wants electronic and aerospace engineers, aircraft mechanics, nurses, tool-and-die makers and head chefs. Ontario's designated occupations include electrical and mechanical engineers, draughtsmen and computer programmers. In order to accommodate those with sought-after job skills, applicants who meet the requirements get a bonus of ten points. As well, those who are willing to settle in the provinces where the jobs are required will receive twenty bonus points. This modern combination of the point system and the occupations list in the immigration selection process has been referred to as high-tech or "designer immigration."

Changes in immigration criteria announced yesterday will make it virtually impossible for people who don't speak English or French to be selected as immigrants, critics say....

The previous emphasis on selecting people according to their occupations has been altered in what officials say is an effort to select immigrants with transferable skills....

Under the new point system, 20 percent of points will be awarded for education or trade certificate, up from 15 percent. Another 20 percent of points would be awarded for ability in English or French, up from 14 percent under the old system....

"It's not a bar (to entry), but it will be difficult," one official said. "We're looking for *immigrants who can hit the ground running* [my italics] (*The Toronto Star*, Nov. 18, 1995).

Summarizing roughly, then, the historical movement of the immigration system in Canada has gone from a closed immigration policy (prior to 1967) to an open policy (post–1967) to a restrictive policy (after 1978) to a designer immigration policy (in the 1990s), where immigrants are expected to "hit the ground running."

Approximately 60 percent of Canada's immigration program is currently in the independent immigration category, based on a "point system" designed to measure labour skills, experience, education, capability of the applicant and other employment-related factors. Entrepreneurs and investors who ostensibly create jobs for Canadians are not assessed on occupation or arranged employment factors. Immigrants who intend to be self-employed are not required to meet the arranged employment factor and may receive extra bonus units. Assisted relatives are assessed against the same factors as other independent immigrants. However, they receive ten bonus units of assessment if they have a relative in Canada who has signed an understanding promising to support them for a period of five years (or fifteen bonus units if they are the brother, sister, son or daughter of the sponsor).

The economic class (entrepreneurs, investors, those with needed skills, and those sponsored by family members with requisite skills and job opportunities) has been and remains the single most important criteria of immigration intake. It accounts for almost two times that of the family class category (spouses, fiancées, dependent children, parents) of the country's annual immigration intake. However, the other so-called non-economic immigration, including the family class category and refugee immigration (which, along with special programs, represents the balance), are also dependant upon economic self-sufficiency. Refugee and humanitarian immigration, for instance, subjects individuals to a "means test" or "solvency test" before permanent residence status is permitted:

> Refugees are not subject to the formal "point system" employed to evaluate the skills and adaptability of independent immigrants.
>
> Nevertheless, the refugee's ability to successfully adapt to Canadian life is taken into account. The applicant's age, level of education, job skills, and knowledge of English or French are used as guides in determining whether the refugee will be able to cope. Also the amount of financial and other settlement assistance available to the applicant may determine admissibility. In some cases, a refugee may not be admitted because of security or health reasons ("Canada's Immigration Law," Minister of Supply and Services Canada, 1989, p.16).

The means test is an economic component for refugee and humanitarian immigration on top of the new $975 "right of landing fee" and other processing incidentals.

This is what irks most frontliners and is the main source of the frustration in their job: While they think in terms of good and bad, the system often boils down to market- and labour-value criteria, which places some individuals at an advantage over others. Moreover, as long as those with resources have a broader access to the system, the moral currency of immigration policy will be brought into question by those without resources.

Challenges regarding the integrity and virtue of the immigration system abound in various social circles, not the least of which is the refugee claimants themselves, many of whom do not feel even ritually compelled to abide by unfavourable decisions, and who register their indignation towards the entire proceedings by going underground. For instance, it is now estimated that fully one-third of refugee claimants ordered to leave Canada have gone into hiding:

> Almost a third of the refugee claimants ordered to leave Canada have gone underground after spending years stuck in a backlog, federal figures show. And after two years of trying to clear 95,000 refugee claims, special tribunals still have about 36,000 cases waiting to be heard.
>
> The immigration department has issued arrest warrants for 4,100 people who disappeared after their refugee claims were rejected. Meanwhile, thousands of people are still in limbo, many after seven years of waiting, New Democrat MP Dan Heap (Trinity-Spadina) said.
>
> "It's worse than failure, it's neglect," said Heap, the party's immigration critic. "They don't care about those human beings, particularly the ones separated from their families by the Canadian government...." (*The Toronto Star*, Oct. 5, 1991).

The typical frontline immigration officer cannot understand how it is possible that the policy bureaucrats and other interested parties do not seem to comprehend the good-guy-bad-guy equation. The disbelief of many seasoned officers is often palpable and disquieting, with their entire comportment suggesting that they would like to grab the big-time guys in Ottawa by the scruff of the neck and shout, "Let's keep the good guys, get rid of the bad guys and don't sweat the small stuff!" It's as if to remind them that if *their* ancestors had been subjected to the same selection requirements and administrative ordinances that are used today, then they probably would not be here in the first place. Moreover, even if their ancestors had a demonstrable market value, today there may not be time for their processing because human and capital resources have to be diverted to other areas, such as tracking down illegal aliens and deportees. (In 1994, the immigration department created a new temporary unit consisting of immigration officers and RCMP officers precisely for this purpose.)

The frontline solution to immigration's myriad of complex problems is simple: lower the admission requirements and streamline the removal process. This is based on the understanding that there are plenty of good people and plenty of good families in Canada contributing to society whose ancestors came from meagre and humble beginnings. In their view, the current situation encourages illegality and creates social chaos. When it is impossible for determined people to achieve their desired goals through normal bureaucratic channels, they will often explore abnormal or extra-normal means. This unfortunate circumstance has conspired to create an untenable situation for the frontline immigration officer—nobody gets in and nobody gets out as advertised.

3

A Skilled Society Versus a Learning Society

The immigration system poses several pertinent questions: Who is best suited to join our regime? What kind of people do we want to invite to Canada? How can we organize our immigration policies and programs in such a way as to produce a good society? The answer to all of these questions—which are really the same question—is actually quite straightforward: society wants to invite people who are in accord with its fundamental principles. What complicates matters, of course, is that these fundamental principles have themselves evolved over time.

Selective Immigration in Historical Context

Originally, the answer to the question of who is best suited to join the regime had to be the "industrious ones." The industrious man was required to do the work of nation building in an untamed wilderness. Immigration programs played an important part, for example, in the settlement of the western provinces at the turn of the century and in providing business and industry with skilled workers in the ensuing years. In this regard, the historical record of Canadian immigration over the last 125 years reveals a marked preference for European settlers of stalwart and industrious stock. Over 12 million European immigrants have entered Canada, most of them from Western Europe, particularly Great Britain. And, of the total European emigration during that time period, about 65 million people, nearly one in six came to Canada to live.

During the early period of immigration in Canada, there was little pretence regarding the cherished ideals of liberal democracy upon which our egalitarian entitlements now flourish. Rather, the huddled masses were brought here to work and not primarily for fellowship or brotherhood or charity or for any other noble or ennobling motive. They opened the West, toiling at back-breaking jobs—ploughing the prairies, laying railway track, mining and hacking down the vast timber lands. Only later, when it became clear the country was in a rather enviable position of possessing plenty of space, abundant resources and a relatively high standard of living, did Canada emerge as a place of least resistance for the actualization of the democratic ethos in the field of immigration. Only after Canada became a model of industry in the Western world was the value of the hard-working, God-fearing, rational and industrious person then challenged by the belief in equal rights of all persons. By the 1970s, immigration in Canada expanded primarily as a family and refugee movement, which emphasized its humanitarian and compassionate aspects, with less emphasis on its economic potential. By the end of the 1980s, Canada had acquired an international reputation as a compassionate and humanitarian society of the first order, with the distinction of being the 1988 recipient of the prestigious Nansen Medal from the United Nations High Commissioner for Refugees.

Accordingly, over the course of Canada's short history, there have been changes of opinion as to what kind of person or persons should be invited to join our society. The country began with the model of the rational and industrious man, who was honest, respected the laws, tilled the soil and was dedicated to his family and clan. Above all, he was to be a lover of freedom and franchise, which translated into the fierce maintenance of ethnic, religious and other cultural differences. The French, Scottish, and Irish originally enforced their separateness from the English, and, in time, they became the pattern for all cultural groups. Eventually, ethnicity became a legitimate form of Canadian identity.

Some groups in the early period, particularly visible minorities and Eastern Europeans, were consistently ridiculed and slandered, but there were no widespread moves or sentiments to expel or eliminate them once on shore. The assorted ethnic cultures that made it to Canada lived in relative peace and security and, above all, isolation. Early Canada was comprised of a disparate people held together not initially by choice but by force of imperial decree and economic incorporation. It is in this respect that the social anthropologist, Suzanne Scorsone, formulated Canadians as "orphans of empire":

> We are a nation of people brought initially together by empire, not by choice. In effect, we have been having one single constitutional conference for a century and a half and more—only the faces, the tables and the dates change. Always there are the same issues of provincial and federal jurisdiction, French and English rights (and what to do about aboriginal rights), assimilation and distinctness, regional balance and population disparity, and the control of resources. Never before, however, have we been required to decide how to deal with them without the external structure (and support) of an imperial government.

Canada is the result of the imperial drawing of common borders around disparate peoples, as surely as were British East Africa, India, and, heaven help us, Lebanon, Yugoslavia and the republics of the former Soviet Union. Once the imperial power withdraws, the peoples within the borders must decide how—and whether—they wish to live together or on their own (*The Toronto Star*, December 28, 1992).

Canada and the United States are both the orphans of the British Empire in some respects. Unlike its North American counterpart, however, nothing was said in Canada about expanding the scope of the public sphere to take in the tired, the weak or the huddled masses, all of whom were self-evidently endowed by their creator with certain unalienable rights among which are life, liberty and the pursuit of happiness. Indeed, many ethnic groups in Canada presumed they were unquestionably better than others, not just as good. Yet, again unlike the United States, Canadian society was relatively free of overt manifestations of ethnicism and racism—free of lynchings, free of tar-and-featherings, free of other forms of aggravated physical violence from the host population and, above all, free of the pressure to assimilate into a dominant culture. In the United States, there was a public openness and private closedness; while in Canada, there was a public closedness and private openness.

Because of an orientation towards preferred settlers, it was relatively difficult for many people and groups to gain admittance into Canada. However, once arrived, for the most part, these people in Canada were allowed to live relatively free of overt persecution within the confines of their ethnic conclave. The general attitude was one of "live and let live," as long as the differentiated cultures remained hard-working in their character, compliant with the laws of the land and non-threatening to their French and English charter group hosts. As a consequence, social life developed a distinct tone of conservativism that caused Kaspar Naegele to suggest that, "compared to the United States, Canada is a country of greater caution, reserve, and restraint" (1965: 501).

Other scholars have also duly noted that Canada seems to have always been less publicly dynamic than the United States and that its early political history from 1776 on involved the defeat of radical reform, and, consequently, some of the traditionalist "Tory" values which declined in the United States linger to this day in Canada. Frank Underhill described the difference in the following terms:

The mental climate of English Canada in its early formative years was determined by men who were fleeing from the practical application of the doctrines that all men are born equal and are endowed by their creator with certain unalienable rights amongst which are life, liberty and the pursuit of happiness.... In Canada we have no revolutionary tradition; and our historians, political scientists, and philosophers have assiduously tried to educate us to be proud of this fact (1960: 12).

There was no specific rights doctrine animating the design and struggle of Canadian life. Rather, in the context of old-world loyalist sentiments, Canada became a "community of communities," united by the structure of work and survival. It stood for the internal preservation of differences, even when those differences despised one another, as they often did. In fact, as Underhill suggested, the strong attachments to the British Empire on the part of those of English origin, and to their former national cultures on the part of those of European origin, were essential if Canada was to remain a separate entity from the United States. The American melting pot, with its radical breakdown of national ties and old forms of stratification into a homogeneous culture, would have endangered the loyalist-conservative tradition of Canadian life (see also Lipset, 1963). So originally, heterogeneity and the preservation of differences in Canada was a more or less calculated move born out of an ethnic chauvinism as opposed to a belief in ethnic equality. It was only later that the preservation of difference, which promoted ethnic segregation and intense ethnic loyalties in Canada, evolved into an official celebration of difference, symbolized in the image of the ethnic mosaic.

A Model of Industry to a Model of Equity

By 1968, Prime Minister Pierre Elliot Trudeau had dubbed Canada "a loose confederation of shopping malls." This rather cryptic remark graphically depicts the diversity he and his colleagues eventually attempted to legislatively define as "a multicultural country in a bilingual framework" (Government of Canada, 1971). Today, Canada as a multicultural country with the bilingual framework of English and French is still dominant in the sphere of the political economy, if not in the sphere of everyday life. We have instituted such things as heritage language programs in our public schools to reinforce the value of others. So, now it is not cryptic in the least to say that the orphans of empire have chosen to live together in a loose shopping mall-like confederation—in the sense that Canada is now a panoply of diverse peoples and languages.

In its best reading, it is now by definition a mosaic of ethnicity based on consensual pluralism, where cultural difference in ethnic modes is positively valued; a multicultural nation that espouses the desire for the harmony of difference, every kind of difference; people who—before anything else and apart from their differences—are unified in their allegiance to equality. Our modern educational system, for example, now teaches us from early on that we are not only to acknowledge the differences of others but we are now to respect and celebrate them as well; we are to be open to all kinds of people, all kinds of life-styles, all kinds of ideologies; and there is no enemy in modern life other than the person who is not open to other persons. In this regard, Canada has become more of a public place for the many than a private preserve for a few. We have come more and more to internalize the belief that, given access to an equal chance, all creeds and cultures will flourish in the public arena and make their unique contributions to the whole.

This change in social psychology is, of course, connected to changes in social conditions. Canada has evolved from an industry-based to a technology-based society—from a society of machines to a society of electronic automation, from human power to information power, from mach speed to electric speed (Benthall, 1976). So, we might say, the model of the rational and industrious person who best suits the regime came to fruition with industrialization. With the rise of a post-industrial, automated society, the country has gradually moved from a model of industry structured by work and survival to a "model of equitable participation" structured by abundance and surfeit resources.

At a time marked by keen international competition, no nation can afford to squander any of its potential human resources. So, for instance, like other advanced societies, Canada has introduced specific domestic initiatives and policies—such as, employment equity, affirmative action, and so forth—designed to remove the obstacles and overcome the barriers that impede the development of skills, thereby helping to bring about more equality of opportunity for this and future generations. The notion is that increasing the equality of opportunity will have a cascading effect in society—enhancing the development of individual skills and at the same time expanding the amount of trained ability that is available. Theoretically, then, we subscribe to the inherent dignity of all human beings regardless of existing circumstances; we believe that, unobstructed, the sons and daughters of the unskilled, helpless "have-nots" of today can become the "haves" of tomorrow.

Social scientists call this phenomenon "intergenerational mobility." We see sons and daughters routinely achieve a higher occupational status than their fathers and mothers. Sons of porters become lawyers and doctors. Daughters of seamstresses become professors and parliamentarians. Intergenerational mobility is a primary factor in economic growth in our society. Of course, intergenerational mobility is contingent upon what social scientists call "life-chances"—that is, the access to opportunities for education, training, portability, and such—where daughters and sons are not only willing but able to activate the achievement ethic of their parents. When high-calibre life-chances exist, we can, and often do, take as much pride in plebeian or unrefined roots as we do in aristocratic ones, for neither is thought necessary to determine one's own fate. Not only isn't there anything wrong with ancestors who were slaves, indigents, outcasts, or fugitives cast ashore by a former imperial power, it's actually thought to add a little substance and texture to one's pedigree, so to speak. The descendants of the slaves and outcasts of yesterday are the premiers, deputy premiers and governor-generals of today.

In connection with this, we have come to recognize the importance of a system of merit where higher occupational levels are open to all social groups on the basis of ability. We promote a system of merit—as opposed to a system of privilege or inheritance—because it is thought to foster human initiative. A system of merit accentuates what Ralph Turner (1960) called "contest mobility," where the most able win the social rewards (i.e., jobs, incomes) of society—as opposed to "sponsored mobility" where an established elite select their own replacements to the top positions. By maximizing life-chance in the form of education and training, we believe we can activate contest mobility, where the ablest people get to the top positions and, therefore, promote intergenerational mobility, where sons and daughters achieve a higher occupational status than their parents. Insofar as this is the case, there may be no greater engine to propel Canadian multiculturalism forward than people who feel they have a vested interest and competitive stake in its structures and institutions, and who can pass this on to their progeny. In this argument, perhaps the best industrial-economic strategy our society could have is to create an environment of equitable participation, where all people are able to go as far as their abilities will allow.

A "Value-Added" System to a "Value-Generating" System

In the past, when industriousness and compliance with the sanctioned Tory traditions of the land was a paramount and indisputable criteria for accepting newcomers, it was effortless to engage in targeted or selective immigration. The welcome mat for newcomers was contingent upon what they had to offer, what need they could fill in regard to national development and how well they were perceived to be able to fit into the country's conservative format. Therefore, preferential treatment was par for the course, and any inequities in the immigration selection process were justified on the grounds of the national interest. Today, however, it is no longer merely a question of what the newcomer has to offer in the mission to build a great nation. Instead, we now routinely believe that part of a nation's greatness can be judged on how compassionate and open-handed it is with its newcomers, as well as other vulnerable segments of society. Thus, the strength of contemporary immigration now lies in the fact that it can afford the opportunity for all who come to our shores from other lands to preserve what they are and to become more than they were previously allowed to be. This, of course, fits well with Canada's modern commitment to its overall principles of respect for cultural diversity. It uses multiculturalism as an instrument to promote equality in the expansion of opportunities for newcomers and to foster anti-racist policies (Multiculturalism and Citizenship Canada, 1991 [a] and [b]).

Over the years, then, Canada has undergone a paradigm shift from a model of industriousness to a model of equitable participation. This required a shift in the paradigm for immigration, as well as a shift from what we might call a "value-added" system, where newcomers are required to add to the national skills-pool, to a "value-generating" system that reaches out to empower people. However, the shifting paradigm has also precipitated a crisis of leadership. The old value-added immigration system was built on the premise of short-term labour market needs while a value-generating system emphasizes life-chances, contest mobility and intergenerational mobility. The old system sought out individuals who had already reached a certain level of technical achievement; a value-generating system relies on individuals who can continually upgrade and develop. The old value-added immigration system produced a skilled society; the new system produces a learning society. In a skills-oriented society, immigration was a centre-piece for social planning and population policy. In a learning-oriented society, a population policy is the centre-piece of the immigration system and social planning.

While immigration policy in Canada originally developed out of the need to target and select industrious types in order to transform a wilderness into a nation, it is no longer constrained by this provision. First of all, competing for skilled immigrants on a global migration market is an uncertain proposition at best, when other societies have more inducements for potential newcomers. Canada would likely lose a global competition for valued skills today to immigrant-receiving societies that are either more affluent, like the United States, or have a better standard of living, like Australia. Furthermore, given the rapid pace of technological change in modern times, and the advent of a cyberspace or information-based economy, the immigration system could be an obstacle to the advancement of Canadian society if it opted to invite only those with preferred marketable skills because many of today's needed skills will be obsolete tomorrow (see Chapter 8). Thus, this country's international competitiveness cannot be ensured by importing talent from without, but rather by developing it from within—within the framework of an overall population plan that maximizes life-chances and mobilizes the creative energies of the whole.

So the rules of engagement with respect to immigration have now irrevocably changed. In the face of advancing technologies and competitive world markets, it could very well be counterproductive to import people with specific skills rather than to develop the skills of the people we import. Indeed, in an age of global migration and technological revolution, Canada's comparative advantage lies in enacting its democratic ethos in the form of an immigration system that can keep pace with an ever-changing environment and by facilitating skills-development through open, continuous education programs and cradle-to-grave learning systems. This not only downplays the need for employment-related admission criteria but also ensures a greater degree of productivity than the present assessment process is meant to achieve. We do not need to bring in skilled immigrants to Canada as much as we need to create a system that is conducive to the continuous cultivation of immigrant skills.

Social Darwinism and Immigration Policy

It is well documented that the British government viewed emigration to its colonies during the pre-Confederation period, especially Canada and Australia, as an extension of its penal system. Canada was a dumping ground for convicted criminals pardoned or banished to the "New Land" as well as a release valve for England's chronic social problems of massive unemployment and poverty. And emigration continued to be the solution to pauperism well into the twentieth century. This prompted the first French-Canadian attack on immigration policy early in this century. It was spearheaded by Henri Bourassa, a French-nationalist member of parliament, who charged that the purpose of immigration was to swamp the French minority in a sea of "drunkards, paupers, loafers, and jailbirds" from England (Petersen, 1965: 41). Thus, for many in Canadian society at the time, immigration raised questions about genetics and the dilution of superior bloodlines by inferior ones and, at the societal level, about heredity, breeding, racial qualities, tribal instincts and their affect on the Canadian social order. This British colonial policy may be linked to the classic joke about the foreign national seeking landed immigrant status in Canada at a visa office abroad: the visa officer asks, "Do you have a criminal record?", to which the applicant responds, "I didn't think that was a requirement anymore!"

Today, of course, we have incorporated distributive justice into our point of view on the proper order and structure of society. In short, there are no inferior bloodlines; there are only inferior opportunities in education, training, lifestyle and so on. This ideological position is not contradicted by the fact that the connection between immigration and biology still lingers in the collective psyche of the nation. On the contrary, the fact that we make anecdotes and jokes about it indicates that this connection can no longer be so routinely accomplished in everyday life. It is no longer good form to give serious expression to illiberal sentiments or to connect quality too closely with genetics. As a rule, we no longer speak of inferior people; we speak of obstacles in life that make people inferior, and there is a practical concern that there be no obstructions to the development of peoples' abilities or to the ability of the ablest people to get to the top levels of society.

Consequently, all things being equal, we have a problem identifying with any perceived inequality between groups or with any perceived discrimination of one group by another. Inequality and discrimination are treated negatively. Even those who still believe that certain groups are inherently superior or inferior to others recognize that their belief is not formally sanctioned by the majority opinion. Majority values are now formally prohibitive of any kind of racial and ethnic ranking. This does not necessarily translate into a commitment to open immigration, however. While migrants are not normally viewed as inherently inferior today, it is still not unusual for immigration to be regarded as a detriment to both the advancement of society and the well-being of its individual members. In this respect, the concerns surrounding immigration are not framed around matters of race and ethnicity, but rather around the matters of volume or scale or other potential encumbrances to the peak performance of society.

This was not always the case. It was the appointment in 1896 of Sir Clifford Sifton as Minister of the Interior, whose department was responsible for lands administration and immigration, that crystallized the original Canadian interest in immigration. The answer to the question of what kinds of persons best suited the regime was relatively straightforward in the mind of Sifton. "When I speak of quality," he said in 1922, in what became a well-known speech, "I have in mind something that is quite different from what is in the mind of the average writer or speaker upon the question of immigration. I think a stalwart peasant in a sheep-skin coat, born on the soil, whose forefathers have been farmers for generations, with a stout wife and half-a-dozen children, is good quality" (Dafoe, 1931: 319).

Sir Clifford's view was actually quite conventional for his day, insofar as he associated biology and biological traits with specific aptitudes. With the creation of The North Atlantic Trading Company, the spreading of information about Canada throughout Europe and arranging for immigrants to travel to new homes in the Canadian West, Sifton ensured the settlement of the empty western frontiers with producing farmers. In the first decade of this century, Canada admitted thousands of Slavic farmers, mostly stalwart peasants, because the country was in need of them to build the wheat economy. At the same time, Italians were shunned and designated undesirable persons by Sir Clifford Sifton instructed his people in the immigration department to keep them out. After World War II, when it was determined that the country was in need of a massive influx of construction workers, Canadian immigration policy was reversed and Italians were cordially invited to join the community of communities (Pierre Berton, "Compassion? Not in Our Immigration Policy," *The Toronto Star*, Oct. 3, 1992).

It was on the basis of a belief in the biological aptitude for nation building that Canadian political leaders first argued for restricting immigration of blacks from the United States and elsewhere. In 1815, for example, the Nova Scotia Assembly protested to the British government against bringing in more "negroes" from Bermuda. It was stated that "the proportion of Africans already in this country is productive of many inconveniences; and [that] the introduction of more must tend to the discouragement of white labourers and servants, as well as the establishment of a separate and marked class of people, unfitted by nature to this climate, or to an association with the rest of His Majesty's Colonists" (Malarek, 1987: 16). This may have resulted in the old joke about the immigration officer who granted landed status to an African: "Welcome to Canada. You'll be happy to know that there's no discrimination here. We treat all of our blacks well. All six of them." The punchline is, of course, markedly different from its patented (southern) United States version: "If there are none in that tree over there, there are none in town." But, they both incorporate a sense of historical duplicity in the topic of race relations.

Interestingly, the only remnants of biological politics that still seem to linger unabated in the Canadian collective conscience lie in the scores of immigration jokes that poke fun at either the social history or the social and ethnic make-up of Canadian society, or both. Jokes can harbour latent beliefs or former beliefs to which people no longer consciously subscribe. In this sense, there is recognition but no embrace; there is understanding but at a loose and comfortable distance. And in some instances, as above, immigration jokes are indications of a rather serious historical circumstance.

Beginning in the 1880s, thousands of Chinese labourers were brought to Canada to work on the Trans-Atlantic Railway, and then they were rebuked and cast aside. By 1885, a head tax was imposed on Chinese immigrants at the rate of $50 per person. By 1904, thoughts of being overrun by the "Yellow Peril" prompted a raise in the head tax to $500 (a humiliating and almost impossible amount for the time). In 1923, The Chinese Exclusion Act was passed by parliament, forbidding Chinese immigration entirely. This prevented many people who were already here from bringing their families over to join them. The Exclusion Act was in effect until 1947, with the proviso the same year from Prime Minister Wilfrid Laurier that Canadian immigration was not intended to change the racial make-up of the country.

Over the succeeding years, prospective black immigrants and expectant black refugees also came to be defined as an "inadmissible class of persons" and were denied entry into Canada by frontline officers. Again, the primary justification for exclusion was that blacks were not biologically equipped to adapt to the Canadian climate (Kruter and Davis, 1978). Even the great immigration period before World War I, when it was announced that any healthy person with $50 was admissible, did not amend this situation. It is well documented in immigration archives that black Americans were commonly subjected to intensive medical examinations—which in some cases were fraudulent—and then sent packing (Pierre Burton, *ibid.*).

No Canadians protested these policies, for the ideas of innately superior and inferior people had not yet been neutralized by the democratic ethos and the institutionalization of equality and multicul-turalism. Thus, by 1952, Canada's politics of exclusion was boldly enshrined in the Immigration Act under the auspice and leadership of Prime Minister Mackenzie King, who declared, in a House of Commons preamble debate on May 1, 1947, that Canada is perfectly within her rights in selecting the persons whom we regard as desirable future citizens. He added, "There will, I am sure, be general agreement with the view that the people of Canada do not wish, as a result of mass immigration, to make any fundamental alteration in the character of our population."

Race theories have justified population control and the politics and policies of exclusion throughout a major portion of Canadian history. This still persists today to a degree. Darwin's scientific principle of evolution was transferred mindlessly to the social context by Spencer and others, who argued that through struggle and conflict certain societies and groups came out on top. Any interference with the process of struggle would have an adverse effect on social development, encouraging poorer quality stock to increase at the expense of the superior. The books of Herbert Spencer, for instance, expounding on what has come to be known as "Social Darwinism," were read by millions of North Americans, and he had many outspoken disciples among writers, scholars, judges, politicians, editors, clergymen and businessmen. Superior races and groups could become polluted by mixing with inferior races and groups or by social policies which did anything to alleviate the struggle. It was the Nordic and Aryan races that were elevated to the highest-ranking human beings by these doctrines. Through such theories, imperialism and aggression were viewed as serving a principle of general social evolution (Porter, 1965: 62).

All of the original points of view with regard to immigration in Canada were dominated by social order and population control issues, in the sense that it was taken for granted that some people possessed a biological aptitude for nation-building work and some people did not. Who these people were was a matter of dispute. The English often had one idea and the French, another. But no one disputed the idea of inherited biological qualities or the now-ridiculous idea that building a great nation was akin to the work of a "stock-breeder." Indeed, two decades into the twentieth century, the very possibility of an assimilation process that could absorb and integrate the mixed multitude of immigrants in Canada was still being questioned. In his book entitled *The Central European Immigrant in Canada* published in 1929, Robert England put it this way:

If we mean by assimilation a process that moulds racial stocks into something else we are flying in the face of what every stock-breeder knows....
No melting pot can make a Slav, an Italian, or Frenchman, an Anglo-
Saxon. Racial qualities, vices and instincts will remain. They may however
be modified by environment, sublimated into some other form (England,
1929: 174).

Social biology, and its connection to racial hierarchy, has historically been a fundamental part of the conventional wisdom and collective consciousness in the Western world. Even the great Canadian J.
S. Woodsworth, who founded the Cooperative Commonwealth Federation (CCF) as the political arm of the labour union movement and
was later to be called the saint of Canadian politics, was not immune
to the social biology of his time. His book *Stranger within Our Gates*,
written in 1908, is a curious mixture of racial ideas and compassion
for the tens of thousands of European settlers who were streaming
into Winnipeg under the most severe conditions of poverty and
deprivation. The book is an important one in Canadian social history
in that it reflects the general attitude of the times regarding racial
taxonomy and racial hierarchy. All racial groups (many of which we
call ethnic today) were analyzed in turn with an account of their
relation to other races or sub-races, their language, the level of their
culture, their diseases and especially their hereditary traits. For
Woodsworth, English orphans and pauper children with their "inherited tendencies to evil" were "a very doubtful acquisition to Canada."
He expressed the fear "that any large immigration of this class must
lead to degeneration of our Canadian people." Woodsworth seems to
confirm the general attitude that Europe was separated into superior
races—Scandinavians, French, German and British—and inferior
ones—Russian, Slavic, Italian and Turkish. The Scandinavians, he
concluded, "accustomed to the rigors of an northern climate, clean-
blooded, thrifty, ambitious and hard-working," would be certain of
success. On the other hand, Woodsworth concluded that, while the
Poles and Ukrainians (then known as "Galicians," imported into Canada to farm the empty prairies and viciously attacked in the Canadian
press as "disgusting creatures," "social sewage" and "human vermin"),
were "distinctly a lower grade," they did possess as a matter of
breeding "a physical endurance bred of centuries of peasant life." Of
Syrians and Armenians, Woodsworth quoted Dr. Allan McLaughlin:
"Their wits are sharpened by generations of commercial dealings,"
but "these parasites from the near East ... are ... detrimental and
burdensome." Of Orientals, there was no question—they could not
be assimilated into polite society. And in the discussion of blacks, he

rejoiced, "we may be thankful we have no 'Negro problem' in Canada" (Woodsworth, 1909: 61–169).

In this latter exaltation, Woodsworth corroborated the conservative thinking of the Fathers of the Confederation, who were determined to avoid the features of the American system which they believed had helped to provoke the bloody Civil War. Indeed, in Canadian history, there was a clear determination and calculated federal agenda to prevent the radical politics that spawned the ominous plague of the American race problem and, at the same time, circumvent this value contradiction of liberal democracy by controlling the make-up of the general population. In other words, they forestalled a Negro problem and the attendant struggle of liberal-democratic consciousness by excluding Negroes.

The conservative Canadian agenda, of course, was played out almost entirely in the arena of immigration and immigration regulations and controls based on the theory of social evolution and reputed biological traits, which allowed the Canadian government to begin to formalize its racial sentiments under the guise of science. Thus, in 1869, two years after Canada entered nationhood, the federal government passed the country's first Immigration Act. This institutionalized selective immigration and would foreshadow the eventual rigid restrictions on entry that dominated the 1952 Immigration Act and the blatant Social Darwinian policies aimed at keeping out various nationalities, especially visible minority groups, on the grounds of absorptive capacity.

Section 5 of the 1952 Act provided a sophisticated update on the prohibited classes, including mental defectives and the mentally ill or those with a history of such illness, epileptics, persons afflicted with tuberculosis, trachoma or any contagious disease and immigrants who were dumb, blind or otherwise physically impaired. Entry by some in these categories was permitted if they had sufficient means of support or were taken care of by family members so as not to become public charges. Also excluded were persons who had been convicted of any crime involving moral turpitude. Barred were prostitutes, homosexuals, pimps, persons seeking entry for immoral purposes, professional beggars and vagrants, persons who were public charges or judged likely to become such, alcoholics, drug addicts and persons who had trafficked in drugs. In addition, persons deemed likely to advocate the overthrow of the system of government by force or subversion, persons who were or had been associated with any subversive organization, spies and saboteurs were denied admission. Meanwhile,

Section 61 of the Act provided the *coup de grâce* of social biology in Canada with a closed immigration program, giving the government power to limit or prohibit the entry of immigrants for reasons of nationality, citizenship, ethnic group, class or geographic area of origin, peculiar customs, habits, modes of life or methods of holding property, unsuitability with regard to climatic, economic, social, industrial, educational, labour or health factors or probable inability to become readily assimilated.

The Fathers of Confederation never had any theoretical doubt about targeting select newcomers on the basis of racial and hereditary traits, because they believed explicitly or implicitly that different groups possessed different biological aptitudes for nation-building work. There was no compunction about registering their complaints when it appeared that the inferior stocks of the world were being unloaded on Canadian soil. Their mandate as political statesmen, conferred by the Constitution, was to institute "peace, order and good government." It was that simple. Nothing was said about welcoming newcomers with open arms; therefore, the struggle of conscience that erupted and transformed the United States never occurred in Canada. Instead, national interests and political expediency automatically overruled any noble or humane sentiment that may have arisen. And this official stance remained intact until the latter half of the twentieth century.

Thus, an internal training session "fact sheet" memorandum acknowledges that immediately following ratification of the infamous Immigration Act of 1952, Miss Philomena Braithwaite, a lady of African descent hailing from the country of Barbados, was denied an immigrant visa to Canada on the grounds that she was "climatically" unsuited and could not adapt to the frosty Canadian environment. With the aid of frontline officers, Miss Braithwaite performed the first full pirouette with a half-twist on the Canadian immigration turnstile, landing right back in sunny Barbados. The biological politics of everyday life in Canada became the full-fledged social policy of exclusion.

Most people in the immigration business today who can actually remember when climate was a criteria for inadmissibility (a policy on the books in Canada until 1967) can hardly believe it possible. But it is only now, with the hindsight afforded by the passage of time, that ulterior motives become crystal clear. It seems obvious now that establishing climate as a criteria for admissibility and inadmissibility effectively limited the migration of blacks and other Third World peoples, including East Indians and Chinese. The agenda was population control and had little or nothing to do with cold weather.

Universal Access and the Recognition of a Common Humanity: The Case of Convention Refugees

Since its highwater mark in 1952, Social Darwinism has been in general decline. There has been a diminution in support for immigration on the basis of race and ethnicity or any other standard of biological aptitude. Conversely, there has also been a general elevation of support for standards of universality in terms of equal distribution of rights and recognition of a common humanity. This transformation in the thought and collective consciousness of the nation has been accompanied by its own special nuances and pitfalls.

Consider the case of Convention Refugees. As a signatory to the 1951 United Nations' Geneva Convention and the 1967 Protocol Relating to the Status of Refugees, Canada now has an obligation to protect refugees on humanitarian grounds and has established formal procedures to give sanctuary to those in need of protection. As defined in the Geneva Convention a Convention Refugee

> means any person who, by reason of a well-founded fear of persecution for reasons of race, religion, nationality, membership in a particular social group or political opinion,
>
> (a) is outside the country of his nationality and is unable or, by reason of that fear, is unwilling to avail himself of the protection of that country, or
>
> (b) not having a country of nationality, is outside the country of his former habitual residence and is unable or, by reason of that fear, is unwilling to return to that country.

The Canadian Immigration Act now also includes the provisions of the Convention definition which exclude from protection those who have committed war crimes, serious non-political crimes and acts contrary to the purposes and principles of the United Nations. Furthermore, the Act provides for the cessation of refugee status when protection is no longer needed.

Persons outside Canada who are in need of protection can approach the nearest Canadian Embassy or Consulate. When individuals make their refugee claims to Canadian officials overseas, the officials act as proctors for the turnstiles. They decide whether an applicant meets the criteria of the Geneva Convention, and they make arrangements for the re-settlement of overseas refugees with a view towards to their eventual self-sufficiency in Canada. (Annual government-sponsored refugee plans to determine the appropriate selection levels are to be made in consultation with the United Nations High Commissioner for Refugees [UNHCR], provincial governments, the Department of External Affairs and interested non-governmental organizations [NGO's] in Canada.)

Theoretically, it works the same way in Canada. In practice, however, the refugee system in Canada has been clogged by people who have left their country of origin in search of greater economic opportunities, and make illegitimate claims to Convention refugee status because they want to jump the regular immigration queue. They know that the wheels of the system turn so slowly that there is little chance they will ever be sent home. In the 1980s, the system was being crushed by the increasing pressure of the economic migrants who claimed refugee status to enter the country. This created a huge backlog of refugees because the system was unable to meet the demand. Under the process, a refugee would be examined by a senior immigration officer under oath, a transcript of the proceedings would be prepared and forwarded to Ottawa to the Refugee Advisory Committee appointed by the Minister, the transcripts would be reviewed and a recommendation as to acceptance or rejection made to the Minister.

In 1985, the Supreme Court of Canada struck down this process in the case of *Harbanjanir Singh* v. *The Minister of Employment and Immigration* ([1985] 1 C.C.R. 178). The court in that decision ruled that the Canadian Charter of Rights and Freedoms applied to all people inside Canada, even if their status had not yet been determined. The clause of the Charter with which the court dealt in that case was Section 7, which states "everybody has the right to life, liberty, and security, and the right not to be deprived thereof except in accordance with the principles of fundamental justice."

After the determination that Section 7 applied to the refugee process, the court went on to review the procedures of the then-existing refugee system. The court held that the procedure adopted by the Minister did not provide adequate opportunity for the claimant to state his or her case and that the opportunity for less than a "full hearing" was being provided. This decision resulted in a further slowing of the ability to process refugees, since it meant that applicants had to be given an automatic oral hearing without a preliminary paper review of their qualifications. At the same time, increasing numbers of people were coming to Canada and claiming refugee status. Because prospective refugees could not be sent back to their countries of origin without first having their claims heard, refugee claimants were allowed to stay and obtain employment while their claims were being processed. Many thousands of people came to Canada, often from countries that *prima facie* did not create refugees, while many thousands more had been in Canada for up to four years without determination of their cases.

In a stated attempt to maintain the integrity of the immigration policies of Canada, and following the advice and counsel of senior officials in Ottawa, the government decided that it would be inappropriate to grant amnesty to those who came here not as legitimate refugees but in order to by-pass the normal immigration process. The decision not to grant amnesty was partially predicated on the philosophy of global migratory awareness—if there were a general amnesty, it would encourage another flow of illegitimate claimants who would again clog the system and wait for the next amnesty (Minister of Employment and Immigration, the Honourable Barbara McDougall, "Press Release," Dec. 28, 1988). After refusing to grant a general amnesty, a process was legislated for dealing with the backlog. At the commencement of the backlog-clearance program in early spring of 1990, the Immigration Commission estimated that there were approximately 85,000 backlog cases, a figure later revised to 125,000. As the numbers of unresolved refugee cases continued to mount during the 1990s, the policy makers were compelled to invent an immigration version of "three-card monte," where they simply hid the backlog of cases from critical public scrutiny by shifting them from under the cover of the Canadian Immigration Commission (CIC) to the cover of the Convention Refugee Determination Division (CRDD). Then, through this slight-of-hand, they were able to close the Refugee Backlog Clearance sweatshops, magically reinforcing their claim to having resolved (or the false impression they have resolved) the immigration backlog problem.

The Backlog Process

The first step in clearing the backlog involved the interviewing of the claimant by an immigration official, who determined if there were reasons to grant immediate landing on the basis of humanitarian and compassionate considerations. The frontline immigration officials were provided with guidelines in order to make this determination. Originally, the guidelines for the initial interview were restricted, so that landing could be granted only in situations where a refugee claimant could claim sponsorship as a member of a family already in Canada or, if the individual were a high-profile sports or cultural figure, could claim he or she came from a repressive country.

On March 5, 1990, the Federal Court of Canada Trial Division, in a case called *Yhap* v. *Canada* (Minister of Employment and Immigration), struck down the restrictive criteria used for the review process and required that the Minister apply the broader criteria developed by the officials in the (I.E. & I.S.) Immigration Commission manuals. These criteria included family relationships (not only blood relatives, but *de facto* family), severe consequences if returned to their country of origin, public policy (which remains essentially undefined), and consideration for those who have established close ties to Canada and have severed ties with their own country. As a result of the *Yhap* decision, it was necessary to re-interview all those who had been rejected during their initial interview. This, of course, meant a further increase in the backlog.

In an attempt to relieve the pressure in the refugee system and re-distribute the numbers, the government as an incentive agreed that those refugees who would leave the country voluntarily would receive a letter which would do two things: guarantee an interview with a Canadian visa officer abroad conducted in a timely manner, and further assured them that they would be given every consideration with regard to their experiences in Canada. Canadian visa officers were to look at the applicant's work history, language skill, general roots and adaption to Canadian society in making their recommendations for landing. What made this option attractive for many claimants, especially from non-refugee-producing countries, was the promise that, from start to finish, they could obtain permanent residence in Canada within six months. As opposed to languishing in the refugee backlog, many people accepted this good-faith option. It is public knowledge that only a few individuals succeeded in doing this—leaving Canada with a voluntary departure letter, attending a visa office abroad, and coming back into the country within a matter of months (while with the Immigration Commission, I met only one). Figures are not publicly available on how many people in this group were denied landing or were still waiting for a determination when the backlog offices were closed.

Those who did proceed with their refugee claims were scheduled for an inquiry before an adjudicator and a member of the Immigration Refugee Board. If one of the panel decided that the claimant had a credible basis and there was no reason not to grant landing, the claimant could apply for landing, and it was granted subject to medical and criminal background checks. The test for credible basis refers in a broad sense to any credible or trustworthy evidence upon which the refugee division might determine the claimant to be a Convention refugee.

The backlog clearance program was to have processed approximately 125,000 refugee claims between 1986 and 1989 at a cost of $100 million, and it was anticipated that 20,000 bogus refugees would be deported. By the end of 1990, senior officials in Ottawa announced that only about one-third of the cases had been heard and less than two hundred fraudulent claimants had been removed, while costs rose to $179 million. At this point, a House of Commons committee estimated it would take at least six years and at least $600 million to clear up the log-jam.

This begged the question as to whether utilizing the backlog program rather than invoking a general amnesty had, in fact, protected the integrity of the system. In many cases, those who entered into the backlog process came to Canada with valid claims at the time of their arrival but, due to the government's inability to process their claims in a timely fashion, events may have changed the circumstances surrounding their claims. An individual, for example, who came to Canada from an East Bloc country in 1987 claiming refugee status on the basis of political persecution, would have had, at that time, a good prospect of having his or her claim accepted. That same person would have little chance of acceptance at a later date, as the relevant time for determining the potential of such persecution is not when refugee status is claimed but rather when the claim is heard.

Under these circumstances, the potential existed not only for the refugee system to be clogged by illegitimate claims but for the system to also clog itself by making otherwise legitimate claims illegitimate. The worst-case scenario is where there is no order or justice—a system that neither prevents manifestly unfounded claims (MUC's) nor expedites the well-founded ones. The issue of how to handle the refugee backlog still lingers as perhaps the most contentious and problematic issue confronting the public-policy process.

The New Refugee Process

Concurrent with the backlog initiatives, the government promised a general review of the determination system and legislative measures to deal with the growing influx of new refugees. In May 1987, the parliamentary Bill C–55 was tabled, which proposed radical changes to the 1976 Immigration Act with respect to the refugee status determination system. Under the terms of this Bill, the refugee process was to be altered so as to deal with the problems associated with the original backlog, while at the same time meeting the challenge of being a more judicious system—the order-justice problem. In particular, the refugee claimant was to be dealt with on an expedited basis.

Bill C–55 introduced a new, two-phased system, purporting to be "streamlined" and capable of combatting the crush of economic migrants who claimed refugee status to enter the country. The tabling of the Bill caused an outcry from the labour movement, churches and immigrant and refugee groups. While most acknowledged that the existing system could no longer cope with the demand, the aid groups maintained that the government was changing its previous policy of "openness."

The second series of events precipitating remedial legislation began in the spring of 1986 with the arrival of the Tamils off the coast of Newfoundland. This caused much consternation and discussion regarding the control of "our" borders. Then, in June 1987, 174 South Asiatics (Sikhs) landed secretly on the shores of Nova Scotia and sought refugee status, causing the discussion to heighten. This resulted in the August tabling of Bill C–84 in which the government claimed increased powers to cope with spontaneous landings on Canadian shores by vessels carrying migrants. It was enacted to combat unscrupulous individuals who profited by transporting people to Canada under false pretences. It increased the penalties for such actions and gave the government broader powers to prevent vessels carrying these migrants from arriving at Canadian ports of entry. Both bills received Royal Assent in 1988 and came into effect January 1, 1989.

Bill C–55 purportedly introduced a new and revitalized refugee determination system. Under the new system, a process that once took years to complete was designed to be handled in weeks. In the first-phase or first-level eligibility and credibility hearing, immigration officials would quickly determine whether there was any merit at all to a claim, preferably right at the port-of-entry or an in-land hearings office. Theoretically, this would quickly weed out all of the manifestly unfounded claims that had previously clogged the system, cutting them off at the pass as it were. Only those claims that met the initial eligibility and credibility standards were to proceed to the second phase or full hearing at the Convention Refugee Determination Division, where Convention refugee status was determined among the claims forwarded by the Immigration Department.

Most refugee claims in Canada originate at a port of entry. The claimant informs an immigration officer of his or her intentions to make a refugee claim and to reside permanently in Canada. In almost all cases, the claimant is not in possession of a visa to enter Canada. Provided the claimants are not a danger to society and it appears that they will attend the inquiry, they will be released. Otherwise they will be held in custody subject to weekly detention reviews. Refugee claims can also be made at an in-land office, before or after the expiration of a (visitor's) visa, and claimants are subject to the same conditions of release.

The refugee process is first initiated by the claimant completing a personal information form. The form is reviewed by a case officer. If there exists a *prima facie* case that the claimant is credible (based upon the written story contained in the information form and the country where the persecution is claimed), the case file will be forwarded to the refugee division for a full hearing before the Refugee Board. If the claim appears not to be credible, an inquiry will be held before an adjudicator and a member of the Refugee Board, both of whom are technically independent of immigration authorities. At the inquiry level, the claimant must establish only that he or she is eligible to make a refugee claim and that there is some credible evidence upon which a Refugee Board might determine the claimant to be a Convention refugee. If the claimant fails to establish eligibility or credibility at the inquiry, he or she will be excluded from Canada and departure or removal will be arranged. If found to be credible, the claim will be forwarded to the refugee division for a full hearing.

The refugee hearing is held before two members of the Immigration and Refugee Board, an independent board established under the new system, consisting of political appointees. At both the inquiry and the hearing, the onus is on the claimant to establish the essential elements of the claim by presenting his or her own evidence, subject to cross-examination, and establishing both subjective and objective criteria for determining persecution. In addition to *viva voce* evidence of witnesses, other evidence in the form of documents are often introduced. This documentary evidence is comprised most often of reports from international human rights organizations such as Amnesty International and America's Watch. Also, the refugee division maintains documentation centres in each of Canada's major cities and compiles profiles on countries that are most often the focus of refugee claims.

The decision at both the inquiry and hearing levels may be brought to the Federal Court of Appeal on arguments of law or law and fact upon leave being granted by the court. The body of jurisprudence for the courts has tended to widen the tests to be applied in the determination of Convention refugee status to include such dangers as domestic violence against women, not specifically addressed by the Convention definition. As these decisions are from courts of superior jurisdiction, the legal principles they enunciate are binding on the boards and upon the inquiry panels.

The "new" Refugee Determination System had a budget of approximately $80 million in 1989, and a refugee claimant arriving at a port of entry in Toronto or Vancouver in January of 1989 could have expected to have a hearing take place within four to six weeks. The same claimant arriving in September of 1990 could not expect a full hearing for at least 6 months to one year, as the new backlog slowly enlarged and gained momentum. By early 1991, however, the new backlog was growing exponentially, and the time frame for the completion of cases was again a matter of years, not weeks, as was intended. By mid–1991, the costs to Canadian taxpayers was $2 billion and still growing (*The Toronto Sun*, May 9, 1991).

There were ancillary costs as well, both material and psychological. Since new refugee claimants who had not had a first-level hearing to determine a credible basis for their claim were not legally entitled to work in Canada while they waited, the social services burden alone was enormous. Welfare costs in Metro Toronto, for instance, skyrocketed by 80 percent, from $456 million in 1990 to $830 million in 1991, because of escalating numbers of people seeking aid. Metro politicians were challenged to consider cutting back on a wide range of items, such as road repairs, homes for the aged and daycare, to pay its portion of the record welfare bill.

From the very beginning, critics feared that the government's attempt to implement a tougher and "mean-spirited" system based on control-oriented legislation would, in effect, also keep out legitimate refugees. And, by 1991, the Refugee Determination System proved to be so cumbersome and time consuming that it began to cause serious psychological stress to refugee claimants and frontline immigration officers alike. Charges were laid against the Refugee Determination System, indicting it with violating individual claimants' rights by jeopardizing their "security of the person," which is in contravention of Section 7 of the Charter of Rights and Freedoms.

Frontline immigration officers were traumatized by the system. Scheduling supervisors, pressured by senior officials in Ottawa, resorted to quadruple bookings of hearings and inquiries to deal with the big numbers. For every boardroom available at any given time, there were four cases scheduled. This became the normal routine. The theory was that if a scheduled case was unable to proceed for whatever reason, another case could be substituted in its place in order to make maximum use of boardroom facilities. In practice, this theory created complete and utter pandemonium, with frustrating delays for refugee claimants lined up for available boardrooms and a back-breaking, impossible workload for immigration personnel—creating a psychic overload for everyone in the trenches.

The system began to be referred to by insiders as "Vietnam in a Highrise." Tension mounted as hearings offices began to resemble war zones, complete with human and furniture projectiles and overflowing with the bodies of refugee claimants, lawyers, consultants, interpreters and various and sundry immigration workers. The Case-Presenting Officers, who represent the Minister of Immigration in the first-level refugee hearings and inquiries, began a job action of work slowdowns and rotating pickets and threatened an all-out revolt. The *Ottawa Citizen* ran the following story:

> Frustrated government officials are threatening to shut down Canada's faltering immigration and refugee processing system.
>
> The internal revolt is being lead by officers who represent Immigration Minister Barbara McDougall at immigration inquiries and refugee hearings.
>
> A committee representing "case-presenting officers" in Ontario and Atlantic Canada warned McDougall in a letter Dec. 11 that they can put the enforcement of the new immigration laws and refugee backlog clearance "in jeopardy."
>
> The committee demanded—so far without success—a meeting with the minister on an urgent basis to discuss the heavy workload placed on officers by the new immigration screening and backlog systems....
>
> An internal government memo written Dec. 21 reveals the frustrations of the case-presenting officers (CPOs) are already adding to the delays in processing immigrants and refugees.
>
> The memo to immigration headquarters from P.W. Pirie, director of hearings and appeals in the Ontario region, reports officers have had to receive written orders to work on a Saturday (*Ottawa Citizen*, Nov. 1, 1991).

When the new process finally broke down in 1991, senior officials in Ottawa shifted the backlog and, therefore, dodged their critics and quelled the growing internal revolt by instructing port-of-entry and in-land immigration offices to automatically transfer the majority of the cases, after intake from the Immigration Commission, to the Convention Refugee Determination Division, technically a separate entity. They were able to forestall public criticism and solve their internal labour problems in one fell swoop. This was accomplished through the Simplified Inquiry Process (SIP), which was a paper-processing shuffle where the initial eligibility and credibility of refugee claims automatically gain acceptance from the immigration department on paper in lieu of a first-level oral hearing (satisfying legal requirements) and they were re-routed straight to the refugee division for full oral or second-level hearing. Theoretically, this move was also designed to further streamline the system and defer costs by getting work authorizations into the hands of refugee claimants quicker; and, of course, this became its major selling point. Meanwhile, it also obscured the fact that while the numbers were off the immigration books, and the refugee crush appeared to be clearing or at least contained, the cases were still active and in the system. This amounted to a bureaucratic method of clearing the backlog by "cooking the books."

In practical terms, this move also necessitated a shift in personnel and capital resource requirements to the refugee division to deal with the burgeoning numbers, leaving the immigration side of the equation with less resources to handle the steady intake of refugee claims at the front end. Effectively this meant that the new system was now being crushed by a frontlog as well as a backlog. Meanwhile, since the time frame for completing refugee claims had not actually changed from the old C–55 system and could still take years to complete once they were returned from the refugee division back to the immigration department for termination, the failed refugee claimants, with work authorizations in hand, could be generally well-established and, therefore, eligible for a "back-end" administrative review to ascertain the undue hardship that removal from Canada might cause them and their families.

Finally, for those who failed to get a positive back-end review in the 1990s, there was always the option of going underground to await a time when the conditions were more advantageous and the chances of receiving a positive decision from immigration authorities were more in their favour. This is substantiated by outstanding arrest warrants indicating that thousands upon thousands of illegal aliens—an estimated twenty-five thousand in Metro Toronto alone by 1994—are underground, still awaiting the omnipresent possibility of "amnesty" (*The Toronto Star*, June 25, 1994).

To avoid declaring an amnesty and therefore admitting system failure, the residence requirement for participating in the Humanitarian and Compassionate Review System was subsequently lowered from five years to three years. On July 7, 1994, the Commission introduced another special program called the Deferred Removal Order Class (DROC). Under DROC, anyone who had resided in Canada for three years or more could apply for humanitarian and compassionate relief, provided they had been working for at least six months and had no criminal record. This move potentially eliminated the burgeoning front-end numbers of refugee claimants who arrived in the early 1990s by administratively re-routing them once again, this time to the more pliant humanitarian review system, and thus shifting the focus of the refugee system yet again to more recent arrivals. In addition, Canada struck a new deal with the United States, the "draft agreement on responsibility sharing"—an arrangement between the two countries in which they recognized each other as a safe destination for refugees. Under this asylum-sharing accord, people with close family members in Canada would be allowed to make their claims here even if they first spent time south of the border. And those who transit to the United States under special circumstances would also be allowed in, as would unaccompanied minors. Along with the asylum-sharing accord with the United States, a new general category for refugee seekers had been drafted to make it easier for deserving cases abroad to be accepted in Canada. The new category sought to identify people who were "seriously and personally affected by civil war, armed conflicts or massive violation of human rights." Theoretically, under the new category more people would be able to meet the lower threshold test. It might be noted, then, that the system continued to be expanded and liberalized, but this was as much a coping mechanism as it was a decisive commitment on the part of the immigration department. Thus, the crisis of the Convention Refugee Determination System had given way to the potentially bigger crisis of the Humanitarian and Compassionate Review System in the 1990s. Policy makers continued to reconcile the principles of order and justice from one crisis to the next, concocting a patchwork legislative history along the way.

The "Revitalization" Motif—Restricting Public Input and Centralizing Decision Making

The issue for the general public today can be formulated in the following way: we want our immigration system to be open and fair-handed with people regardless of race, creed, colour or sex; however, at the same time we want the system to be effective in furthering the goal of building a strong society. These two things are not necessarily compatible. An open and equitable immigration system that is also economically sound must be strategically nurtured through a comprehensive long-term social planning and population policy that ensures the universality of our immigration programs while facilitating social integration.

It is interesting to note that, subsequent to the 1952 Immigration Act, one of the most persistent motifs of successive government approaches to immigration is the expression of a need to revitalize the immigration system through comprehensive and long-term planning. "Long-term planning" is a bigger catch-phrase in the immigration business than "streamlined immigration procedures," which is now also a current rage. What both have in common, however, is that, since 1952, successive governments have set conditions that have made their achievement virtually impossible.

When the 1952 Bill was before parliament, some opposition members wanted to use the occasion for a detailed discussion of the role of immigration in Canadian society. However, government spokesmen at the time pointed out that, since the Bill merely revised administrative procedures, such a full debate was inappropriate (Canada, House of Commons, *Debates*, June 23, 1952). Every subsequent change to the Immigration Act from this point on was defined as merely a revised administrative procedure. Therefore, truly extensive and informed public debate became either inappropriate or discretionary (that is, at the discretion of the governing party).

In 1973, the federal government of Canada once again announced plans for a comprehensive review of immigration policy. Following the example of the *American Commission on Population Growth and the American Future* (United States Congress, 1972) and the *Australian National Population Inquiry* (Borrie, 1975), immigration was placed in a broader context. Demographic factors influencing the growth and distribution of population in Canada and future population projections were related to the immigration question. Unlike the American and Australian studies, however, the *Canadian Immigration and Population Study* (the "Green Paper on Immigration") was undertaken by a small group of senior officials in the Department of Manpower and Immigration and not by an independent or comprehensive commission. Moreover, from this point on, immigration policy in Canada became the growing preserve of senior policy makers, until they nudged out both the public and the transient politicians (see Chapters 4 and 5).

On the whole, then, the post–1952 revitalization motif consolidated two trends in the immigration business: restricting public input, and centralizing the authority and decision-making powers of the immigration bureaucracy. Furthermore, as the system has broadened in complexity and scope, it has also moved quite naturally towards improving its industrial-efficiency quotient. Because the true bureaucrat believes that the revitalization of the system is achieved by adjusting efficiency levels, senior officials continue unabashedly to suggest that the way to achieve an open system that is also economically sound is through efficient service and streamlined immigration procedures. From 1952 onward, all the major criticisms and subsequent changes of the Canadian immigration system are the result of evaluations of program delivery and admission and control procedures, rather than a focus on bringing immigration programs into balance with the guiding tenets of society. In a word, senior officials have mistaken the efficacy of the system for the integrity of the system. Consequently, our immigration programs—while undoubtedly becoming more and more refined and precise—are continually falling out of step with our fundamental principles.

Gender Inequality in Immigration Policy

In the post-1952 era, senior immigration officials have continually had to catch-up to, or be dragged along by, some major forces of change in society. Immigration policy makers have typically responded to the challenges by adjusting administrative techniques— coincidentally precipitating the difficulty they have had over the years in synthesizing the humanity of immigration with the economics of immigration. For example, one of the major challenges of the Canadian immigration system relates to "gender issues." This was highlighted internationally at the United Nations Conference on Women, which convened in Beijing in September 1995. At that conference, Canada's record on helping refugee women was harshly criticized in a report written for the Ad-Hoc Working Group on the Status of Refugee Women in Canada, co-authored by Wenona Giles of York University. The report, which was quoted in part in the Canadian press, criticized Canada's system for sponsorship of refugees from abroad, saying that its emphasis on job and language skills and economic criteria worked to the disadvantage of refugee women: "Although women and children make up about 80 percent of the world's refugees, women comprise only 27 percent of the refugees who arrived in Canada between 1979 and the end of 1994" (*The Toronto Star*, Sept. 1, 1995).

There was some question as to whether the extenuating circumstances and contributing factors related to these statistics would help to clarify the picture and mitigate this criticism. For instance, according to the 1988 United Nations Procedures and Criteria for Determining Refugee Status, refugee claims must be based on fear of persecution for reasons of race, religion, nationality, political opinion or membership in a social group. Therefore, it is usually the person in the family whose activities occasioned that fear who initiates a refugee claim. In most refugee-producing countries in Africa and South America, for instance, which are also patriarchal societies, that person is the husband. In addition, it is often the case in refugee-producing societies that, while a person may have an acute fear of persecution or death for political or other activities, that person's family (who may not have participated in political or other activities) may not be in imminent danger. In such cases, which are many, while the family is ravaged and the women and children can become displaced, it is the husband, whose life is in immediate jeopardy, who has a stronger impetus to flee first and to make the initial refugee claim, often without being able to contact or arrange departure for other family members. This is clearly a phenomenon that goes beyond Canada's refugee determination process.

In addition, even in cases where members of a family are in a position to file a refugee claim at the same time, for procedural purposes, immigration officials often defer the claims of individuals whose case relies on the spotlighted activities (that is, activities that came to the attention of authorities in the country of origin) of other members in the family. Again, the spotlight activities are often undertaken by the males in the family in patriarchal, refugee-producing countries. In such cases, a woman's claim may be deferred and not logged into the system, pending the results of her husband's claim. If the husband's claim is successful, he is in a position to sponsor the entire immediate family for permanent residence, thereby foregoing any further refugee hearings for family members. Hence, the successful refugee claim of a husband eliminates the need for his wife to make a claim, which, of course, leads to misleading statistics. Children's claims are always included and attached and dependent on one or the other of their parents' claims, which in effect means children cannot actually initiate a refugee claim in the Canadian refugee determination system, although they are taken into account in the process. (Orphaned children are usually sponsored for residence by a community group or non-governmental organization or adopted by private citizens.)

Meanwhile, it is to be further noted that Canada is the first country officially to go beyond the UNHCR Handbook on Procedures and Criteria for Determining Refugee Status and include gender as an additional or sixth criteria for determining refugee status. And, to date, a number of cases have been decided favourably where a woman has feared returning to her country of origin because of spousal abuse.

Nonetheless, it is important to ensure that gender is included in Canada's immigration standards of universality and equitable participation. It has been noted, for instance, that since immigrant women, more often than men, are sponsored into the country by family members, and as such are not considered market bound, they have not enjoyed equal access to such things as language-training programs and, therefore, their integration into society has been hampered (Belfiore et. al., 1985; Boyd, 1987). Like the other issues involving disaffected sectors of modern society, gender issues now challenge the industrial-efficiency measures of the immigration bureaucracy in ways that go beyond merely enhancing program delivery or admission and control devices. It is now increasingly recognized, when gender is not taken into account and women's issues are not put on the immigration table, that half of the world is underrated, undermined and undervalued. And this goes against our deep-seated belief that an inclusive society is the foundation for modern progress. So, the actual challenge to the immigration bureaucracy is to bring what we stand for into line with what we actually do (or into line with the way we actually construct society). Hence, gender equality is a new recurrence of, and variation on, the same discussion that has existed since 1952—of revitalizing the system in order to bring it into a balance for optimum functioning.

Gender inequality is a breach of the immigration system because it violates what we all know is integral to an enlightened, democratic society. It indicates that the forces of democratic society are out of sync—resulting in a social order that is not inclusive and, so, is antithetical to the uniform dispensation of social justice. Gender inequality in the immigration system reflects the negative correlation of social order and social justice. It follows that the solution to the problem of gender inequality lies not only in developing an immigration system that reflects gender inclusiveness in its policies and programs, but also, and more consequentially, an immigration system that serves to pro-actively empower women in society.

Combatting the Fear of Immigration

While the objective of immigration in Canada is no longer to build a country on the backs of stalwart peasants, the system continues to engage in selective immigration as a major policy directive. The difference is this: whereas originally Sifton's "stalwart peasants in sheep-skin coats" were all the rage, now, in the age of designer immigration, it seems to be "electronic engineers" and "computer programmers" who are the favoured settlers. Immigration in Canada, as it is reflected in the independent immigration stream, remains largely designed to import quality people rather than enhance people's qualities—it is a value-added system rather than a value-generating one. Bill C–44, the latest ten-year plan (implemented in 1995), once again advises the Minister of Immigration to be more selective about who gets into Canada:

> The report by top bureaucrats urged Marchi (Minister of Immigration) to cut immigration levels by 50,000 next year to 200,000, restrict family class, cancel the Live-in Caregiver program and to be more selective about who gets into Canada.
>
> And *The Globe and Mail* quoted Marchi this week as saying Canada should more actively recruit independent and business immigrants from Europe (*The Toronto Star*, Sept. 17, 1994).

And Madison Avenue advertising techniques are being used to woo upscale immigrants from around the world through overseas ad campaigns in trade journals and newspapers (complete with toll-free numbers and mail-in coupons), trade fairs and information seminars, and even the Internet:

> The newspaper ads play on time-worn images of Canada—a modern city, a mist-shrouded lake, a scarlet maple leaf. But these promotions are more than mere travel brochures. They aim at persuading professionals to leave cities in the Middle East, Asia and the United States and move to Canada.... The ads specify that only those who speak French or English fluently, are well educated and have several years professional work experience need apply. Business immigrants are wooed through trade fairs and smaller seminars set up by Canadian immigration officials (*The Globe and Mail*, June 7, 1995).

The importance placed on recruiting economic immigrants is reflected in the budget for overseas promotion. While other departments are facing cutbacks, the promotions section of the Immigration Department received a budget increase in 1995 to $2 million, up from $500,000 in 1994. This increase makes Canada the biggest international spender in a competitive field. Australia, for instance, spends about $1 million annually to attract immigrants. Among immigrant-receiving countries, only the United States has no promotional budget and relies solely on spontaneous applications.

Most of the promotion being conducted today takes place in Asia, Western Europe, the Middle East and western United States, with an emphasis on regions that specialize in high technology. In India, for example, much of the recruitment has occurred in Bangalore, the hub of the country's software industry. This "designer immigration" orientation is the ultimate in the fetishization of humans as commodities. And one of the ironies is that Canada has continued to serve over the years as a reception centre for highly skilled immigrants on their way to the United States. As John Porter once put it, "Canada has resembled a huge demographic railway station ... harbouring the 'birds of passage' who have stopped over in Canada while making the move from Europe to the United States" (Porter, 1964: 33). In strict economic terms, the U.S. clearly has more to offer newcomers than does Canada. (This accounts for a prevalent response at the port of entry to the question "Why do you want to come to Canada?": "Because I couldn't get into the United States.") Once newcomers have landed in Canada, they can begin their plans for the exodus to the land of the free and home of the brave. And some estimates place the annual number of emigrants leaving Canada at approximately 50,000. The one thing that can be said for sure about the independent immigration stream today is that the end of the high-tech underground railroad is likely to end in the United States, not Canada. (The Department of Immigration keeps detailed records of all immigrants who come into the country, with data on their birthplace, age, sex, occupation, destination, and so on, for the past thirty years of immigration. However, the government does not collect information on those people who leave the country, and only by examining records of other nations would it be possible to get an exact determination of the numbers of people who leave Canada each year. Fifty thousand emigrants yearly may be a highly conservative estimate.)

The point can be made that it is not immigration *per se* that is the drain on the Canadian economy, but rather the lack of an overall population policy based on a human-resource and human-capital strategy. When a wide-based population policy is in place, oriented towards the development of human capital in conjunction with the expansion of the technological-industrial base of the nation, the continued pressure to compete for skilled immigrants from the world queue in order to bolster the economy is alleviated. Comprehensive population planning in Canada can secure a competitive edge in the global arena through national training and educational initiatives for residents and newcomers alike, and Canada's destiny is placed in its own hands.

There is, of course, no wish here to portray a learning-oriented society as a cure-all for the enormous population pressures and emigration problems caused by chronic economic crises, political upheaval and ethno-cultural conflicts around the world; rather, only a learning-oriented society can provide some measure of flexibility in a highly volatile world. Skill-oriented societies that engage in selective immigration policies based on changing versions of "the right stuff"— and that take defensive admission and control measures to prevent external transgressions and the impingement of "the wrong stuff"— actually underwrite further population pressures around the globe and, therefore, increase the propensity for the afflicted to migrate. Restrictive and defensive national immigration policies are truly in-adequate to meet the challenges and requirements of the new world order; and they create what Anthony Richmond (1994) called "global apartheid," where people who earlier may have been welcomed either as useful workers or as escapees from oppressive regimes are now part of a global system of social stratification and "eth-class" conflict.

In 1991, an Angus Reid survey showed that 61 percent of all Canadians (with percentages ranging from 68 percent in Quebec to 54 in Alberta) support the multiculturalism policy in Canada (Multiculturalism and Citizenship Canada, 1991). Further, 70 percent of the sample believe that multiculturalism will enrich Canada's culture. However, it is now one of the ironies of modern life that while Canadians are able to believe in multiculturalism, they are at the same time coming to fear immigration. Current economic, social and identity problems seem so huge that many Canadians are not ready to accept the reality of increasingly polymorphous interethnic and inter-racial relations (Dorais et al., 1994: 401). Canadians may believe in pluralism, but they still perceive it as a threat to national cohesion and the future of the country (White and Samuel, 1991). As Dorais, Foster and Stockley put it,

> public opinion exhibits a growing wariness towards immigration and cultural pluralism. This wariness is compounded by unfavourable economic conditions and a high rate of unemployment for which immigrants are often blamed. It is not surprising that a large part of the public, whose opinions find an echo in newly established popularist political parties (the Reform Party in Western Canada and Ontario, Bloc Québécois in Quebec and the Confederation of Regions in the Atlantic Provinces), consider multiculturalism a threat to national cohesion and identity (Dorais et al., 1994).

The growing fear of immigration that is beginning to take political shape today—in the Reform Party in Western Canada and Ontario, Bloc Québécois in Quebec and the Confederation of Regions in the Atlantic Provinces—begins with an inadequate or inept response to international migratory pressures on the part of the immigration policy makers. This, in turn, sets into play a chain reaction that generates a climate of uncertainty and growing wariness of the mixed multitude in everyday life towards one another. This fear of immigration, and the invocation of new dubious tribal instincts, is coterminous with the failure of policy makers to recognize that immigration must be a part of a broader population policy, and not the reverse.

To begin to address the 1990s immigration quagmire of implementation and expenditure, the democratic ethos in our modern life must be matched with an open immigration system that actively reaches out as an "enabling technology" of empowerment. However, this idea of empowering newcomers requires a transformation in our thinking—a change that our contemporary policy makers not only often fail to achieve but often fail to conceive.

Since 1952, rarely have more than a few years gone by without the events of the day enticing some new amendment to the immigration law or adjustment to the regulations and procedures that is meant to redress a perceived imbalance between Canada's own national self-interest and its moral pledge to those from other lands seeking protection and safe sanctuary. In the last ten years alone, the remedial legislative work ranges from Bill C–55 and Bill C–84 to Bill C–86 and C–44—all designed to streamline the immigration system and redress inadequacies. This incoherence has been acknowledged by immigration officials themselves. The Annual Report to parliament for 1990 by the Public Affairs and Policy Group Employment and Immigration Canada summarized the previous twenty years of immigration history this way:

> In the late 1970s and early 1980s immigration declined, falling from 140,000 in 1980 to 85,000 in 1985. *Immigration became largely a family movement, and no longer realized its full economic potential* (my emphasis). When the present government took office, it placed an emphasis on revitalizing the immigration system. In a Special Report to parliament 1985, the government outlined a balanced approach to immigration, supporting objectives in three areas: family reunification, a commitment to refugees and humanitarian activities and economic development through the selection of business immigrants and skilled workers.
>
> These objectives have been pursued successfully, through a policy of growth in immigration since 1985. The bulk of the increase took place in

the economic stream of immigration, but there was a significant increase in all categories.

In the Speech from the Throne in 1989, the government reaffirmed this policy of increased immigration. (Employment and Immigration Canada. "Annual Report to Parliament. Immigration Plan for 1991–1995," October 1990: 7).

A useful distinction can be made here between what the American Sociologist Robert S. Lynd (1957: 6) called a "liberal democracy" and a "thoroughgoing democracy." The Canadian immigration system co-incides with a liberal democracy which "yokes together a professedly democratic social structure and political system with a capitalist economy and division of labour." In this regard, the immigration system is sometimes about economics and sometimes about the ethics of equality, because it reflects the hybrid order of our society as opposed to contributing to overall or distributive justice. Since the emphasis on one means the failure to maximize the potential of the other, all human and capital resources do not come into play in the same way at the same time.

As noted in the Annual Report to parliament above, accentuation of one aspect of Canada's immigration system has historically led to the failure to maximize the potential of the other. The emphasis on the economics of immigration in our society can contradict, suppress or close off aspirations towards an open-door policy, and, of course, the reverse is also true. This is distinguished from a thoroughgoing democracy, where the immigration system would be designed to contribute to the coherence in expressing and implementing democratic values by promoting optimal use of human resources and facilitating social development through an agenda for nation building that maximizes the life-chances of individuals and mobilizes creative energies of society as a whole.

The policy makers aspire for balance, but there has been a continuous state of imbalance or disequilibrium in the system; and, throughout it all, from the White Paper to the Green Paper and beyond, they are left echoing a hollow refrain regarding the "revitalization of the immigration system." In conjunction with the purported significant shift, the Report stated that

> immigration planning must strike a balance between our desire to respond generously and compassionately to [these] people, and our ability to respond to their needs effectively. It must reflect a due regard for our own national interests, and the interests of provincial governments. It must also address longer-term measures to maintain the desired balance, through a process that is efficient and well-managed (Employment and Immigration

Canada. "Annual Report to Parliament. Immigration Plan for 1991–1995," October 1990: 12).

Insofar as the principle of social order is segregated from the principle of social justice, modern policy makers have an inherent inability to effect coherent goals. Moreover, without such a solid foundation for major goals and values, it is difficult to engender a sense of shared purpose or cultivate a common commitment to immigration in the nation as a whole.

In a thoroughgoing democracy, a comprehensive long-term plan to build a nation would include maximizing the life-chances of individuals and mobilizing the creative energies of society in general. Yet, for contemporary policy makers, the idea of identifying appropriate longer-term measures to maintain the optimum balance of Canada's immigration program suggests "examining management systems used by other countries, such as direct controls on issuing visas." The Annual Report to Parliament for 1990 further stated that

> a review of the management system is now taking place, to identify appropriate longer-term measures. This includes an examination of the management systems used by other countries, such as direct controls on issuing visas. However, the universality of our immigration programs—which guarantees equal treatment for all source countries—will be preserved. *No measures that interfere with universality or our fundamental humanitarian principles will be considered* (my emphasis). ("Annual Report to Parliament," Public Affairs and Policy Group Employment and Immigration Canada, Ministry of Social Services Canada, 1990: 12).

Of course, those countries which have the most direct control on issuing entry and exit visas, such as China, are totalitarian dictatorships and repressive regimes that are anything but democratic. And, in Europe, where they are attempting to develop a sophisticated lattice-work of regional and multinational control systems, migrant workers and refugees are increasingly being beaten, stoned and swarmed.

So far the only clear outcome of these policies is that democratic governments that respond to the phenomenon of global migration solely or primarily by tightening immigration controls seem to unwittingly provoke patterns of illegal migration (by definition and by response) and precipitate violent protest and attacks on foreigners in their countries. Professor Anthony H. Richmond (1994: xi) has pointed out that "Western European countries have taken severe measures to deter and exclude spontaneous arrivals of asylum seekers. As a result, the numbers arriving fell from 693,100 in 1992 to nearly 543,200 in 1993"; however, "the actual numbers crossing international borders, legally and illegally, rose substantially." This might suggest that countries that have the most inviolable immigration management systems are not necessarily the most progressive societies; and that when you start looking to identify appropriate long-term measures by way of reviewing the immigration management system of control-freak societies, you substitute the goal of system competence for the goal of social progress. But this nuance is left out of the bureaucratic equation.

While it appears to be clear to everyone involved, including those who actually make the decisions, that comprehensive long-term planning is required (to ensure that the "universality of our immigration programs—which guarantees equal treatment for all source countries—will be preserved") as we move into a new century, it is now the style of policy makers to seek to preserve this universal access in the immigration system by increasing regulatory control—that is, tinkering with the occupations list, revising the refugee determination system, limiting family class sponsorships, actively recruiting business immigrants, and so on.

The result of this is that policy makers have subscribed to a world of "progressive proceduralism" (Spencer, 1976: 203). They routinely and unproblematically treat the integrity of the immigration system as merely a matter of correct calculations and procedures. Therefore, the present assignment of the experts is continually to repair or prevent breaches in the immigration system. The question of whether or not the goal of Canadian society should be to import a highly skilled workforce rather than create one is not even an issue of public discourse. The question of whether, in the long run, selective immigration measures based on occupation lists, point systems and other measures of labour value strengthen or inhibit the development of society in an age of advancing technology has never been a public policy consideration. And last, but not least, there has never been any serious deliberation at all as to whether the attempts to control the quality or type of people that come to Canada may actually be an obstacle to a rich diversity and thus eventually prevent the country from becoming a truly enterprising force.

4

The Cult of the Expert

tacey Merkt is an American church worker who helped undocumented Salvadoreans enter the United States. She was convicted of "transporting and conspiring to transport illegal aliens." She was sentenced to eighteen months in prison in January 1987 but was released from prison in April to serve the rest of her sentence under house arrest. She was released from house arrest in July 1987.

In many circles, and especially among the Salvadoreans she tried to bring to safety, Stacey Merkt's crime is viewed as an heroic act. Amnesty International adopted her as a "prisoner of conscience" as it believed that those she helped could have been in danger of imprisonment, torture or extrajudicial execution if returned to El Salvador.

Stacey Merkt is what Professor Joesph Campbell would call an old-style hero—someone casting light on the dark places in the human soul. "The hero" according to Professor Campbell, "ventures forth from the world of common day into a region of supernatural wonder; fabulous forces are there encountered and a decisive victory is won; the hero comes back from this mysterious adventure with the power to bestow boons on his fellow man" (1973: 30). Moreover, Campbell declares, "the great deed of the supreme hero is to come to the knowledge of this unity in multiplicity and then to make it known" (Campbell, 1973: 40).

No More Heroes

Of course, Stacey Merkt is also an American. There are no Stacey Merkts in Canada ready to "put it all on the line and do hard time" if necessary, out of conviction. In Canada we share the metaphor of the hero, but we cannot see its reference. So, while it might be argued that some individuals have tried to put it all on the line and have been sentenced to hard time—like Dudley Laws, for instance, who was convicted of the same crime (or Canadian equivalent) as Merkt— these Canadian equivalents tend to be designated simply as criminals, or worse, avaricious criminals, rather than "prisoners of conscience." It is also true that Canada does not lack in vocal fighters, as evidenced by the outspoken human rights lobby during the immigration debates in 1988 leading to the C-55 refugee legislation in 1989; Rabbi Gunther Plaut has an important status in Canada among human rights activists. In addition, there are professional associations that perhaps attempt to advance and buttress the heroic spirit in the great white north, like the Centre for Refugee Studies at York University that gives out an annual award to a notable person in the field of immigration and refugees. However, in the traditional sense of the term, there are no actual or bona fide immigration heroes in Canada, challenging the system at any cost on a mission to find the unity in our multiplicity.

Arguably, this country hasn't had, or abided, a bona fide immigration hero since Harriet Tubman, the abolitionist and fugitive slave, who in the decade preceding the American Civil War conducted her daring runs on the Underground Railroad (the secret network of safehouses and people that helped black slaves to escape to the Dominion of Canada). During the period in Canadian history from 1763 to 1885, about 30,000 escapees were surreptitiously transported from the United States. It is reported that Ms. Tubman personally escorted more than 300 slaves on their road to freedom. Like Stacey Merkts, Harriet Tubman answered the call for action in her time.

The United States and Canada are both examples of liberal democracies that emphasize tolerance and pluralism. However, unlike the United States, no one is allowed the status as a champion of the oppressed and downtrodden in Canada anymore. This is partly due to the fact that, unlike the United States, immigration is not directly linked to Canada's national mythology. Indeed, Canada does not have a distinctive national mythology as such. And this may be indicative of the fact that the Citizenship Act only came into being in Canada in 1947. There is no recognized folklore emphasizing rugged individualism and sanctioning the "luck and pluck" of an Horatio Alger. Nor are there monuments to freedom or statues to liberty beckoning the clamouring hordes. Like their American counterparts, Canadians have been known of late to exhort the "vision of founders" and to extol a "love it or leave it" or "it's the greatest place in the world" ideology. But, it is fair to say, Canada is not as unambiguous for Canadians as the United States is for Americans. Hence, where the citizens of the United States tend to imagine themselves in terms of a clear national profile and distinct national identity and act strongly in accordance with this imagination, Canadian citizens tend to be a little less directed by a national image and identity and more reticent and taciturn in their actions. So, while ordinary Canadians believe in the democratic tenets of freedom and equality like Americans, they lack the myths, symbols and folklore that could support and sustain a decisive or impassioned commitment to immigration. Thus, psychologically, at least, Canadians are inclined to take up a position at a loose and comfortable distance from the full gravity of the topic.

If Americans still believe in the ruggedness of individualism, then Canadians tend to believe in the smoothness of bureaucracy (Lipset, 1963 and 1989: 130-47). Anyone remotely resembling the likes of a Harriet Tubman or a Stacey Merkt would commonly be viewed with suspicion as either a crook or a crazy, because it is routinely taken for granted that our system for immigration and refugee determination is eminently fair and enlightened in its judgement of needs and protection against persecution. In Canada, the subject of immigration does not herald the call to action or compel ordinary citizens to take a stand on the principles by which we live. "The system" is charged with the responsibility of bestowing boons on our fellow humans. Our generosity and compassion, our pluralism and tolerance, our freedom and equality are thought to be built into the modern immigration system.

Thus, where once citizens of Canada may have been enticed to act on their principles as a matter of conscience, now they act to maintain the functional efficiency of the system. The system is responsible for our order and our justice—our regulations and our virtues, our excellence and our refinement, our progress and our equality. Thus, the resolution of the order-justice equation in the pursuit of the good life and the best possible regime is routinely consigned as the administrative responsibility of bureaucrats in a system-delegated division of labour.

In 1994, for instance, speaking of the new ten-year immigration plan introduced by then-minister Sergio Marchi, the immigration department's director-general of policy, Laura Chapman, was quoted as saying, "I think it is a turning point; it's an effort at a degree of coherence that no minister has ever tried before. So things will no longer grow like topsy; they'll grow, it is hoped with some direction or purpose or goal in mind" (*The Toronto Star*, Sept. 23, 1994). What Ms. Chapman did not say, but what is *a priori* knowledge, is that she and her colleagues had more of a hand in formulating the ten-year plan than Sergio Marchi. However, when the "effort at a degree of coherence" sputters or fails, it will, of course, be the politicians' problem, and the politicians will face the major repercussions.

While the Minister of Immigration is the democratically elected representative of the masses, and assumes certain statutory duties connected to that office, it is select administrators who actually craft the statutes. The Minister of Immigration may make an annual announcement to parliament and the country regarding an official global-planning level, but the minister does not make the plan. It is the professional bureaucrats who are responsible for establishing the complex criteria and framework for the analysis of immigration and population needs, for working out the complicated formulas and stratagems of immigration planning and last, but not least, for instituting a systemic regime of regulations and procedures. In this respect, the complexity of modern life and the rise of bureaucracy has made politicians interchangeable, if not optional; while the professional bureaucrats are often able to escape both public scrutiny and political responsibility.

To use a more modest analogy, the field of immigration in Canada is now generally accepted as a technical field of endeavour, like auto mechanics is a technical field, beyond the range of the average citizen's knowledge. In the same way that the average citizen cannot put together a car engine, they are also not seen as being able to put together society's engine—nor, it is thought, should they even try. And in the same way that the average citizen is at the mercy of the auto mechanic when it comes to repair costs and the quality of repairs, the average citizen is also at the mercy of administrative bureaucrats when it comes to the quality of society. The difference is, however, whereas the average citizen has the option of shopping around to get a second opinion or a second estimate on car repairs, in the field of immigration the bureaucrats at the Immigration Policy Division are the only mechanics in town.

The Age of the Immigration Specialist

Immigration is a field of endeavour that now seems to demand the technical and administrative proficiency and the specialist appraisal of full-time experts, who are perceived to have the machinery and technical wherewithal to compute immigration needs and population goals. They control the frame of reference and complex criteria by which the success of the immigration system is gauged. Therefore, both the public and the politicians rely on the hired experts to interpret the issues calling for public policy and to work out the technical calculation for immigration targets. Colin Campbell and George Szablowski (1979) were perhaps the first to characterize the elite functionaries or administrative men of government who manipulate its large central agencies as "superbureaucrats," whose coming of age roughly coincided with the 1960s- and 1970s-era of Prime Minister Pierre Trudeau:

> During the four years of Trudeau's first mandate the machinery of the federal government underwent unprecedented surgery. The cabinet was remodelled into a system of interlocking, functionally defined committees. New bureaucratic organizations were created to break down the monopolies of older departments. Task forces and interdepartmental committees sprang up bridging the gap between executive and bureaucratic decision making (Campbell and Szablowski, 1979: 8).

Once a system of interlocking elites was in place, bridging the gap between executive and bureaucratic decision making, it eliminated the tension between our democratic values and our democratic participation, the tension between our theory and our practice. Now the system was responsible for the conservation and achievement of what we stand for. It relieved us all of the burden of a bad conscience by relieving us of the responsibility of addressing our own principles of nation building.

Of course, reference to the bureaucratic elite, or the superbureaucrats, as a single-minded bloc is somewhat misleading at the everyday level, where all kinds of minor and major coups lead to career victories and shattered careers. There is serious in-fighting and jockeying for position from time to time among this elite. In the late 1980s, to take one classic example, a Deputy Minister of Immigration, who took over the policy direction at the EIC, openly repudiated the policy perspective of his predecessor. Subsequently, the chastened predecessor is reported to have been shifted far from the policy arena after an internal audit revealed a plethora of chronic managerial, frontline and client service deficiencies in the immigration system. A 1986 internal audit resulted in the following conclusions: (1) senior immigration officials at national headquarters had failed to ensure that policies, procedures and guidelines were being followed in regional and local immigration offices across Canada; (2) the entire immigration system lacked firm direction and control from senior officials in Ottawa; (3) management had not been innovative in improving and streamlining service to the public at the point of contact; (4) frontline staff were inadequately trained and morale problems were severe; (5) the quality of service to the public was unsatisfactory and the system caused long delays for clients, involved excessive paperwork, and was bound by outdated procedures that made little effective use of modern technology; and (6) as a result, the basic conditions required to provide high quality service to the public had suffered significantly, and the image of immigration had been seriously tarnished (Malarek 1987: 44–57).

To date, the only substantive structural result of this report, apart from a musical-chair (or musical-career) shuffle at the senior management level, is the institution of regular client service training sessions for frontline staff. Of course, in the 1990s, this focus on high quality service to the public has been off-set by increased automation (in the form of mail-in centres and electronic file systems) that eliminate face-to-face contacts, offload the responsibility for informing and helping clients to the private sector and community-based organizations, and increase the financial burden on clients through escalating processing fees and service costs.

The upshot is that the image of immigration is still seriously tarnished, and this can still precipitate some serious in-fighting and nasty office politics. But there is a level at which all elite immigration bureaucrats are the same; that is, they all blame the politicians for the topsy-turvy world of immigration, and they all treat every new political regime as an occasion for their own absolution.

The subject of immigration in Canada tends to elicit sometimes passive and sometimes strident responses to the extant policies and procedures. Ordinary Canadians are inclined to shrug with bemusement, and then accept the official immigration policy as it stands—or shriek with anguish, and then accept the official immigration policy as it stands. Neither response is a call to action. Rather, both are induced by a capitulation to the bureaucratic powers-that-be—capitulation, of course, being a conditioned response and not a necessity.

Again, it was Joesph Campbell who informed us of our historical task in the age of bureaucracy: "The hero-deed to be wrought is not today what it was in the century of Galileo. Where then there was darkness, now there is light; but also, where light was, there now is darkness. The modern hero-deed must be that of questing to bring to light again the lost Atlantis of the coordinated soul" (1973: 388). Heroes, like Harriet Tubman and Stacey Merkt, are essentially driven by a quest for the integral. The hero, as Joesph Campbell would say, is challenged by the question of what is essential and necessary and is animated by the spirit of adventure. But the very idea of heralding a call to action seems ludicrous in a bureaucratic state, and it strikes the pledged citizens of bureaucracy as a primitive or uncivilized response to the social environment. We still value the hero-passion for order and justice in Canadian society, but it has been removed from the personal jurisdiction of individuals, and converted into a function of the competence of our institutional arrangements.

The Structure of Immigration Bureaucracy

Large-scale bureaucracy was first explored systematically in the work of Max Weber, who isolated a confluence of factors—social and material prerequisites, such as a money economy, the increasing division of labour, and the increasing scale of organization, improved transportation and communications, and so on—that aided the relentless development of centralized administration in the modern world. He noted that this type of organization is characterized by a hierarchical apparatus of control, and an emphasis on discipline, technical knowledge and impersonal procedures. And as he predicted, institutional bureaucracy is now *the* major organizing unit of our society and a particular form of legal authority in the Western world. But Weber was more concerned with its social-psychological consequences than its organizational dynamics. He saw in the world around him all the phenomena that have become famous or infamous under the labels of "red tape" and "Parkinson's Law"—the tendency for officials to see rules as ends in themselves rather than as means to an end; the difficulty of finding responsible decision makers amid a maze of rules and regulations; the tendency for organizations to drift, to expand mindlessly, making their own survival the highest value; and the tendency of administrative bureaucrats, hoisted into the lead power roles of society, to cover up failure, hide disasters and avoid prying eyes. All of this caused him to remark that "the dictatorship of the official is on the march."

In its relation to modern society, Weber wrote that "bureaucratic administration means fundamentally the exercise of control on the basis of knowledge" (1964: 311). He envisioned the dangers posed to democratic government by the powerful keepers of a rising bureaucracy with their penchant for secrecy and contempt for the public, a theme common to contemporary political studies. He suggested that a fully developed bureaucracy always overshadows its erstwhile political superiors, confronting elected politicians with the imposing image of the trained and knowledgeable professional (1978: 232).

Bureaucracy, of course, is an abstraction or, to use Weber's term, an *ideal type*, which actual formal organizations only approach to varying degrees. Thus, no social system or formal organization is ever completely rational, efficient and formalized in its organization and operation but, insofar as these ideals are dominant in practice, the system or organization is usually regarded as a bureaucracy. With the contemporary growth of a great many very large, formal secondary groups established to attain specific goals, bureaucracy has become the characteristic form of organization in the modern world.

Bureaucracy is based on the goals of centralized planning where orders come from the top down. Yet, the administrative aspects of a formal organization—that is, the hierarchical apparatus of control—is distinguished from the formal organization itself. Thus, there has been some question raised in modern times as to who is and is not a bureaucrat. The workers in a factory, because they are not part of the administration, would not be considered part of the bureaucracy even though they are part of the formal organization. Yet, as we have seen in Chapter 2, this distinction is blurred in the case of service organizations like the Immigration Commission, where the frontline personnel may take on varying administrative responsibilities that either overlap or are part and parcel to their daily tasks. This has lead analysts to distinguish "line bureaucrats" from "superbureaucrats" in order to signify the rise in importance and gradations of administrative decision-making power and technical expertise.

Social scientists have also attempted to differentiate the status and personality types within a bureaucracy on the basis of their involvement in their professional group versus the bureaucracy itself. They are: "the functional bureaucrat"—oriented to a professional group; "the specialist bureaucrat"—also oriented to a professional group but has some identification with the bureaucracy; "the service bureaucrat"—somewhat oriented to a professional group but primarily obtains satisfaction by serving the bureaucracy; and "the job bureaucrat"—entirely immersed in the bureaucracy with his or her profession providing only the qualifications and skills for his or her job (L. Reissman, *Social Forces*, March 1949, in Theodorson and Theordorson, 1969: 34); and "the superbureaucrat"—the elite functionaries of government who actually manipulate its large central agencies, bridging the gap between executive and bureaucratic decision making (Campbell and Szablowski, 1979).

Individuals in the Immigration Commission have a relationship to their office or position that helps define their personality type, and they also have a relationship to power in the organization and society at large. From a sociological standpoint, all of the designations above regarding bureaucracy are meant to be collective and descriptive and to counterbalance the departmental designations and titles in a way that adds more depth than the officialese or bureaucratese of the institution—i.e., Deputy Minister of Immigration, Director of Hearings and Appeals, Manager of Greater Toronto Investigations, Program Specialist, Senior Immigration Officer, Immigration Officer, Escort Officer, Counsellor, Administrative Assistant and so forth. These official titles hold little in the way of explanatory potential, but the difference between a functional bureaucrat and a service bureaucrat, or a specialist bureaucrat and a job bureaucrat, or the generic difference between a line or frontline bureaucrat and a superbureaucrat, can help to illuminate the individual and power dimensions of the immigration commission.

Still, to the public it may appear that modern immigration bureaucracy is an undifferentiated monolith, dominated by dispassionate ticket punchers and hall monitors, consumed by thoughts of procedure and career. This, of course, is connected to the fact that the Commission job titles and designations are not explanatory, but are internal classifications that have little relevance to the outside world. It is also connected to the fact that modern bureaucrats have a reciprocal orientation—the lowly ones and lofty ones alike are often a lot better at rules than principles. Frontline immigration workers, for instance, can recite rules of entry and exit (a requisite knowledge for acquiring the position) without ever having to analyze their fidelity to the attending principles of the society they serve.

Indeed, big bureaucracy prevents it from being otherwise. It demands a fealty to itself. It wedges its way into the relationships between people and demands organizational competence and individual loyalty to regulatory roles and obligations. This is why modern bureaucrats tend to be viewed as "apolitical" and commitmentless. They are identified by the public with their function as rule producers and rule enforcers. All bureaucrats, and especially the lower level ones, become synonymous with rules and regulations in the public consciousness.

In this sense, modern government bureaucracy is perhaps more than even Weber imagined. Like Franz Kafka's allegory of *The Trial*, it seems to the modern public that at every hall there is another door keeper, each one more powerful than the last. All are subject to an elaborate machine order, set in motion although no one knows quite how. Like the Great Wall of China, one can no longer see the whole design or even know there was one. Yet, as with the court functionaries, the hangers-on in *The Trial*, some small portion has become the stuff of the officiators' daily lives, and they, in turn, keep the machine going even though they have lost all sense of what the whole meaning might be.

Amalgamating Authority in Immigration Bureaucracy

In the modern-day atmosphere of "economic restraint and fiscal responsibility," as it is often called, the current trend is towards the rationalization of resources in the form of streamlining, amalgamating and de-layering operations and downsizing the workforce. During the reign of Brian Mulroney and his Progressive Conservative Party, and under the rubric of streamlining, downsizing and amalgamating government, the Immigration Commission was officially adjoined to the Public Security Ministry, along with the Royal Canadian Mounted Police, the Canadian Security Intelligence Service, Canada Customs, the National Parole Board, the Correctional Services of Canada and the Passport Office. As a practical advantage, a new superministry could share one computer network linking the data of the formerly separate agencies. This would facilitate the inter-agency exchange of information—something that was strictly prohibited in Canada because of privacy laws. Presumably, bringing all the enforcement agencies "under one roof" not only added to greater efficiency, but it also reflected a corresponding decline in the need for political guidance and supervision, and permitted new and deeper intrusions into individual lives that threatened further alienation.

When the liberal government took office in October 1993, the Public Security Ministry became the Ministry of Citizenship and Immigration, perhaps less intrusive but still under the streamlining, downsizing, amalgamating and de-layering banner, this time (as the nomenclature suggests) with an orientational emphasis on admission rather than control. Indeed, the name and orientation of the federal department dealing with immigration has always reflected the admission or control emphasis of the government of the day. Since Confederation, for example, this department has undergone the following changes in designation: Canadian Immigration and Quarantine Services—1667–1892; Immigration Branch, Department of the Interior—March 14, 1892–1917; Department of Immigration and Colonization—October 12, 1917–1936; Immigration Branch, Department of Mines and Resources—December 1, 1936–1950; Department of Citizenship and Immigration—January 18, 1950–1966; Canada Employment and Immigration Commission—August 15, 1966–1993; Department of Public Security and Human Resources (dividing immigration into two departments)—June 25, 1993—November 4,

1993; Department of Citizenship and Immigration—November 4, 1993 to present.

Ironically, there is another unwitting consequence that attests to the relentlessness of bureaucratization that even the big-time bureaucrats have found somewhat unsavoury. As immigration was subsumed by the Public Security Ministry and then the Ministry of Citizenship and Immigration, many senior management positions became redundant and, therefore, subject to an operations reassessment. In an effort to streamline and amalgamate authority, many superbureaucrats sacrifice themselves as well as others on the altar of bureaucracy. (Of course, the immigration grunts and foot-soldiers get the pink slip, and immigration superbureaucrats get the golden handshake.) In August 1993, the government announced plans to cut forty-five Deputy Minister and Assistant Deputy Minister positions from the payroll, albeit with a healthy severance package (an internal audit conducted in mid-1993 suggested that the government spent up to $350 million giving public servants special golden handshakes, with lump sum payments of up to $127,000 apiece—*The Ottawa Citizen*, Jan. 12, 1994).

The Francophone and Anglophone Agenda in the Immigration Debate

In 1988, the Canada Employment and Immigration Advisory Council report on the "Perspectives on Immigration in Canada" concluded that the Canadian population had not exhibited much interest in discussing immigration issues and, on the whole, still remained uninformed about all questions related to immigration:

> For reasons difficult to define, immigration has not generally received particular attention from the public in Canada, although it is part of the national mythology of the United States. Except perhaps for a few periods in our history, including the past couple of years, Canadians do not seem to have had much interest in discussing immigration policies ("Perspective on Immigration in Canada." Canada Employment and Immigration Advisory Council, August 1988: v).

The reasons for the general ignorance regarding immigration policies may have been difficult to define, as the Advisory Council submits, but they probably had more to do with acquiescence than indifference. It was originally suggested, for instance, that the general public's lack of interest in and knowledge of immigration issues stemmed from the fact that, from the beginning of the country's history, and particularly since Confederation, national debates had focused on the relations between Francophones and Anglophones. Consequently, ethnic groups that did not belong to either community had found themselves on the sidelines.

In an often-quoted phrase by John Lambton, the first Earl of Durham, Canada is described as "two nations warring in the bosom of a single state." Lord Durham's pre-Confederation report in 1839 on the British North American "problem" focused on the struggle between French and English Canadians. He noted "that dissensions which appear to have another origin are but forms of this constant and all-pervading quarrel: every contest is one of French and English in the outset, or becomes so ere it has run its course." In his opinion this quarrel had produced a political paralysis. "It would be idle," suggested the Earl of Durham, "to attempt any amelioration of laws or institutions until we could first succeed in terminating the deadly animosity." He saw a resolution in British immigration and complete Anglo ascendancy. This, of course, proved impossible. By the turn of the century, it was observed that "the dominant race suffers the presence of the French because it cannot do otherwise" (Siegfried, 1978: 15).

William Petersen later commented on the original immigration dynamic in the formation of French-Canadian nationalism in Canada:

> The most obvious division in the Canadian nation, as well as the one most clearly relevant to the issues of immigration policy, is the sub-nation of French Canada. The present French population of Canada is descended almost entirely from the approximately 65,000 persons settled there by 1763. The political separation from the homeland effected by the Treaty of Paris became a complete estrangement by the revolution of 1789, with which French Canada had little sympathy. Without immigration, the population increased from this slight base to more than 1,000,000 at the time of Confederation.... While a certain antagonism had existed between Quebec and English Canada ever since the establishment of British rule, French-Canadian nationalism in its present form dates from 1885, the year Louis Riel was executed (Petersen, 1965: 40).

The birth of a French-Canadian nationalist movement is generally recognized to have taken place in 1885 at a meeting protesting the execution of Louis Riel. Riel had led the *métis* of Manitoba's Red River Valley in an attempt to set up a rebel government in opposition to the coming of English-speaking settlers and union with Canada. Since Riel, the French and English "charter" groups have had conflicting ideas about who should enter the country—an antagonism that has been exacerbated over the years because, in large part, immigrants to Canada have come to adopt the English rather than the French-Canadian way of life, and so immigration has periodically been perceived and treated as a threat to French survival.

There is no doubt that the agenda for Canadian immigration was originally controlled by the cross-cultural contest between the French and English—insofar as they represented the dominant ethnic and political constituencies of the country. This duality of the so-called two solitudes largely dictated the federal institutional form of the country and necessitated the enshrinement of two official languages. However, in more recent years, the increasing ethnic heterogeneity of the Canadian population and the growing numerical strength and voting power of other ethnic groups, as well as the rise of Aboriginal activism, have caused a shift away from the official image of a bicultural country towards a recognition of Canada as multicultural.

With the extension of the Canadian mosaic and the current policy of multiculturalism, one might have expected a gradual and more expansive national debate on immigration. Yet this period also coincides with the rise of large-scale bureaucracy and new configurations of administrative power and technical expertise. Hence, the contemporary agenda for immigration in Canada is no longer the political prerogative of the French or the English, or any particular high-ranking ethnic group. Now it is the top bureaucrats who are at the tip of the societal heap, and the top bureaucrats are graced with the ultimate power of coordinating the heap. Top immigration officials elucidate the public interest in immigration matters, and then guide the public policy development in relation to the matters they have elucidated. However, this has neither translated into a more expansive debate nor or a more inclusive citizen democracy, because the agenda is increasingly being filtered through a bureaucratic lens that increasingly obscures the competition between ethnic cultures and the conventional politics of Canadian society.

Vertical and Horizontal Dimensions of Social Life

The above interpretation actually fits well with John Porter's (1965) exploration of Canada's *Vertical Mosaic*. He observed that Canadian society was not developing along horizontal lines like a truly open and egalitarian state, but rather it was developing along vertical lines of differential wealth and status. In terms of Porter's horizontal and vertical dimensions of society, a horizontal order is inclusive and a vertical order is exclusive; a horizontal order is integrated and a vertical order is stratified. And it was his thesis that the vertical order of Canadian society was shaped, in large part, by ethnic group competition and class conflict. So, as he pointed out, by the mid-1960s the antagonism and asymmetry that had long existed between the

French and English was applicable to other groups as well. The national dualism and cultural resistance of immigrant minorities led to multiculturalism. In addition, he was also able to identify the early dynamics of administrative bureaucracy and the beginning of the rise of administrative men as a collateral force. As he put it,

> Bureaucracy is the concentration of administrative power within the machinery of hierarchical co-ordination. It is the product of two processes of social development: the increasing division of labour, and the increasing scale of organization. Jobs in the productive sense and offices in the administrative sense are narrowly defined. The individual is limited to his job or office, and his work is governed by a set of rules. Control is exercised through a series of supervisory offices which become fewer as the heights are ascended until it is centralized in a very few offices at the top. The proper functioning of these bureaucracies depends on the carrying out of the goals of centralized planning. Thus orders come down from the top. Success depends on carrying out orders, so that bureaucratically organized workers are predisposed to obedience. The bureaucratic structure of offices also represents the career avenues for those who want to rise. Obedience and the observance of rules improve the chances of promotion. Sanctions and rewards, like orders, also come from the top down. (The opposite would be the case where workers "controlled" their supervisors and managers by electing them, after making judgements about their performance. This is the principle underlying trade union organization, but, as we shall see later, it works out only in a limited fashion.) Bureaucratic organization is therefore a power instrument *par excellence*" (1965: 220).

While the bureaucratic management of government and major institutions was often purported to prevent the centralization of power, Porter pointed out that it actually becomes an instrument for the entrenchment of power. First, the complexity of modern life and mass society necessitates systematic organizations of people whose job it is to organize life systematically. Second, accompanying the technical operations associated with modernity and mass society, there are activities of pure administration as well, which require expertise in the organization and control of people. This accounts for the rise of the bureaucrat. The effect is that bureaucratic authority is increasingly entrenched and verticalized.

In 1983, for example, an internal memorandum on (what is known in the trade as) "functional authority" was issued by the Deputy Minister and Chairman of Employment and Immigration Canada in perfect bureaucratese. The vertical authority relationships of the Immigration Commission still stand:

> Functional authority, applied within the [department], is based on the principle that the level of authority must be consistent with the office of accountability. Correspondence originated by a region or NHQ [national

headquarters] at the level of chief would be considered as requesting or extending advice; under normal circumstances, and with prior consultation, regions would be expected to follow that advice. If the advice offered adversely affects regional operations, yet is required in the interests of standardization, or as a result of central agency requirements, the matter is to be referred to the next higher NHQ and regional level for resolution. Guidance requested by a regional director or extended by a NHQ functional director general/director should be viewed as expert, and prudence suggests that it should be followed; however, in the judgement of regional management, when such guidance does not act in the best interests of the public, or if it contravenes instructions previously received, it must be referred to the next higher NHQ and regional level for resolution. Direction requested by a regional executive head, or extended by a NHQ functional executive head, should, under normal circumstances, be accommodated quickly and in an appropriate manner. However, executive heads may refer any matter to the deputy minister/chairman for consideration or decision (found in Malarek, 1987: 44–45).

The vertical mosaic of ethnic group power and class conflict, precipitated by the French-English struggle and identified by Porter as the dominant force in Canada, has not become a horizontal mosaic and classless society in the 1990s. Instead, a kind of discretionary authority has been increasingly consigned to officials to manage old class conflicts and the rest of the complex social environment, and then this authority is further centralized hierarchically within the bureaucratic organization itself. So, while Porter's vertical mosaic has perhaps been abated somewhat in recent years, a vertical society remains, generated and represented by "big bureaucracy" itself (see Lipset, 1989).

This was again identified in its nascence by Porter as the "managerial revolution" concept and the escalation of the hierarchical apparatus of control:

> It has been suggested that knowledge has become so important in power competitions that hired experts actually run the bureaucratic organizations for which they work. This "managerial revolution" concept is often overdrawn, but there is no doubt that in all bureaucratic organizations there are conflicts between the elective and bureaucratic principle ... it is often argued that these elected heads fall into the hands of hired officials who control the flow and application of knowledge (Porter, 1965: 222–223).

In Porter's way of thinking, from early on the democratic ideology of ethnic equality and multiculturalism was a fraud perpetrated primarily by the British upon all other Canadians, including the French, in order to maintain social control over the dominion (Burnet, 1983: 240). Marxists similarly see multiculturalism as a means used by those in the corporate ruling class for dividing the working classes, through insistence on their cultural and linguistic differences rather than on their economic similarities (Bernier, 1979; Dorais et al. 1994: 397). However, the administrative sector of modern society now vies for social power and control with the more traditional elites in business and politics. The bureaucrat elite no longer merely mediates group conflict and power competitions; they are part of the dynamic. The idea of multiculturalism in Canada can no longer be seen as merely an ideological tool of British hegemony or the wider corporate elite. It is actually characterized by the dominance of government rather than any grassroots or social group articulation of its definitions and reality (Dorais et al., 1994: 402).

The social conflict theory and model of human behaviour assumes that society is created out of the competition between vocal interest groups to influence the national agenda and impact public policy (see Olson, 1965). The original French-English conflict, as well as the subsequent recognition of multiculturalism and reconstitution of the Canadian identity along pluralistic lines, was conducive to and illuminated by social conflict theory (Brimelow, 1986). Today, however, we live in a world where institutional bureaucracy and its elite administrators are increasingly taking charge of negotiating the problem of heterogeneity and diversity for the state and the public interest. As a result, it could be argued that our immigration system today is not so much about the social conflict and effective lobbying of interests as it is about the cult of the expert.

The managerial revolution concept, identified by Porter, is no longer a mere concept; it is now a full-fledged bureaucratic coup. The machinery of society is now run by clusters of administrative government officials who often comprise, with their corporate and political counterparts, interlocking elites (Clement, 1975). In the field of immigration proper, the matter goes even further. Here, it is now not "overdrawn" at all to say the "elected heads fall into the hands of hired officials who control the flow and application of knowledge." Indeed, in the public policy sphere of immigration, the bureaucratic principle has now fully usurped the elective principle.

For instance, a survey by the Immigration Department's Research Unit, which looked at the 1988 tax records of independent (economic) immigrants who arrived in 1981 and 1985, found that on average they earned considerably more than family-class (non-economic) immigrants and even the Canadian wage earner. This, of course, was a foundational study for the new ten-year immigration plan for 1995. On the basis of the Research Unit's finding, and despite Immigration Minister Sergio Marchi's and his cabinet colleagues self-professed pro-family immigration impulses, department officials convinced the Liberal government to put a greater emphasis on attracting economic immigrants rather than on family reunification. The day after the announcement of the new immigration policies, *The Globe and Mail* noted:

> This view was espoused at length by Mr. Marchi when the Liberals were the Opposition and for several months after they took office last year. At that time, he declared family reunification a priority.

> But his department advisers apparently have persuaded him that the issue isn't so much the quality of family-class immigrants as the wide gap between them and economic immigrants (*The Globe and Mail*, Nov. 2, 1994).

The fact is that administrative officials in the Immigration Commission are now in such complete control that they are often no longer inclined to defer their decision-making authority to elected officials as they may have done in the past, nor are they inclined to play a dutiful role of giving away their expertise to the public.

In this context, while arguments in support of immigration as a essential component of nation building have been generated by the enlightened professionals for some time, and have been continuously fed to politicians to be repeated in one Speech from the Throne after another in the House of Commons, many citizens remain unconvinced, as an ever-widening gulf emerges between public opinion and official immigration policy. As a result of this, the scale of immigration in Canada is far ahead of general public support. It is clear that this is at least partly due to the fact that the public-at-large have been inhibited from fully understanding or impacting the immigration system and have been subsumed by an agenda that is not identical with their stated attitudes or preferences.

From Spin Doctors to Policy Moguls

In the beginning, the rise of large-scale bureaucracy in Canada in the field of immigration created a parallel universe of sorts that first aligned itself with the established Anglophone and Francophone elite bases of power in Canadian society, reinforcing the traditional (political) authorities, the Tories and the Grits, by becoming the answer-man or articulate-mouthpiece for the installed (political) party. The elected officials and representatives of the people first made (political) decisions based on party platform, while administrative officials or senior civil servants did all the spade-work. The bureaucrats provided information and executed the policy initiatives of the political elect.

In its fuller bloom, the administrative decision-making process of the bureaucrats began to dominate the executive decision making of politicians, and new bureaucratic organizations were created to break down the monopolies of older departments. Task forces and interdepartmental committees sprang up to bridge the gap between partisan politics and effective management. Here, bureaucracy and the top bureaucrats actually began to commandeer some state institutions, putting words in the mouths of the elected authorities—stealing their thunder, as it were.

In this regard, today we have the term "spin doctor," which has come into being as part of our everyday vocabulary, signifying the bureaucratic skill of advancing a compelling argument for an otherwise seemingly partisan (political) position. More and more, bureaucracy turns the established political authorities into puppets or frontmen, mouthing words provided for them by their "spin doctors" until, in the final analysis, the superbureaucrats are providing the (political) questions as well as the answers, shaping the very thinking and decisions made by elected officials. Here is where the spin doctors become "policy moguls," formulating and writing the immigration scriptures.

Of course, the unique French-English acrimony that originally drove state politics in Canada still intrudes into all aspects of Canadian society, including immigration policy. Indeed, it is built right into the system. Section 109 of the Immigration Act provides a legal basis for federal-provincial agreements on immigration policy and programs. The most comprehensive of these is the Canada-Quebec Accord, which came into force on April 1, 1991 (replacing the former Cullen-Couture Agreement). It prescribes the sharing of responsibilities between the federal government and the province of Quebec in all areas relating to immigration, demographic and employment questions, as they apply to Quebec. But it is the bureaucratic organization of experts that provides the advice and consent on how the ethnic mosaic and political regimes should govern. They are responsible for informing the cooperative efforts in all areas related to demographic and employment questions as they are related to distribution and settlement patterns. Thus, Canada and Quebec now participate jointly and equally in immigrant selection, albeit according to criteria established for each party by a new and improved bureaucratic elite.

Under the Canada-Quebec Accord, much of the thrust of the Cullen-Couture Agreement was maintained regarding the selection of independent immigrants and refugees, but, in addition, integration services were completely taken over by Quebec, and a transfer of federal money was made to the province for this purpose. Canada agreed to transfer money to Quebec for integration and settlement programs in the amount of $75 million for 1991–2, rising to $90 million by 1994–5 (Young, 1994: 20–1). According to government figures, the current transfer payment for 1997-8 is down to $80 million.

Quebec's independent immigrants are selected pursuant to its own points system (subject to the federal statutory criteria relating to medical, criminal and security requirements). Quebec also selects refugees destined to the province. Although members of the family class are not "selected" in the same sense as independent and refugee applicants, Quebec immigration nevertheless plays a role in interviewing applicants abroad and providing counselling. Quebec also sets the financial criteria that sponsors in Canada must meet.

Under the Canada-Quebec Accord, Quebec's most significant role is with regard to independent immigrants. Both the Canada and Quebec selection processes are parallel, having many of the same features, with points for education, employment, specific vocational preparation and so on. The Quebec grid, however, rewards knowledge of French significantly more than knowledge of English. The Quebec grid also contains a number of factors not present federally. Applicants to Quebec can receive five points for having relatives or friends who reside in Quebec in the settlement area (two points if they reside elsewhere in Quebec). Spouses can also boost applicants' points if they speak French or have an occupation for which there is at least an average demand in Quebec. Finally, there are points available for families with children under twelve years of age, with a maximum of four points for three children.

In order to fulfil its objectives relating to the selection of immigrants, Quebec has established offices in nine countries. These offices are in Bangkok, Brussels, Buenos Aires, Hong Kong, London, Mexico City, New York and Paris. In three cases, the offices are located in the Canadian Embassy, and in the other six, the offices are in separate buildings (Young, 1992: 6).

Today we have expert sets of Canadian bureaucrats and Quebec bureaucrats, Francophones and Anglophones, in a parallel reality, collectively engaged in the technical task of computing population and labour market needs in the light of social, economic, demographic and, of course, cultural criteria. So the field of immigration is an example of an area of public policy where the technical operations and formulas are arrived at and applied by bureaucratically organized officials in overlapping cultural regimes. In both (or all) instances, these officials are related to the public and its elected representatives in the same way that knowledge is related to mere opinion or enlightenment is related to ignorance.

As time and bureaucracy move forward, the bureaucrat elite are becoming less and less inclined to defer any authority at all to outsiders—Francophone, Anglophone or otherwise. For all intents and purposes, even high-level politicians and party leaders can be bureaucratically out-manoeuvred today, as the following article (on the highly contested "bond system" for immigration sponsorship) reveals:

> Former immigration minister Bernard Valcourt says the Liberal government is creating one system for the rich immigrants and another for the poor.
>
> He said he was "flabbergasted" by Immigration Minister Sergio Marchi's proposal last week to force people to post bonds if they wanted to bring relatives to Canada.
>
> "I couldn't believe it," Valcourt said. "I remember that position being made to me (during Mulroney's term) and we rejected the suggestion (as) … unwieldy and unnecessary. We saw no reason to penalize the overwhelming majority through a bond system. Marchi noted that taxpayers are shelling out $700 million a year for people who fail to live up to their sponsorship agreements (*The Toronto Star*, Nov. 6, 1994).

Much to their consternation, even today's transient politicians are now "flabbergasted" about being essentially out-of-the-loop in the policy development agenda when they don't conform to bureaucratic rationality.

We can see that contemporary immigration bureaucracy approaches the dimensions of the Weberian ideal type more closely, perhaps, than any other institution in Canada. It has become its own unit of analysis, framing the question of who gets into the country in terms of a matrix of efficiency gains, and then vetting the answers so as to hear only what it wants to hear.

5
Containment Strategies

The public may be ill informed and alienated about Canada's immigration policy, but it is now wide awake with opinions and anxieties. As the Canada Employment and Immigration Advisory Council observed, there is an escalating public interest today in the field of immigration:

> Immigration is a misunderstood subject, until recently it has been left to experts. Otherwise well-informed opinion leaders often have little knowledge of immigration issues. Few newspapers pay regular attention to immigration issues, with the exception of covering special events. However, the last two years are an exception to that rule. Immigration, and especially refugees, have become a fashionable reporting subject for the media ("Perspective on Immigration in Canada," Canada Employment and Immigration Advisory Council, August, 1988: 8).

This renewed interest has been precipitated by a media-blitz awareness of the global population crisis and of increased urbanization and metropolitanization within Canada, along with the accompanying problems of traffic congestion, housing shortages and environmental pollution. Further, recessions, stagflations and energy crises, together with a rapid growth of the labour force as a consequence of the high birth rate of forty years ago and combined with high labour force participation rates by women, have helped to create a general climate that is not particularly favourable to more immigration.

However, it was a series of events beginning in 1986 that actually marked the great immigration awakening in Canada. The Canada Employment and Immigration Advisory Council noted the following:

> [A] series of events began in the spring of 1986 with the arrival of the Tamils off the coast of Newfoundland. This caused much discussion, most of which was sympathetic to refugees. In June 1987, 174 South Asiatics (Sikhs) landed secretly on the shores of Nova Scotia and sought refugee status. In August the government recalled parliament and tabled Bill C–84 in which it claimed increased powers to cope with situations such as the Tamil and Sikh landings ("Perspective on Immigration in Canada," Canada Employment and Immigration Advisory Council, August, 1988: 1).

With the surreptitious arrival of the Tamils off the coast of Newfoundland in 1986—followed by the clandestine landing of the Sikhs on the shores of Nova Scotia in the following year, followed by a plane load of Turks, followed by the Trinidadian queue-jumpers, followed by the Sri Lankan insurrectionists, and so on—immigration has been more and more in the forefront of the news, finally achieving an almost equal footing with such matters as free trade, the Meech Lake Accord, and the constitutional referendum initiatives. Furthermore, now that the global issue of international terrorism has been added to the mix as a new subscript to the debate, immigration is likely to remain an eminent public policy issue in Canada for some time to come.

Bureaucratic Strategies for Containing Public Sentiment

For their part, immigration administrators have developed a number of effective strategies for containing the dismissive public sentiments and disruptive racial attitudes in the wider society, while continuously asserting their bureaucratic authority. I will discuss these bureaucratic strategies here in succession.

1. *Restricting Direct Input from the Voters into Policy Development.* Firstly, in regard to the containment of negative public sentiments, it is notable that the public are allowed no direct input into the immigration system. The public can vote for the political party they want to lead them, which, of course, is indirectly connected to immigration policy. The public can also consult with special committees of the Senate and House of Commons, who periodically conduct hearings, conferences, seminars and opinion forums before they report their findings to parliament. But the public has no direct input into the clause-by-clause policy, which is for the most part crafted by the professional administrators behind closed doors in departmental and interdepartmental committees. Thus, the functional authority of the bureaucracy mitigates against public participation in policy development and inhibits political mobilization and other collective action.

2. *Utilizing Bureaucratese.* Bureaucratic jargon or bureaucratese reflects the belief that the sloppy thinking and unrefined interferences in everyday life and speech can be a nuisance and hinderance in the attempt to create proper institutions for people. Therefore, for the true bureaucrat, bureaucratese is a way of being obscure for the public's own good.

Consider the following, which translates into meaning "Sorry, you have to leave the country."

Dear Miss Sanchez:

This is in reference to your request for consideration under subsection 114(2) of the Immigration Act to seek an exemption from the Governor-in-Council from the requirements of subsection 9(1) of the Immigration Act.

The individual circumstances of your request have been carefully reviewed and it has been determined that your case does not warrant referral to the Governor-in-Council either for reasons of public policy or humanitarian and compassionate considerations.

You have not established that under-served or disproportionate hardship would result if you were required to leave Canada, nor have you demonstrated that your presence in Canada is in the national interest.

Embedded in the bureaucratic jargon of this rejection letter are criteria such as "for reasons of public policy" and "in the national interest" that have never been specified and, so, cannot be challenged.

The notion is, by excluding ordinary citizens from the dialogue and decision-making process, proper institutions can be created both faster and better for those same citizens. Of course, the public do not see the obscurity matter in the same way. The public's definition of bureaucratic jargon is the result of partly not understanding the bureaucrat's language and partly due to the fact that the bureaucrat's talk is incongruous. In the mind of the general public, incongruity is covered over by incomprehensibility. In other words, bureaucratese is a private language that covers the mistakes of officials. In both cases, in the public arena and in the bureaucracy, however, bureaucratic jargon is seen as an interactional tool for the bureaucrat that prevents the intrusion of the uninitiated into the discussion of policy issues and, thereby, protects against public interference into bureaucratic decision making.

In this interactional process, it is also logical that over time the bureaucratic elite can come to believe that they know what is best for both the public and the politicians, and they can begin to exercise their authority independent of the citizen democracy they purport to serve. It is in this regard that bureaucratic authorities are able to speak of ethics and democracy but take unethical and draconian measures to preserve the competence of the system—such as the recent overtures to automation designed to eliminate all human points of contact:

A total overhaul of the immigration department will result in most face-to-face service being replaced by telephone centres and electronic client cards and the lay off of as many as 1,200 department staff by 1997.

Under a "renewal" blueprint delivered to all office managers yesterday, the department hopes to eliminate almost all face-to-face service with its thousands of clients—and save $54 million from its annual budget by April 1997.

Most immigration applicants would be issued plastic cards, like bank cards, that would allow them to get access to their files from remote locations.

Virtually all applications would be handled by mail at remote processing centres and all inquiries would be channelled through central telephone centres. Only complex cases would be dealt with in person at immigration offices (*The Toronto Star*, Sept. 9, 1995).

Hence, the ultimate immigration management action plan, as we enter the twenty-first century, has finally been crafted, and it aims to eliminate all human-to-human, or face-to-face, immigration service entirely. The Case Processing Centre in Vegreville, Alberta, which opened in 1994, was supposed to process all immigration applications from inside Canada in a more thorough and expeditious manner. However, boxes of applications were unopened for months because initially there was no system in place to monitor all applications on arrival to ensure they were complete. In addition, the increased automation of the system posed barriers to people who had not mastered English or French. Responsibility for answering people's questions immediately began to be off-loaded to the private sector—with the immigration department requiring that people pay huge amounts of money for services (the processing and landing fees are in excess of $3,000 for a family of four)—all while continuing to provide less and less service.

3. *Obfuscating the Notion of the General Consensus.* On behalf of the prevailing government, senior officials tend to justify immigration policy on the grounds of seeking a "general consensus"—which, of course, does not correspond to any particular opinion and therefore affords policy makers (who have already effectively distanced themselves from direct public input) the luxury of not abiding by any. However, the usual tactic is to seek out and promote only those public sector opinions that are in accord with the already preferred direction. These chosen opinions are then referred to as the general consensus. The 1985 Task Force on Program Review (The Neilsen Task Force) wrote the following with respect to the immigration program and emerging public sentiments:

> Review is also made more difficult by the fact that it is hard to obtain an unambiguous representation of public preferences and attitudes concerning immigration. On the one hand, available polling data suggest, and have for some years, that increased immigration is opposed by a majority and incidental material suggests some degree of tension and resentment, possibly racial in origin, in Toronto, Vancouver and Montreal. On the other hand, virtually the entire body of organized opinion (lawyer groups, refugee sponsoring and church groups, immigration aid groups, etc...) tends to favour more immigration, relaxation of criteria and amnesties for particular groups. It is understandably the more organized views which are sought out by the press and represented by parliamentary committees, and it is these which tend to appear most frequently in media coverage of immigra-

tion matters ("Improved Program Delivery, Citizenship, Labour and Immigration," a study team report to the Task Force on Program Review, 1985: 132).

To paraphrase the authors of the Neilsen Task Force, public opinion on immigration in Canada falls into two general categories—disorganized and organized. Within this opposition in the public arena, as is duly noted, the immigration bureaucracy will not usually support negative sentiments among the general population in regard to the nature of immigration policy. However, it may, and often does, accommodate the more organized opinion in Canada from church groups and the like, which tends to favour more immigration, relaxation of criteria and amnesties for particular groups—that is, insofar as this organized opinion falls within the bounds of potential productivity or efficiency gains and provided those who hold to such opinions are willing to pay the requisite processing fees.

4. *Providing the Immigration Vocabulary for Public Use and Consumption.* Since immigration is now commonly viewed as a major concern by both the elected representatives of government and the general public, the immigration authorities have provided (or made available) a vocabulary for both groups to express their concern and defined such current migratory phenomenon as "economic migrants" (those coming to Canada mainly because of better employment prospects than in their home country), the phenomenon of global "asylum shopping" (which refers to refugee claimants who scout out countries with the best social services package), "passport babies" (which refers to children born in Canada but rendered stateless by non-resident parents), "criminal element immigration" (which refers to a general class of individuals fleeing prosecution rather than persecution), and, last but not least, the phenomenon of the "family-class echo" (where increased migration from refugee source countries by individuals claiming refugee status is numerically compounded by the reunification of family members). By allowing the public to become privy to the immigration vocabulary and defining the terms, the experts also act to delineate the public discussion and deflect potential ethnic tensions that can arise from increasing diversity. So, for instance, the dramatic increase in Sri Lankan migration to Canada doesn't suggest that a red flag be raised in regard to Sri Lankans or any particular ethnic group, but rather it echoes an alarm in regard to a growing migratory phenomenon that puts a strain on the resources and poses a threat to program delivery and the competence of the system. The vocabulary is designed to conceptualize immigration problems without marginalizing individuals or groups. So it allows the public to

address its anxiety—without, up to this point at least, resorting to outright hostility against any single culprit or scapegoat.

5. *Preventing Scapegoating*. Scapegoating refers to a phenomenon of blaming one's troubles, frustration or sense of guilt on some convenient but innocent person or group. (Once a year the ancient Hebrews symbolically placed their sins on a goat and then drove the goat into the wilderness—hence the term.) In the words of the Canada Employment and Immigration Advisory Council, scapegoating is connected to racial attitudes:

> It is extremely difficult, based on polls conducted in the last five years, to draw conclusions about the attitudes of Canadians towards racism. An August 1987 poll sought to identify Canadian attitudes towards non-white immigrants. Results seemed to indicate that opinion distribution is almost the same for immigrants belonging to visible minorities as for other immigrants. However, it can be assumed that racial attitudes of Canadians are affected by a number of external and changing factors, for example, the economy, so that it would not be so much a fundamental behaviour, but rather attitudes which are modified by circumstances. Immigrants, and by extension all visible minorities, may therefore become scapegoats ("Perspective on Immigration in Canada," Canada Employment and Immigration Advisory Council, August, 1988: 8).

Scapegoating has been largely avoided in Canada in the latter part of the twentieth century, despite extended bouts of economic recession. This is partly because of the democratic ethos in the Canadian collective consciousness and, perhaps, also because the immigration authorities have succeeded in enforcing a vocabulary that has prevented immigration from being consistently framed in a racial context. As a result, Canada has a relatively low incidence of acts of violence against immigrants and other ethnic minorities. Anthony Richmond noted the following:

> However, the overall incidence of violence in Canada, including cases that have a clear racial component, is much lower than in the United States. The rate of serious violent offences known to the police is five times higher in the United States than in Canada. The rates for Britain and Germany are also lower than those of the United States. One thing all four countries have in common is a trend in the past decade towards more crimes of violence and more individual acts of violence specifically directed at immigrants or other ethnic minorities. Racial and ethnic harassment is not a new phenomenon, but the number of reported cases in Britain and Germany has been rising. In the latter country, Turkish immigrants who were long-term residents were singled out. Attacks on homes and hostels resulted in some fatalities. Governments in several countries, including Britain, Germany, France, and Sweden, reacted to heightened racism by tightening immigration controls and threatening to deport illegal immigrants (1994: 112).

At present, immigration issues are still centred on the integrity and abuses of the system and not against any particular ethnic or racial group. However, if the current debate about immigration escalates in Canada beyond the issues of system abuse into a wider domain faster than a vocabulary of system abuse can be created to accommodate it, the possibility of mounting conflict leading to racial antagonism and wholesale scapegoating increases. It is not out of the realm of possibility for ethnic and race relations in Canada to deteriorate into a downward spiral, particularly if the Canadian public is kept uninformed. In this regard, it has been argued quite forcefully that Canada's racial problems may be only a generation away (Reitz, 1987; see also Reitz & Breton, 1994).

6. *Controlling the Question-Answer Sequence in the Immigration Debate.* The ultimate technique for containing public sentiments and asserting bureaucrat authority is to gain control of the very nature of the popular immigration debate by controlling the question-answer sequence. An example of this occurred at the planning meetings held in Montebello, Quebec, in March 1994, organized by the Public Policy Forum. The meeting consisted of the Minister of Immigration and Citizenship, senior department officials, and thirty other people selected from across Canada from various fields of endeavour, ranging from business leaders, trade leaders, social services, health and welfare and so on. This planning meeting is attributed with providing the basis for the ten-year immigration plan *Into the 21st Century—A Strategy for Immigration and Citizenship* (Immigration Consultation Report, Citizenship and Immigration, 1994), and for providing the framework for the Minister's $1 million coast-to-coast consultations prior to the tabling of Bill C–44 in the fall of 1994. The groundwork laid prior to public consultations with the Minister consisted of developing

(a) a discussion document which provided basic information on Canada's immigration program, introduced the ten issues identified at Montebello and posed questions to incite discussion;

(b) an organizer's guide which offered some basic information and suggestions for hosting a consultation meeting;

(c) a tabloid which presented a condensed version of the Discussion Document; and

(d) a reporting form to invite and assess Canadians in reporting their views to the department.

Thus senior immigration officials not only formulated the (ten) legitimate issue-questions that were to be discussed in the cross-country consultations with Canadians, they also provided these Canadians with organizer guides, basic information and suggestions, a synopsis of the issues and a report-form questionnaire to be filled out and returned to the department (to monitor the public temperature, and monitor the success of their guidance). It is to be noted that, inadvertently—before the Minister's $1 million coast-to-coast public consultations were officially over, and while they were being hailed as the most extensive public consultations ever—some enterprising members of the media happened to uncover a pre-existing policy paper on Bill C–44, drafted by senior department officials, complete with purposed changes to the existing legislation and with long-range strategy recommendations on how and when to introduce the proposals to the Canadian public. In other words, "the fix was already in."

Containing a Backlash

Policy officials will not ordinarily indulge the man-on-the-street who inquires if immigration is "white enough"—although polls seem to indicate that this question is at the tip of many ordinary tongues—because such a question conforms neither to democratic values nor to bureaucratic reasoning. For example, a public opinion poll conducted by Angus Reid Polling Company and *The Toronto Star* confirmed that many Canadians are now inclined to believe immigration in general, and non-white immigration in particular, is threatening the root fabric of the country:

> One in four Canadians believe non-white minorities are threatening the fabric of the country, a poll suggests. One in three Canadians hold intolerant views and attitudes towards ethnic and cultural minorities and 12% were found to be highly intolerant, according to the Angus Reid-Southam poll. The phone poll of 1,501 adults conducted Feb. 16–22 (1993) also found:
>
> - 57% of Canadians believe minority groups should try to be more like other Canadians rather than maintain their native culture and language,
> - 26% believe non-whites could damage the fabric of Canadian society,
> - 47% said Canada is taking in too many immigrants,
> - 42% don't believe recent immigrants should have as much say in Canada as people who were born and raised here,
> - 24% said more white and fewer non-white immigrants should be taken in by Canada,
> - 13% believe Canada would be better off if all recent immigrants went back to their home countries. Eight-nine percent of highly intolerant respondents agreed with the proposition that Canadian society is being threatened by non-white minorities. This group has "some difficulty in terms of tolerance," says Darrell Bricker of the Angus Reid polling com-

pany. "They tend to be older, they tend to be disproportionately rural and they tend to be less educated," he said. These people overwhelmingly agree that new immigrants are taking too many jobs from other Canadians. The poll is considered accurate within 2.5 percentage points, 19 times out of 20 (*The Toronto Star*, April 11, 1993).

Asking "Are there too many?" and "Is it white enough?" may be everyday questions from some Canadians, but they are officially delegitimized as not only illiberal and inequitable but also—and most importantly—potentially detrimental to the overall industrial performance of the nation as a whole.

Since the Liberals came to power in 1993 on the heels of their "Red Book" promise to aim for annual immigration levels of one percent of the population (soon to be about 300,000), the economic-class category has grown from being approximately equal to the size of the family-class category to the point where the economic class is now almost twice that of the family class. The current public disaffection for immigration has effectively curtailed intake targets and restructured the breakdown—preventing immigration officials from increasing intake beyond 220,000 in 1997. Citizenship and Immigration Minister Lucienne Robillard, who tabled the annual report to parliament entitled *Staying the Course* (October 1996), claimed a social backlash against immigration in recent years has induced the Liberal government to "hold the line" on immigrant levels for 1997. "Right now in Canada, I must tell you that the population is divided," Robillard said. "I think that to have more immigrants in this country, we need the support of the population of Canada." Robillard further asserted, "We head towards the one percent but we have to take into account the reaction of the people of Canada." With such high disapproval ratings for immigration, the ability of the policy officials to contain the potential political backlash resulting from any immigration intake policy at all is no mean feat.

From the perspective of big bureaucracy, the question is not whether immigrants in general, and non-white immigrants in particular, are taking jobs away from real Canadians and eroding the social fabric. The question is how many and what type of immigrants are conducive to the maximum industrial and other efficiency levels in society. Rather than make a concerted effort to advance public awareness and mobilize their support, the response has been to raise the economic component in the immigration-intake equation, to downplay the effect of immigration and hope thereby to placate public fears.

6

Immigration and Economic Prosperity

Canada's early immigration program was organized around a theory of social evolution and reputed biological traits. Today, however, this outlook has been reduced to a crank view, along with anti-Semitism, the Vatican conspiracy, and the gnomes of Zurich. The historical contingency of this movement eventually unmasked its claims of scientific authority as a kind of self-serving racialism, which established a marked preference for settlers of European stock.

Immigration as a Mutually Compensatory Exchange

Contemporary social theory in the field of immigration has moved far away from any racial taxonomies that tie the biological to the social, but history may reveal it is no less self-serving. Social theory is now routinely oriented towards helping to organize Canada's immigration program around the macro-myth of immigration and economic prosperity. In 1988, for example, the report on "The Perspectives on Immigration in Canada," issued by the Canada Employment and Immigration Advisory Council, acknowledged the growing professional preoccupation with the economics of immigration:

> In the last few years, studies have assessed the economic role of immigration from two view points. The first one examined, from a "macro" point of view, the effects of immigration on the Canadian economy as a whole. The second dealt with the more specific contributions of entrepreneur and investor immigrants to the economy ("Perspective on Immigration in Canada," Canada Employment and Immigration Advisory Council, August, 1988: 13).

The economics of immigration has come to the forefront as a public policy issue and as the major focal point of professional literature (Simon, 1989). By promoting the idea of a mutual reciprocity of economic and other gains between newcomers and citizens, it is hoped that the general public's anxiety over the immigration issue will be alleviated. In 1993, for example, Public Security Minister Doug Lewis, speaking to the Law Society of Upper Canada, claimed:

> We are eager to get the message out that just as immigrants realize new opportunities when they settle here, Canada and Canadians likewise benefit.... I happen to believe that immigrants are absolutely necessary on an economic basis, as well as social. We have had studies that show that immigrants, in proportion to the number of people already in the country, are more likely to create jobs when they come here (*The Toronto Star*, Oct. 2, 1993).

Immigration, as a mutually compensatory exchange between Canadian citizens and newcomers, is now a standard political refrain and dominant paradigm in Canadian society, propped-up by the studies that "show" immigration means jobs and prosperity.

Public Dissatisfaction with the Immigration System

In the 1990s, every major politician associated with immigration, Liberal and Conservative, has lent support to the link between immigration and economic prosperity:

> We, as Canadians, must do everything possible to ensure that we understand both the challenges and the opportunities that immigration provides for all of us. And we must each play a part to ensure that we provide a genuine welcome to those who have chosen Canada as their new home— Barbara McDougall, Minister of Employment and Immigration (St. Paul's Report Number 21, November 1990).

> It is fundamental to the future of this country that we have increased levels of immigration and the federal government is committed to this goal— Gerry Phillips, Ontario Minister of Citizenship, 1991 (Ryerson College).

> We continue to see immigration as a way to achieve our demographic goals, develop our economic base, enhance our world economic contribution, meet the demands of family and community, and provide help during international humanitarian crises—Doug Lewis, Public Security Minister, 1993.

> Canada's role within the family of nations is to try to continue to be— within our means—a voice of compassion (Sergio Marchi, Minister of Immigration and Citizenship).

Yet the hypothesis that increased immigration leads to prosperity is more and more of a hard sell from the point of view of everyday life experience. On the surface, it appears to many that exactly the opposite is true—that it is primarily the prosperity of Canada as a society that affords the possibility of increased immigration, and not the reverse. To the ordinary citizen it increasingly appears that immigrants have not created our good fortune, but rather that they flock here in droves on the waves of global migration to share in our good fortune, as it were. Accordingly, many people now find it difficult to swallow the "prosperity pill" that immigration expands the economy and the job base; if anything, they tend to see immigrants as taking jobs away from other Canadians.

If a significant number of Canadians have perhaps always felt this way, it is only now that they are beginning to let these feelings be known. A telling development took place in the wake of the tabling of Bill C–44 in June of 1994. In the federal parliamentary debate, the right-wing Reform Party, critical of the proposed Bill, put forward a platform advocating a moratorium on immigration in Canada—in the face of what was presented as "the hard evidence" from professionals inside and outside the department that independent (economic) immigrants as a group are a greater net contributor to society than Canadian citizens—for the stated purpose of allowing the public to regain its confidence in the immigration system. What is interesting about this, however, is not the formidability of the challenge—Bill C–44 was legislated in the fall of 1994, despite opposition, with a focus on attracting high quality independent and business immigrants. Rather, what is interesting is the suggestion that it may be possible to raise the issue of "validity" in the field of immigration by going beyond the mere compilation of economic data.

The issue of validity has been effectively raised in the past as an issue that does challenge the mere compilation of data. In the now-infamous 1986 internal audit of the immigration department, for instance, the departmental authors concluded (among other things) that, while the immigration department is heavy on figures, charts, graphs and percentages, there was very little in the way of statistics on just how *well* the work was being carried out. In other words, they pointed out that the correct procedures for the compilation of data is separate from issues of meaning and value. The report said that national headquarters placed strong emphasis on monitoring, but the question of just what was monitored arose, since current methods were directed mainly at measuring quantity activities rather than the quality of the results. The report concluded that, unless headquarters were to institute a formal and effective monitoring system to inform itself about service quality, the current system would continue to yield "vast amounts of data and very little useful information" (Malarek, 1987: 44–57).

In the area of policy development, the best and brightest of Canada's early ground-breaking social scientists, such as E.A. Forsey, John Porter and William Petersen, had already questioned the possibility of effective immigration planning, arguing that the absorptive power of the country is impossible to determine precisely over any substantial period; and, insofar as this is the case, it is difficult to see what is meant by an immigration "plan" in the first place, other than the continuous adjustment of the number of immigrants to current economic needs, as judged by current unemployment figures (Porter, 1965: 60–103). Meanwhile, many researchers, in total disregard of their predecessors, continue to conduct "optimum number" studies showing how many people can be let into Canada to be metabolized by the political economy at any given time and to build macroeconomic models that correlate immigration more closely with "labour market demand" (Bodkin and Marwah, 1987). What they do not address is the question of how immigration should serve society.

Much of the research literature supports the liberal view that says "yes" to immigration on the basis of its positive economics, while organizing the task for researchers of finding the optimum measures and breakdowns at which it is most cost effective. Paradoxically, this literature has now given birth to its own nemesis—a whole new 1990s branch of "no" literature. What are now popular are offerings by independent investigators, who question the present and future impact of substantial immigration, maintaining that soft entry requirements are damaging the economic infrastructure of our society (cf. Globerman, 1992), and others who challenge the current economic viability of immigration in Canada. Charles Campbell, a former and long-time member of the Immigration Appeals Board, suggests that Canada's immigration system is a time bomb ticking:

> The economic benefits of immigration have for years been a recurring defence of policy. Statements, usually by Ministers, are based on academic studies which deal with immigrants as a "mass." They are not a "mass." They are individuals and should be so selected and assessed. No one questions the contributions, often outstanding, of many of today's immigrants included in that "mass." Their successes are not by themselves a defence of the whole policy but it is clearly the intent of the Public Affairs Branch to use them for that purpose (Campbell, 1989: 33).

Other critics are also beginning to challenge the positive economic benefits of immigration. One of the more forceful critiques was offered by Daniel Stoffman in a series of "specials" to *The Toronto Star* (September 1992), where he argued that immigration adds little to the economy. Mr. Stoffman, among a growing number of other investigators and independent research organizations, argues that economics is a feeble foundation on which to construct an immigration policy in the first place. As he put it, immigration doesn't make you richer.

It makes immigrants richer if they came here from a poor country. It makes a few Canadians, such as immigration lawyers, richer. It makes other Canadians, especially those who compete for unskilled jobs, poorer. But for the majority, it makes little or no difference.

That is the opinion of most economists who have studied immigration. Whether the studies are done in Canada or elsewhere, they come to the same conclusion: neither immigration, nor population growth in general, has any impact on the income of the average native-born person.

In Canada, this old news has been kept as secret as if it were a formula for building a nuclear bomb. The federal government does not like to hear it because it justifies the world's largest per capita intake of immigrants by saying it makes us all better off.

Meanwhile, politicians representing ethnic ridings and other advocates of wide-open immigration cling to the nonsensical idea that "immigration creates jobs" (Of course immigration creates jobs because it makes the population larger, thereby increasing demand for products and services. But that doesn't mean unemployment is reduced by immigration. The new jobs are offset by the newly arrived immigrants who join the workforce.) (*The Toronto Star*, Sept. 22, 1992).

Thus, we now have a kind of investigative corroboration for the commonly held belief that outlanders and immigrants have not created our good fortune, but rather have a negligible "impact on the income of the average native-born person."

The Parallel between Capital Migration and People Migration

The formulation of the macromyth linking immigration to economic prosperity stems from the notion that the migration of people is somehow analogous to the migration of capital. It has even been suggested that research bearing upon the impact of immigration may garner insights relative to research surrounding foreign direct investment and free trade (Globerman, 1992). In principle, it is thought that the range of restrictions on the international movement of products and financial capital has a correlation to a country's economic efficiency and, ultimately, the economic welfare of its people. To the extent that trade liberalization and the migration of capital is an unrestricted stimulus for domestic and foreign market growth, individually and collectively nations grow richer.

When this principle is applied to human dimensions, the suggestion is that the range of restrictions on international immigration also has a relationship to the fortunes of individuals and to nations. Accordingly, to the extent that individual migration is for the purpose of maximizing individual skills, levels of wealth in the world will

increase. Furthermore, to the extent that immigration stimulates domestic workers to achieve higher levels of efficiency, there will be a
secondary wealth-enhancing effect. There are, of course, provisos
related to this augmentation of wealth, as economist Steven Globerman points out: "If the increased wealth generated by migration is not
repatriated, at least in part, to the country of emigration, the gains
from international migration may be captured entirely by the immigrant and the countries of immigration. Of course, this is also true in
the case of capital migration" (Globerman, 1992: 3).

The importance of the analogy between capital migration and
people migration is that it theoretically postulates direct and indirect
economic benefits from immigration, and this provides an attractive
foundation for much of the professional research literature in support
of a large-scale immigration program. However, one of the problems
with this analogy is that, despite the escalating phenomenon of global
migration in the last two decades, borders around the globe are
closing against economic migrants and assorted displaced and disaffected persons (Bean, Edmonston and Passell, 1990; Matas, 1989).
Regional economic communities, such as the EEC and the proposed
U.S.-Canada-Mexico free trade area, are facilitating movement within
the region while more severely restricting access to it (Richmond,
1994: 195). All in all, the borderless economic world has not been
conducive to a borderless peopled world. In fact, the reverse has
been true. As borders come down economically, they are erected
cognitively and politically to keep undesirables at bay and claims on
national sovereignty secure. So, while international migration is theoretically an integral part of the world capitalist economy, the repres-
sion of the flow of refugees and other displaced and disaffected
persons throughout the modern world reflects the lack of political
integration and instability of that system (Petras, 1981; Zolberg, 1989).

People migration in the global age is more like the antithesis than
the analogy of capital migration. It is true that, whereas nation-states
were once treated and analyzed as closed systems, we must now
address the reality of an interconnected global society; therefore,
comprehending the world as a total system (Giddens, 1985) is essential to any form of contemporary theory (Robertson, 1990). However,
to comprehend the world as a total system today means we have to
further recognize that the corollary of the globalization of the world
economy is the retribalization of civic life (McLuhan, 1962 and 1966).
Trade liberalization and the worldwide migration of capital is carried
out by increasing degrees of social and political regulatory constraint.
So the global economy lead to migratory pressures, which in turn

lead to an increased intensification of immigration admission-and-controls measures on a global scale.

Social Science as a Service Industry

In his analysis of Canada's immigration program in the 1940s, William Petersen argued that economic contingencies in Canadian society have a pervading effect on the political mobilization of the public or the masses, which in turn necessitates constant revisions to the immigration plan.

> The fact that opposition to large-scale immigration has been neutralized does not mean, however, that it is not a factor in the present programme, for its administrators know that their range of action is very limited. At the first indication of an economic recession, for example, whatever doubts arise about the wisdom of continuing the immigration programme will be mobilized into political action much more quickly because of this powerful, temporarily quiescent opposition. In the long run, a sizable immigration can bring Canada important benefits, but it is utopian to suppose that it will not cause short-term disturbances, and it is by these fluctuations that the programme is guided. Many resolutions demand a long-term immigration plan integrated with the future development of the rest of the economy; but this is not feasible partly because just the opposition of, among others, those who demand planning makes it necessary to adjust the present programme on a week-to-week basis (Petersen, 1965: 38).

With this sociological theorem in mind, finessing the public, or at least containing its potentially volatile sentiments regarding increased immigration, has grown from a preoccupation into a kind of science of behavioural engineering.

For their part, social scientists have been employed by the government for their quantifying skills in preparing studies on mobility, integration, attitudes of new immigrants and labour adjustment, rather than addressing the qualitative goals and interests of the country. The bulk of the professional literature on immigration consists of statistical and census analysis of international and domestic profiles and trends. It is produced, directly or indirectly, by the Immigration Department Research Division and the Policy Analysis Directorate, Immigration Policy Branch (internal divisions are subject to restructure and rename), as well as the government-funded studies undertaken by respected researchers associated with various universities across Canada, who may also be cross-associated with the major research "think tanks," such as the Centre for Refugee Studies, York University; the Institute for Behaviour Research, York University; the Fraser Institute, Simon Fraser University; the C.D. Howe Institute, and the Institute for Research on Public Policy in Montreal. These studies in the last thirty years number in the hundreds, if not thousands. For the most part, the appraisals emanating from these studies are contained within the overall policy parameters set by the immigration department. This, of course, may not be the intention or claim of the authors or the studies. However, at a social interaction level, they clearly have a symbiotic relationship with the established authorities. They are often entirely funded by, and funded at levels determined by their utility to, senior departmental officials.

The most popular studies in the field of immigration, and the studies that receive the support or recognition of government and other funding agencies, are studies in the areas of global migration trends (e.g., Hersak and Thomas, 1988; Simmons, 1988; Beaujot, 1989; Blackburn, 1990), immigration net profit areas (e.g., Samuels, 1988; Denton and Spencer, 1987; Simmons, 1988), integration and adaption studies (e.g., Herberg, 1989; Newwirth, 1987), and immigration and criminality studies (the latter being the newest of the new—for example, Samuels and Faustino-Santos, 1991; Borowski and Thomas, 1994). These are the hot topics of the 1990s and the age of global migration. And one can safely speculate that, as we move into the twenty-first century, illegal migration and criminality studies will take over the field, with the marriage of professional research literature and professional bureaucratic interests. As worthwhile as these studies undoubtedly are, the divisive forces surrounding immigration in society, fostered in part by the bureaucratic control of immigration knowledge, will remain untouched (and the general populace will remain mystified, bewildered and alarmed).

This body of research fits well within what has been called the civil service definition of the social scientist:

> This service includes positions the duties of which are to advise on, administer, supervise, or perform professional work requiring a knowledge of sociology and sociological methods, relating to the culture, structure or functioning of groups, organizations or social systems; to the relationships between groups, organizations or social systems; to the demographic characteristics, and ecological patterning of communities and societies; or to human behaviour in social situations (N.Z. Medalia and W.S. Mason, *American Sociological Review*, April 1963) (Theodorson and Theordorson 1969: 401).

In the civil service definition, theorizing is conceived to be a service industry, and social theorists provide a service like other service-oriented workers in our society. The notion is that you pay the theory practitioner and add his or her services to the pot, or to the whole, like any other practitioner in the modern industrial complex. These conceptual products are for sale to government departments directly. In the field of immigration, for example, social scientists are typically designated as significant professional practitioners if they have the tools to conduct studies of Canada's absorptive power and cost effectiveness at various points in time—in accord with the bureaucratic strictures of efficiency gains and cost-benefits analysis. Social theory becomes another technical skill and specialty, like other specialties within the differentiated division of labour. Theorizing is viewed as just another practice, not one that gives meaning to practice. And the theorist becomes a scripted bit player or contract player in the drama of life.

Of course, true social theorizing is more than a method or technique. As Randall Collins and Michael Makowsky (1985: 4) put it, true social theory is imbued with the spirit of discovery, and has "progressed by disengaging the web of everyday belief" through the process of asking "some previously unasked question" in order to "uncover sources of bias that we did not know existed." This is what Alan Blum and Peter McHugh (1984) identified as the foundation of the tradition of self-reflection in the social sciences. However, too often the contemporary job description requires that one not ask awkward questions (Collins and Makowsky, 1985). As C. Wright Mills once bluntly pointed out in an analysis of the analyzers, many modern social scientists have forfeited sociological imagination and have become institutional lackeys:

> I want to make it clear in order to reveal the political meaning of the bureaucratic ethos. Its use has mainly been in and for non-democratic areas of society—a military establishment, a corporation, an advertising agency, an administrative division of government. It is in and for such bureaucratic organizations that many social scientists have been invited to work, and the problems with which they there concern themselves are the kinds of problems that concern the more efficient members of such administrative machines (Mills, 1959: 115).

In Mill's projected view, many social scientists today are no longer engaged in the search for the reality "of" society, because they reflect the reality "in" society. They don't have a calling, but rather a career. So, the words *radical, critical, analytical* and *revolutionary* are no longer applicable, and the theorist is no longer a catalyst for change. As far as the immigration bureaucracy and power structure is concerned, social science is considered in its totality as merely a technical and quantitative task.

Much of the existing literature in the field of immigration, apart from statistically based studies (on a vast array of international and domestic profiles and trends) commissioned by the government, is oriented to unearthing the abuses of the system. Literature and research has focused on racism and race and ethnic tensions in Canada (beginning most notably with Abella and Troper, 1982; Adelman, 1982; Avery, 1979; Ramcharan, 1982; Li, 1988a, 1988b, and 1990) and the history of racism in immigration policy (e.g., Winks, 1971 and 1977; Schachter, 1984; Henry and Ginzberg, 1985; Billingsley and Muszynski, 1985; Li and Bolaria, 1985; Samuels, 1987; Nash, 1989; Richmond, 1990). This does not mean that concerns of equality have been resolved. In a multicultural society like Canada, the issue of equality is always front and centre in its evolution towards a more inclusive society. The equality issue of the 1990s is to ensure that gender is included in Canada's immigration standards of universality and equitable participation (e.g., Belfiore et al., 1985; Boyd, 1987; Basavarajappa and Verma, 1990; Seward, 1990).

The most uncompromising of the professional studies sponsored by the Department of Employment and Immigration (now Citizenship and Immigration) or Statistics Canada (see Richmond 1981; Samuel and Conyers, 1986; Beaujot, et al., 1988) tend to be census and profile studies, detailing useful statistical information in regard to the demographic characteristics of Canada's population. There are, of course, early seminal studies of immigration by Canadian researchers (such as Porter, 1965; Naegele, 1965; Petersen, 1959), but I am unaware of any government-funded or government-sponsored studies or non-government funded studies that actually give a critical analysis of contemporary immigration policy. They all may disagree with specific aspects of immigration policy, and present supporting evidence and recommendations for a system realignment or alteration, but they do not take the system or policy agenda to task, so to speak, by questioning and taking apart the contexts within which the system functions and the policy agenda is formulated. For the most part, researchers have chosen to help the bureaucrat elite in their mission—to compute the minute and technical calculations of Canada's population size, rate of growth and demographic structure, measured against labour market needs and population goals, in order to arrive at an operative plan. A concerted effort at a truly independent interaction between social research and policy development in the field of immigration has yet to be mounted with any consistency.

Intake Levels

The important public policy studies in immigration literature have been primarily focused on the question of the average level that immigration into Canada should take (e.g., Marr, 1975 and 1992; Samuels, 1989). Should intake levels be at 100,000 or 200,000 per year? Or should intake levels be even higher? Should Canada move to higher levels, for example, 330,000 per year, as immigrated in 1911, or even 400,000 per year, as immigrated in 1913 (Marr, 1992: 39)? How should intake levels be determined? Should they be raised in good economic times and lowered in bad times? Or are there other factors to consider?

The question of intake levels has been a key issue throughout the history of Canada's immigration program among policy-oriented researchers. It was observed early on, for instance, that Canada has been prone to tap-on/tap-off levels of inflow, which in a modern context has made long-range planning more difficult and causes problems for the administration of Canada's immigration policies (Petersen, 1965; Porter, 1965; Samuels, 1989). It has been further suggested that this volatility may be unnecessary (Samuels, 1989). If it is shown that various levels of immigration have only minor effects on Canada's economic and population structure, then there is little to be gained by continually changing the level of the inflow. Also, if considerations of population size and structure become more important factors in setting the level of immigration, they are by nature long term and add further to a rationale for a constant level of inflow rather than the cyclical one that is closely tied to the state of the Canadian economy (Marr, 1992: 39).

However, underlying the observable problems created by the volatility and cyclical nature of immigration flows, and the possible remedial rationale or amending formulas, is the matter of determining what the objectives of Canada's immigration policy should be. And the answer to this question depends entirely on the social goals of the country. Without the commitment of societal members, it does not matter how rational or sound immigration policy is, since it will always be problematic and divisive. In an age of global migration, an unsound immigration policy is a potential disaster that reverberates far beyond national boundaries. However, even sound and sensible immigration programming can have adverse effects in everyday life if it is not made compelling to Canadians. Canadian people need to see the rationale of their immigration policy or the body of professional research will continue to grow, while attitudes towards immigration in society become increasingly problematic and rancorous.

The Efficiency Gains Perspective of Bureaucracy

The disenchantment with and divisiveness caused by the immigration system is spreading. Many people, from all sectors of society, are becoming more deliberate in their accusation that the immigration program fails to deliver the goods and, so, poses a threat to the future well-being of the nation. In the face of opinion polls that suggest broad public displeasure with high levels of immigration, and the political ramifications that have resulted, the administrative officials in charge of Canada's immigration policy have been forced to redouble their efforts, converging full force and with intense specificity on the common economic themes of interest to the general Canadian public: Do immigrants displace native-born workers and lower wage levels? Do immigrants' earnings exceed or fall short of previous immigrants or Canadian-born workers' earnings? Do immigrants earn enough to keep off the dole? Has the quality of immigrant changed over time? (DeVoretz, 1992). The purpose of these rudimentary economics questions is not so much to mollify public anxiety as it is to entice or nuzzle public sentiment down the sanctioned bureaucratic pathways, since there is still a significant and unspoken gap between public preferences and attitudes concerning immigration and contemporary immigration policy.

However, after an exhaustive review of the professional literature on the earnings of immigrants, Arnold de Silva (1992), a Senior Researcher for the Economic Council of Canada, suggested that the investigation into the comparative economic performance of immigrants is inconclusive, and there is no expert consensus on the subject:

> Even on the broader question of the economic performance of immigrants, the evidence from existing studies is patchy and inconclusive. Some of these studies claim that immigrants have done quite well by pointing out that within about 20 years after their arrival, immigrants have been able to match the earning level of the native-born. However, other studies argue that this is not true of all immigrant groups, especially of some of the new groups who came during the 1980s. Thus there is no consensus on the subject (de Silva, 1992: 1).

In actuality, if the general public is typically concerned with economic gains and losses, the immigration bureaucracy is typically concerned with efficiency gains and losses. These concerns are similar but not exactly identical. The efficiency benefits of immigration may be incurred in ways that are quite apart from its manifestly economic benefits and in ways that are not immediately economical. So, for example, increased immigration may add to the enhanced creativity and flexibility of a diverse society as opposed to one that is homogeneous; or, it may stimulate the international penetration of markets through exports by firms with multilingual and multicultural salespeople and management; or, as some claim, immigration may imbue the receiving country with a sense of entrepreneurial spirit (Samuel and Conyers, 1986; Wattenberg and Zinsmeister, 1990). All or any of these would have a beneficial impact on society and industrial efficiency that, in the long term, is likely to dwarf all other short-term effects. As one study sponsored by the Policy and Program Development Immigration noted,

> there are other factors which do not render themselves easily to analysis, such as the entrepreneurial ability of immigrants. The immigrant entrepreneurs, both those who come under the business immigration program and others who become entrepreneurs either because they cannot find employment in their intended occupations or because they wanted to become self-employed, are well known to have added new jobs to Canada's economy. As Joseph Schumpeter pointed out decades ago: "The immigrant entrepreneur may innovate: the introduction of a new good or a new quality of a good, the introduction of a new method of production, the opening of a new market, the usage of new sources of supply of raw materials and industrial organization" (Employment and Immigration, "The employment effects of immigration: A balance sheet approach" by T.J. Samuel and T. Conyers, Policy Development, Policy and Program Development Immigration, 1986: 14).

Indeed, the Economic Council of Canada (ECC) itself has determined that the economic argument for immigration is weak at best. The EEC released a study in 1991 entitled *New Faces in the Crowd: Economic and Social Impacts of Immigration,* which concluded that there is no sustained correlation between immigration and economic growth and that immigration does not create unemployment.

On the first count (economic growth is not significantly affected by immigration), the ECC notes that there have been periods when per-capita income has grown rapidly while net immigration rates were quite low and other periods when the reverse was true. There have also been periods when both real incomes and immigration grew rapidly. On the second count, unemployment is not created by immigration because the number of firms will expand steadily to create the needed new jobs; however, sudden increases in immigration might strain market adjustment processes creating a temporary burst of unemployment.

The Economic Council of Canada also considers the economic argument that the aging Canadian population will cause dependency costs to rise, including health and social security. It concludes that a higher rate of immigration will provide at least part of the financial wherewithal to fund these spiralling dependency costs, but the contribution will be quite modest. Moreover, this contribution could be more than offset by the costs of social assistance and language training that would have to be provided for the influx of immigrants. Nevertheless, in the final analysis, it recommends that immigration should be gradually increased above the average levels of the last twenty-five years on the non-economic grounds that it will make Canada a more dynamic and exciting society.

The ECC also postulates that one of the major sources of economic gains to immigration is related to economies of scale. Specifically, immigration could improve real income levels in Canada if a larger population size contributed to greater efficiency. For every additional million persons above Canada's current population of 27 million, it is estimated that the Gross Domestic Product per capita would be higher by about 0.3 percent. This translates into $71 annually per present resident and $1894 annually per immigrant forever into the future. These are all gross amounts, since costs associated with immigrants have not been netted out (1991: 8). In this regard, immigration is a minor economic vehicle. The foregoing benefits of immigration are applicable to present residents and immigrants alike, albeit more so for the latter.

However, the reason for immigration in Canada is not that it is directly economical according to the ECC, but rather that it is enriching in many indirect and social ways: "the positive effects on native-born Canadians of emulating the industriousness of immigrants; the attraction and dynamism of cosmopolitan cities; greater export penetration by firms with multilingual, multicultural salesmen and management; the beneficial effects of having to spell out human rights objectives and commitments; and the enhanced creativity and flexibility of a diverse society as opposed to one that is homogeneous" (1991: 31). Accordingly, the ECC notes explicitly that non-economic issues are likely to be of greater importance than economic issues in the ongoing debate. In particular, worries about the erosion of cherished traditions and values, about problems in schools swamped by pupils learning English or French as a second language, and about an immigration processing system that sometimes seems out of control outweigh worries about job losses (1991: 1). In addition, given the changing population base in Canada, a focus on non-economic issues associated with the ethnic intermix is an important part of any overall analysis and control of the impacts of immigration. On this point, whether significant social conflicts will be associated with the immigration of diverse ethnic groups is contingent in large measure on how well immigrants integrate into their communities (1991: 28).

New Questions

In the final analysis, expert opinion still prevails in the field of immigration, and the expansion of popular debate has actually had little impact on the current statutory practices and programs. As Canada's ethnic mix is moving from one that is overwhelmingly European in origin to one that includes substantial minorities from outside Europe, the bureaucracy continues to try to rein in negative public sentiments by broadening the immigration debate and emphasizing the short-term gains from immigration. Yet the narrow economic argument is weak at best.

This, in turn, opens up supplemental lines of thought and questioning: Should potential immigrants be selected according to universal standards which assess their ability to adapt to Canadian life and to settle successfully? Does Canada have a moral obligation to accept the persecuted and disaffected? Should immigration be used simply to import skilled labour and build a strong industrial base? Should the reunification of families have a high priority in the system? Is immigration only a tool for relieving job shortages and fulfilling domestic labour market requirements? Are there important human rights objectives and commitments? Do the interests of stability and security offered by a homogeneous society outweigh the advantages of enhanced creativity and flexibility that come with a diverse society?

These kinds of order and justice questions, which underlie public policy in the area of immigration as well as the country's future, still remain to be investigated systematically by researchers. Unfortunately, the public has not had an opportunity to reflect on these issues either, even though such a discussion would help to alleviate unfounded fears about continued immigration.

7

Democratizing the Administration of Immigration

L ack of accountability is at the core of every problem in the field of Canadian immigration. However, when all is said and done, it is generally and begrudgingly acknowledged by the mystified and the nonplussed alike that bureaucracy seems to be the price we all have to pay for a "workable" society. Without a massive bureaucratic machine, especially in the case of government institutions, it is difficult to imagine how modern complex societies could function.

Reinventing the Bureaucrat

Echoing this concern, some observers have advanced the new proposition of reinventing the Civil Servant:

> Public servants seem to be the public's favourite target these days—according to conventional wisdom they're overpaid, they're unsympathetic to the public's needs, and they're completely uncompetitive compared to the private sector....

> What our democratic institutions need, people seem to be saying, is a lot more democracy and a lot less institution (*Profiles*, Vol. 3, Issue 5, 1993: 9).

In this view, the way to a kinder and gentler society is to create a kinder and gentler bureaucrat, "one who doesn't rely on management techniques for everything, one who sees the advantage of involving people from start to finish" (*Profiles*, Vol. 3, Issue 5, 1993: 10). Of course, the immediate problem with this proposition is that bureaucrats aren't the cause of bureaucracy; bureaucracy is the cause of bureaucrats. Therefore, the idea of reinventing the civil servant is not only anathema to the established ways of doing things, it is irrelevant to the root causes of alienation and the fractured wholeness of modern life. Insofar as modern bureaucracy focuses on the technical achievement of goals, over and above those for whom the achievements are for, widespread attentiveness and accountability to the public goes against its very nature. Accordingly, the call for a civil servant that downplays "management techniques" and "sees the advantage of involving people from start to finish" is a call for a form of life that values participation over achievement and is a transaction altogether different from the bureaucratic form of procedural rationality that now exists.

There is, for example, a major push in some circles to require mealy mouthed bureaucrats to speak in ways that ordinary people can understand. This, in fact, was recently an injunction of The Nova Scotian Education Minister, who asked his staffers to be more succinct by "thinking of the best poets":

> The people who do all the writing for Nova Scotia's education department are going back to school—to learn how to write.
>
> Recent departmental reports have been loaded with jargon and bureaucratese, and Education Minister John MacEachern wants staffers to learn how to be succinct.
>
> "I asked them to think of the best poets," said MacEachern.
>
> In January, department employees will be given a two-hour introduction to plain writing, followed by a seven-hour course in communicating ideas in a way easily understood (*The Toronto Sun*, Dec. 18, 1994).

Learning how to write plainly and communicate ideas well is admirable, of course, but it does not spell the beginning of public accountability in our institutions. Plain-talking bureaucrats, or even poetic ones, are not necessarily at one with the public. In fact, quite the opposite may be true. With no bureaucratic jargon to hide behind and obscure their actions, officials may be merely easier targets for public wrath.

Thus, the idea of reinventing the civil servant fails to comprehend the nature of public accountability. Alienation is signified in modern times by social erosion and fragmentation. The solution for de-alienating society has to entail the reintroduction of community involvement into community affairs—not teaching officials to think like poets. Only by making the administration responsible to people is it possible to repair the social ruptures in the fabric of our everyday life.

Reinventing Government and Capitalism

In a political context, both Liberal and Conservative pundits intercontinentally acknowledge modern alienation as a structural problem that requires a structural solution. Hugh Segal, for example, the former Progressive Conservative Party chief-of-staff for the Mulroney administration turned political pundit, put the matter this way:

> Neo-liberals in the United States have spoken for some years about re-inventing government—a debate of value and promise. But more important is the need to re-invent capitalism—based on an enterprise that is as much humane and fair as it is free—on an economics that views profit as an

instrument for both economic growth and social justice in a truly balanced society (*The Toronto Star*, June 11, 1993).

And for both Liberals and Conservatives, the recognized conceptual challenge is to create a dynamic balance in society between our capitalist economy and democratic values in a way that "views profit as an instrument for both economic growth and social justice."

Yet, to say we should reinvent government or reinvent capitalism begs the question of what structures could be introduced to achieve the peak performance of society. The mere fact of a new government or a new capitalism does not in itself guarantee harmony or wholeness. In order to effectively create "a truly balanced society," as Mr. Segal aptly designates it, our institutions have to be participation driven, because it is impossible to harmonize the whole without the concerted thought and action of the citizenry. By logical extension, the key is a design focus in the immigration system aimed at democratizing administration through:

(a) enhancing interaction between the parties in the system, members of the public and the members of the administration;

(b) emphasizing informed consensus by compulsory public education and participation-driven decision making;

(c) creating effective receptors for transmitting information and for feedback; and,

(d) creating a culture of innovation that encourages and incubates new ideas.

If we were to use the financial investment analogy of portfolio management, we might say the asset mix of our investments has to be determined by our strategic long-term position. From this perspective, balancing the immigration system, and optimizing human assets or resources, is actually a matter that cannot be decided (in all detail) beforehand, but the proper means of arriving there can be established. And like a portfolio manager in capital markets, the goal of the asset mix is to achieve a result that is more than the sum of its parts.

Democratizing the administration of the immigration system is a constructive alternative to the status quo. The details sketched below may be viewed as examples of how to get there.

Enhanced Interaction and Informed Public Consensus

The question posed in this book is: How can the immigration system in Canada maintain a balance between social order and social justice in the context of a commitment to multiculturalism? The answer, put simply, is: (1) to liberalize admission requirements at the front end of the system by phasing out occupation lists and adjusting the point system to give greater weight to basic skills; (2) tighten settlement guidelines through comprehensive training and educational opportunities; (3) ensure maximum intake levels through mechanisms for social adjustment within the system; and (4) accelerate the removal process for malefactors, miscreants and felons at the backend of the system.

The problem is, of course, that this regime will not necessarily resolve Canada's multicultural problems—insofar as it fails to engage and engender a common understanding among Canadians, and advance the general immigration debate in society-at-large, it would merely perpetuate ethnic disorientation and disequilibrium in society. Today, many Canadian citizens actually feel powerless in regard to Canada's immigration policy and, therefore, are typically threatened and anxiety-ridden about any distinguishable influx of immigrants. This anxiety and alarm is heightened in an age of global migration when those wanting to come to Canada are believed to be a threat to Canada's territorial integrity and privileged lifestyle, and it culminates in a special "made-only-in-Canada" brand of low-voltage racism. This problem of new faces in the crowd needs to be addressed head-on.

The often-made assertion that Canadians have the primary say when it comes to immigration policy is prompted by a seemingly endless series of public consultations conducted whenever a new political party takes over the government. However, insofar as public consultations are considered at all, they are not viewed as a means of building consensus among the citizenry; rather, they function as a barometer as to how far the experts can actually go without causing political upheaval or, more often, as a smoke-screen to mask administrative decision making. In reality, public opinion is merely one factor in the senior management's decision-making process—for senior policy makers are not interested in observing the general consensus as much as they are in defining it.

Public anger and disillusionment stem from the fact that Canada's immigration program is an archetype of efficiency and precision and not a model of democratic participation. Notwithstanding staged consultations alleging to take the pulse of the people, senior immigration officials draft policy-position papers and anticipate public objections to those positions before any public discussion takes place in meeting halls around the country. So, to the dismay of millions of Canadian residents, the bureaucratic goal is to make the system meticulously complete within itself and capable of negotiating any exigency; the goal is not to make it publicly accountable, and success is measured on the basis of system competence, not on the basis of system accountability. In the end, this has an exacerbating effect on social relations and precipitates a growing racialization of the immigration debate in the public arena, where Canadians appear to be deeply ambivalent about the public recognition of other cultures, the freedom of non-white and non-European cultural groups to maintain their unique identities, and the rights of minorities to function in a society free of racism (Henry et al., 1995: 2).

The paucity of informed public debate threatens to devolve Canada into what Manning Nash (1989) called a seething "cauldron of ethnicity in the modern world"—a diversity resembling a sometimes dormant, sometimes boiling, pot more than it does either a melting pot or a pressure cooker. It would seem that in order to eliminate the fear of "otherness," a liberal democracy not only has to enshrine pluralism in legislation, it has to introduce mechanisms that bridge the gap between the public policy process and the public consultation process. In order to get the best out of an immigration system, Canadians have to be committed to it. If immigration policy is to be guided by a general consensus, it must be an informed consensus.

In the field of immigration, an informed consensus requires two things: (1) compulsory public education as a part of policy development and decision making; and (2) an immigration department that is oriented towards empowering people and entrusting the public with authority. This, in turn, will pave the way for a situation where anxiety about immigration is a thing of the past.

Public Participation and Public Accountability

The serious questions that are now being raised about the accountability of large-scale bureaucracy indicate that the most pressing need today is to bring Canadians into the decision-making process. More democracy and less institution is the silent rallying cry of over-bureaucratized Canadians.

In this respect, publicly accountable immigration policy begins with democratizing administration:

> Increasing public participation at all stages of public policy is one of the keys of democratizing administration. Public input should be sought not only at the policy agenda stage where the broad outlines of policy are set, but also at the stage where specific policies are turned into legislation and then implemented. Even at the final stage, citizens should participate in

determining the criteria for assessing a program and have the opportunity
to take part in improving or even cutting it ("Reinventing the Civil Servant,"
1993: 10).

Democratizing administration means ensuring that immigration policy
is developed in the public arena at open venues rather than in the
backrooms of Ottawa and behind close doors. This, of course, entails
increased public participation at all stages of policy development.
Immigration policy development can be democratized without being
reduced to chaos, but it requires creating institutions that function as
vehicles for public input and societal unity.

Receptors for Informed Public Debate

Since the immigration department, like other large bureaucracies,
acts automatically on its bureaucratic reflexes to cover up failure, hide
disasters and avoid prying eyes, the system is not conducive to public
scrutiny and evaluation, or effective public action. In this respect, the
general clarification of public policy issues related to immigration is
inadequate. As its first order of business, the Canadian public needs
receptors for (1) the dissemination of information and (2) interactive
consensus building. A true receptor, of course, transmits information
and processes feedback.

Although some university and research institutions attempt to serve
in some ways as receptors, public information and feedback conduits
are not built into the research system. Public information and feedback entail an active relationship with society and reflection on the
impact of social research. University and other research institutions in
Canada can function effectively from time to time in the capacity of a
policy counterbalance, contributing to a professional dialogue as opposed to merely echoing the monologue of the bureaucrat elite. But
they are more often contracted by the federal government or are
affiliated with federal labs and think-tanks, which can compromise
their exchange. Here, too often the task of the researcher becomes
one of preserving the stated objectives and terms of reference of the
bureaucracy, rather than investigating them.

To my knowledge, there is no centre for independent immigration
research in Canada that assumes a primary role as a receptor—actively seeking to be the intermediary between the public and public
policy or to bridge the gap between the public consultation process
and the public policy process. There is often a pointed effort to
strengthen and energize the network of decision makers and researchers by bringing the academic community into the life of gov-

ernment, but not to involve the public actively in policy formation. The Metropolis Project is a case in point.

The Metropolis Project is a six-year, international undertaking to investigate the effects of immigration on the world's cities, including those in Canada, the U.S., Israel, France, the UK, the Netherlands, Argentina, Germany, Sweden, Denmark, Norway, Italy and New Zealand. The Canadian arm of Metropolis established four Centres of Excellence on Immigration and Integration in March of 1996—in Toronto, Montreal, Edmonton and Vancouver—involving fifteen Canadian universities and approximately three hundred researchers. The project's stated aims are: (1) to integrate research more systematically into policy development, and (2) to develop an inventory of best international practices for managing global migration by identifying the most effective responses to the many practical challenges that face all countries which have significant numbers of migrants entering their large urban centres. To bring the academic community into the life of government by involving it in specific policy-research areas is all to the good. However, uniting the public policy process with the research process, rather than uniting the public policy process with the public consultation process, mitigates against its potential status as a receptor. As a true receptor, social research must supplement and reinforce the dissemination of information with interactive consensus building. This means a research organization that can contribute to the scholarly literature in the field and also one that can mobilize the public in the pursuit of common goals. In this way it would contribute to an informed public debate while stimulating democracy.

Similarly independent government organizations like The Auditor General of Canada and The Economic Council of Canada (now defunct) provide objective evaluations of such things as the cost-effectiveness of immigration programs and the economic and social impact of immigration on society-at-large. These evaluations are "priority straighteners" and "fat trimmers," and are often crucial in re-focusing a bloated bureaucracy on its own goals of efficiency and system competence and crucial in protecting the public taxpayers from potential financial imprudence and other indiscretions. However, no matter how effective these institutional protectors are, they are not receptors; they do not interact with the public in a concerted effort to counsel and promote understanding.

The fact that there are no independent research organizations currently functioning as receptors for transmitting information to the public and processing feedback attests to the extent to which conventional social research has abandoned its pedagogic role. Practitioners tend to provide tools for the compilation of data to serve bureaucratic ends and are no longer inclined to indulge the spirit of discovery by asking original questions. The difference between a collaborator and a receptor is the difference in the questions "How do we make this or that program cost-effective?" and "How can the immigration system bring people together to move forward as a nation?"

An Advisory Service within the Immigration System

Another way to ensure public accountability is through the formation of an Immigration Advisory Service within the immigration system that could function as a systemic unit bridging the gap between the bureaucracy and the Canadian people, and designed to gather and inform the public consensus on a daily basis. Its mandate would be: (1) to advise the public about programs and services, and (2) to advise the bureaucracy about public needs.

An Immigration Advisory Service should be a fixed feature and also a medium of institutional self-reflection in the sense that feedback loops between various segments of the society and the bureaucracy could be fixed and tightened. An Advisory Service, so described, could be both cost effective and make significant inroads in addressing the deficiencies of the bureaucracy. Standing in the system between administration and advocacy groups would afford it the opportunity for meaningful strides in the areas of public education and performance monitoring.

Creating a Culture of Innovation

In the field of immigration, the main task of government bureaucracy is to provide incentives to immigrants. This includes making settlement support services central to its operations. In the final analysis, the economic attainment of Canada's immigrant population is either facilitated or inhibited by the "settlement and integration" incentive structure of the existing society. A comprehensive incentive structure entails a dedication both to settlement-support programs and to institutional mainstreaming, integrating immigrants to improve representation, access and equitable treatment (Fleras and Elliott, 1992: 179–82). If Canada's immigration system provides no sustained, positive incentives, then it will lessen the expectations and eventual performance of immigrants and, therefore, curtail the long-term economic growth of society and as a result foster social strain. Rather than expending all its energy sorting and measuring prospective immigrants, society should be thinking about what new measures are required to ease the adjustment of new immigrants and bring them into the mainstream of Canadian life as effectively as possible.

Immigration policy should facilitate newcomers in their course of creating a life of meaning and value. Canada's immigration system needs to shift from an emphasis on selection criteria to a wider focus on maximizing human-resource potential through the life-long learning model of service delivery. This is a more enlightened action plan for a modern democracy in the twenty-first century.

8

The Immigration System as an Enabling Technology

In the 1960s, social scientists prophesied that modern education systems would need to produce specialized technical experts in considerable numbers (Durkheim, 1964; Weber, 1964). This proposition undoubtedly rings true as a general pattern for developed societies. In fulfilling the needs of specialization, our education system has been supplemented by an immigration system that emphasizes the international importation of highly skilled labour—"designer immigration"—a brain drain where developed countries like Canada siphon off the talented individuals of the less-developed ones.

Even if these early scientists could have predicted that the complex division of labour in modern societies would be supplemented by intensive intake policies, they could never have anticipated the subsequent development: that the accelerating forces of technology would de-specialize labour and, therefore, navigate the modern educational needs away from a predominantly technical orientation. Modern economies are becoming acutely aware of the liberal arts as a necessary framework from which to negotiate any environment—or, as a means of perceiving the environment itself (Innis, 1971).

The Global Village

The structure of the division of labour in modern societies is not fixed but flexible, and one of the most important challenges facing Canada will be its capacity to adapt to the rapid pace of change. In this regard, Canada doesn't need to import skills as much as it needs to be able to adapt quickly and effectively to new labour-market needs. Many jobs that exist today did not exist yesterday; and many jobs that will exist tomorrow have not yet been conceived. Worker flexibility is at least as important as worker skill, and worker flexibility depends, in part, on the quality and scope of educational opportunities available and the access that the people have to those opportunities. Canada needs technical expertise, but its workers must also possess the knowledge needed to negotiate a changing world;

this means workers who have not only learned a skill or a trade but have also learned how to learn.

Today, it is not the technical heights of achievement that are reached that matters; rather it is the breadth or range of education. Merit is no longer identical with an acquired market skill, because market skills are being continually revised. Talent is no longer identical to a specialized occupation, because occupational specialties are being constantly updated. In this regard, our modern education requires adaptable systems that allow for continual upgrading, long after traditional schooling has been completed.

The revolution associated with advanced technologies in communications, transportation, automation and "fourth-generation" computerization is an acceleration of trends that go back to the beginnings of the Industrial Revolution itself (Kumar, 1978). What is new is the restructuring of the global economy and the transformation of our life-world from a skills-based to a learning-based paradigm. As Marshall McLuhan put it, "After three thousand years of specialist explosion and of increasing specialism and alienation in the technological extensions of our bodies, our world has become compressional by dramatic reversal" (1964: 20). The very same process of automation that causes a withdrawal of the present workforce from industry causes learning itself to become the principal kind of production and consumption: "Paid learning is already becoming both the dominant employment and the source of new wealth in our society. This is the new role for men in society, whereas the older mechanistic idea of 'jobs', or fragmented tasks and specialist slots for 'workers', becomes meaningless under automation" (McLuhan, 1964: 304).

Much of the capital market that is the engine of the Canadian economy today already exists without a physical component in cyberspace, as part of a borderless world. (Some securities markets, such as national and international bond markets, are markets without a marketplace or "virtual" marketplaces, consisting of a computer and telephone-based network of dealers who may never see their counterparts' faces). New modes of production are being created through satellite communications, information processing and computer-linked financial networks. Canadian society is now in a state of technological flux—where high-tech and high value-added industries are beginning to be re-tooled by the information economy. The future of Canada and other rich nations does not hinge on targeting or importing choice stocks of skilled labour as much as on the capability of developing and elevating skills once they are here.

In 1989, twenty-five years after McLuhan's initial probe into the phenomenon of technological flux, it was finally officially opined by government-supported researchers in the joint study *Job Futures* (1989), conducted on behalf of Employment Canada and the British Columbia government, that there is an ever-increasing need in Canada for improved levels of basic skills, and that those with greater general knowledge are more adaptable to change for tomorrow's jobs. This was the first study of its kind in the political sphere to advocate a liberal arts education as mandatory for the future well-being of society. This opinion has been wholly reinforced, in some detail, by the authors of *Inventing Our Future*. One of the specific recommendations proposed by the "new" federal advisory committee for stimulating economic growth and global competitiveness calls for "an overhaul of Canada's education system to ensure that the country's young people have the basic skills that they need: The ability to read, write, work with numbers and operate a computer" (*The Toronto Star*, Oct. 17, 1992). From this perspective, Canada's economic competitiveness requires increasing expenditures in the public education system, not increased cost-cutting measures; it requires the creation of more teachers, not eliminating existing teaching positions; and it requires reducing class sizes, not increasing them.

Sociologist Sharon Carere (1987) calls this back-to-the-basics orientation to eduction the new pencil/paper technology. In a state of technological flux—where the knowledge base is expected to double every eighteen months—the modern world has activated a fundamental form of mind-and-will over matter-and-desire, which is applicable to both modern educative practice and to society at large. The challenge of the modern education system is not knowledge *per se* but rather to prepare the person-student to learn. What is important is the bases of knowledge, not the particular information itself. In this model, a liberal arts education takes its place today in a vision of the educated person because it equips serious students with tools to understand their place in a complex world and to create a life of meaning and value for themselves and their community. The idea is not only to participate in society but also to create meaning in society (Frankl, 1978).

Still, in the field of immigration, the back-to-the-basics education movement has had a negligible impact on the experts. Arguments for designer immigration not only continue, but many suggest that the selection policies are not rigorous enough. For instance, a study commissioned by The Fraser Institute, entitled *The Immigration Dilemma* (1992), questions the future impact of immigration in Canada, maintaining that soft entry requirements are damaging the economic infrastructure of our society. Poorly skilled migrants have displaced the indigenous population at the low end of the job market, causing massive and chronic unemployment and placing a heavy burden on social services. In addition, the trend towards accepting more refugees and other immigrants selected for their non-economic attributes suggests that future economic benefits from immigration will be consistently loweer than in the past. Meanwhile, problems with integrating new Canadians will be greater given that, as well as possessing more limited job skills, they are less proficient in the official languages than earlier generations of immigrants.

There are other considerations suggested by the authors of the study as well:

> Specifically, changing economic and political conditions inside and outside of Canada suggest that immigrants to Canada will be increasingly less skilled than earlier generations of immigrants, at least relative to the indigenous population. These changes include more aggressive "competition" for skilled immigrants from other developed countries including the U.S. and Australia, lower real after-tax disposable income levels in Canada compared to other developed countries relative to distribution of real after-tax disposable income levels in earlier years and the increasing weight of refugee immigrants in the total immigrant population. Increased competition for skilled immigrants will directly reduce the supply of such immigrants willing to come to Canada given existing economic and social conditions in Canada. Relative decreases in real disposable income levels in Canada will also discourage immigration of skilled people to Canada, especially with Canada's relatively high marginal income tax rates (1992: 11).

The proposition here is that the former lack of a national focus on skilled immigration has had a deteriorating effect on the economic and social conditions in Canada, and this, in turn, has affected Canada's ability to attract highly skilled immigrants now and in the future.

With a rapidly changing industrial base, however, the possibility exists that the skill that is imported could immediately become obsolete. The situation now dictates that Canada begin to think in terms of developing people from within as much as importing skills from without. The idea of a skilled society must give way to the idea of a learning society—and this requires a shift in immigration policy from improving the quality of immigrant allowed into Canada to improving the quality of education and training immigrants receive once they arrive.

To McLuhan's way of thinking, in modern societies there are new rules of human engagement:

As electrically contracted, the globe is no more than a village. Electric speed in bringing all social and political functions together in a sudden implosion has heightened human awareness of responsibility to an intense degree. It is this implosive factor that alters the position of the Negro, the teenager, and some other groups. They can no longer be contained, in the political sense of limited association. They are now involved in our lives, as we in theirs, thanks to the electric media (McLuhan, 1964: 20).

Technological proliferation decentralizes modern living, turning the globe into a village. As John O'Neill put it,

Nothing can be more curious than the annual flocking of American immigrants to their former homelands to discover the omnipresent toilet roll, toothpaste, central heating, hamburger, and Coca Cola signs for which their ancestors displaced themselves and with which they identify America as the ultimate trip. What is sad in all this is that the real history of immigrant labour and political refugees recedes into the background of canned cultures created for the international tourist who travels as nearly as possible with the same technosphere as he or she enjoys at home (O'Neill, 1988: 20).

The television jingle "I'd like to buy the world a Coke" implies that the world would like to have one, or a Pepsi, or a Seven-up or another commercial beverage of their choice. Psychologically, as citizens in McLuhan's electronic global village, we do not now know exactly where our village ends and others begin. We are wired into each other. The people and the nations of the world are now involved in our lives, as we in theirs. The globalization of the world economy defies national inclinations towards isolationism and closed borders and promotes a greater emphasis on internationalism and cooperation.

Yet, the new globalism, like the back-to-the-basics learning movement, has not received focused attention in the formation of Canada's immigration policy. Designer immigration is the case in point. The lingering ambition to recruit specialized skills and technical aptitudes is one of the biggest forms of cultural lag that exists in the immigration system today. While society has moved from a model of industry to a model of equitable participation, immigration policy makers have not forsaken the last remnants of the old Social Darwinian axioms regarding nation building. Contemporary policy makers still treat immigrant labour largely as a selection process where only the fittest survive the roster cuts.

Meanwhile, since it is no longer good form to give conscious expression to illiberal sentiments, or to connect quality too closely with genetics, suppression and circumlocution abound. The fiction is that, apart from the crucial question of whether it is economically feasible, everyone wants as large and diverse an immigration as possible. William Petersen (1965: 52) called this "the official fiction" of Canadian immigration. In this fiction, the only important issue is the economic-geographic one—but which economic-geographic points are accepted as valid depends on the person's predisposition to the whole matter. Meanwhile, what is required is a shift in emphasis from a pro-active recruitment process to a pro-active settlement process.

The Federal Integration Strategy

Canada has undergone something of a paradigm shift, from a model of industriousness to a model of equitable participation that requires a shift in the paradigm for immigration as well—from what I have called a skills-based society to what I have called a learning-based society. The difference between these two is perhaps best exemplified by The Federal Integration Strategy of the 1990s. The federal initiative set out to: (1) provide a policy framework to guide settlement and integration programs across federal departments; (2) ensure greater collaboration with the provinces, the private sector and non-governmental partners in the delivery of settlement and integration services; (3) set new directions for language training and increase funding to make a more flexible range of options accessible to a greater number of immigrants; and (4) place a new emphasis on helping immigrants understand and accept Canadian values and on helping Canadians understand the diverse backgrounds of newcomers (See "Annual Report to Parliament," Public Affairs and Policy Group Employment and Immigration Canada, Ministry of Social Services Canada, 1990: 13–15). The problem is that the policy sets out to integrate newcomers rather than empower them.

The integration of immigrants in Canada implies the ability to settle and adapt, harkening back to Robert England's stock-breeder, whose metaphorical rule is "You can't make a silk purse from a sow's ear."

> If we mean by assimilation a process that moulds racial stocks into something else we are flying in the face of what every stock-breeder knows.... No melting pot can make a Slav, an Italian, or Frenchman, an Anglo-Saxon. Racial qualities, vices and instincts will remain. They may however be modified by environment, sublimated into some other form (1929: 174).

Like the stock-breeder, policy experts still have limited expectations in the field of immigration. They are not inclined to attempt to mould immigrant stocks, they simply want to be able to integrate them into Canadian society without too much ruckus or rancour.

Canada's Federal Integration Strategy thus comprises measures to attempt to eliminate social tension and conflict, and preserve different cultural life-styles (through language instruction, adjustment assistance, reception and orientation services, job-finding clubs and activities, and friendship and mentor associations) by ensuring that newcomers adapt to the established order and do not become a public charge, or otherwise burden the host society.

This is, and it is not, a pro-active strategy. It is mindful of the public good, but it is not forward looking. It is not guided by the goal of activating human resources or investing in human capital; rather, it is guided by the goal of insuring that the gains from immigration outweigh the losses. Further, the actual responsibility for providing newcomers to Canada with an internal compass and support networks is, for the most part, delegated to the provincial and local service providers and ethno-community organizations.

To be specific, $357 million (excluding $80 million to Quebec) has been allocated by the Canadian immigration department for settlement and integration services in 1997-98, invested in four programs: The Adjustment Assistance Program (AAP), which provides transitional assistance to indigent government-assisted refugees for up to one year; The Immigrant Settlement and Adaption Program (ISAP), which provides funds for organizations to accord immigrants with the essential bridging services to facilitate their access to community services; The Host Program (HOST), which provides funds to assist organizations in recruiting, training, matching and monitoring volunteers who help newcomers adapt, settle and integrate into the Canadian life; and The Language Instruction for Newcomers to Canada Program (LINC), which provides basic language instruction in one of Canada's official languages to adult immigrants. The eligible service providers in all of the above programs are educational institutions, non-governmental organizations, businesses, provincial/territorial or municipal governments and individuals. Over the years, the Canadian immigration department has meticulously refined ways of measuring prospective newcomers' chances of adapting to society by appraising such criteria as their age, occupational demand, vocational preparation, arranged employment, location, education, relatives in Canada, official-language competence and personal suitability. But this fastidious attention to details declines once residency is assumed.

The report by the Immigration Legislative Advisory Council, released in January 1998, is the latest official call for a more measured and restrictive admission policy for immigrants. While, on the one hand, the report recommends adequate funding for settlement and integration services, on the other it suggests that new immigrants pay for their own language training (a fundamental variable in settlement and integration) and that financial penalties be imposed on those who bring children over six who are not proficient in one of the official languages (Legislative Review Advisory Group, *Not Just Numbers: A Canadian Framework For Future Immigration*, Ministry of Public Works and Government Services Canada, January 1998).

Traditionally, strong family ties have been the primary indicator of immigrant performance and success. The most successful immigrants have not been those with the greatest initial financial wherewithal or even official language skills, but rather those who have the incentive to improve the quality of their lives and the future lot of their family. In this respect, the vitality of Canadian society, past and present, has been strengthened by the broad mix of immigrants who contribute to our economic growth and quality of life in very different ways. So, the real task of modern nation building is not filtering the flow of global migration in order to select choice candidates, nor erecting punitive financial barriers to keep out the have-nots; but rather the real challenge is in managing ethnic diversity and immigration dispersion in a way that actualizes our mixed endowments through the development of genuinely dynamic settlement processes.

The language requirement in particular fosters racial and ethnic divisions, and this proposal has not been well received by ethnic communities in Canada. Making language a base requirement places a question mark on the legitimacy of those immigrants already here whose language facility is not up to par. It also undermines the foundation of successful multicultural initiatives, such as heritage language programs, that have helped bind the country together into a distinctive mosaic.

While there is a highly coordinated recruitment policy in place— complete with federal interdepartmental coordination, international embassy and visa-office outreach and an extensive overseas promotional budget—there is no comparable pro-active approach to, or managed supervision of, the settlement policy. The contemporary immigration policy provides intensive quality control in the pre-immigration phase (the period prior to reaching the nation's borders), but provides virtually no managed quality control in the post-immigration, settlement phase. Within the context of this policy framework comes the preference for immigrants who "can hit the ground running."

Of course, the idea behind the Federal Integration Plan is that a highly coordinated recruitment process can relieve the immigration department of the onus of an elaborate, ongoing monitoring program of support services. By being policy intensive on the recruitment side and selecting high-caliber immigration candidates, the federal immigration department can conceivably reduce the urgency of providing comprehensive settlement for newcomers and is, therefore, ultimately relieved of the onus of any responsibility for the performance of society.

In everyday life, the general responsibility for filling the huge gap in the human-services delivery system for new immigrants is assumed by provincial and community agencies. Non-governmental organizations have developed into a Canada-wide network, originally with volunteer coordination, in order to lobby on behalf of their different constituencies in refugee and immigration matters (Lanphier and Lukomskyj, 1994). And when the Bulgarians land in Gander or the Gypsies fly into Toronto en masse from the former Czechoslovakia in search of the promised land, the boundaries of the support system and the limitations of project-specific funding are brought clearly into view.

Unlike mainstream provincial agencies whose services have universal applicability and accessibility, the ethnic-community agencies act as brokers and advocates for minority populations, providing settlement and integration services, language interpretation, family counselling and so on. These ethnic-community organizations usually maintain more flexible hours, with evening and weekend services; serve as drop-in centres; have locations in accessible, informal settings, such as community centres; provide home visits and community outreach; advertise their services in the multicultural media; and provide group counselling (Bridgman, 1993).

All this has resulted in what has been called a "two-tiered system" (Chan, 1987), where service providers exist side by side with little interaction and coordination in the planning and delivery of services (Doyle and Visano, 1987). Mainstream provincial agencies offer services to anyone in the community who meet general eligibility criteria; and local ethno-community agencies provide services to people on the basis of membership in a particular racial or cultural group. This two-tiered format creates a situation where the two delivery systems are generally isolated from each other and compete for resources to serve the needs of a diverse immigrant population. Some studies suggest that this clash between provincial-mainstream and community-based agencies may be reflected in the view of funders that ethnically or racially specific services for immigrants are an unnecessary duplication of the programs and services offered by mainstream agencies (Henry et al., 1995). Consequently, racial bias and discrimination can be a requisite by-product of the Federal Integration Strategy and the current method for the allocation of resources. For instance, the findings of numerous task forces and consultations, undertaken to appraise the quality and accessibility of care and services provided to racial and ethno-cultural client groups, have produced evidence of the failure of mainstream social and health-care agencies to provide services that are racially sensitive, culturally appropriate and linguistically accessible (Canadian Task force, 1988; Radford, 1989; Bergin 1988; Medeiros 1991; James and Muhammad, 1992).

This is further compounded by the fact that funding has generally been in the form of time-bound projects rather than operational funding. Therefore, the security of continuous support for immigrants cannot be absolutely relied upon by any particular service provider (see Fernando, 1991), placing both mainstream provincial agencies and ethno-specific agencies in a permanently vulnerable position and limiting the kind of services they can provide.

A number of studies have also drawn attention to problems and barriers that exist in all the traditional, mainstream, human-service delivery organizations across Canada, related to the training and education for service providers, the allocation of resources and the access and participation of people of colour as clients, managers, staff, and volunteers (Doyle and Visano, 1987; Chan, 1987; Sanga, 1987; Bergin, 1988; Bambrough et al., 1992; Henry et al., 1995: 15). Other research has disclosed that the theories, methodologies, and skills taught in many educational programs for social work, medicine, nursing and other human-services professions around the country bear little relation to the needs of clients from diverse racial and cultural backgrounds (Allodi, 1983; Agard, 1987). The disempowering effects of an Anglo-centric pedagogy is a great disadvantage for immigrants and refugees (Thomas, 1987).

In 1987, the Social Planning Council of Metropolitan Toronto publicly reported on an extensive study it commissioned on "access to the health and social services for members of diverse cultural and racial groups" (Doyle and Visano, 1987). The study's findings suggest that while access to basic social and health services is a universal entitlement, mainstream agencies have failed to provide accessible and equitable services. The researchers identified many linguistic, cultural, and racial barriers and discriminatory practices, as well as an absence of strategies to address these obstacles. They found institutional discrimination reflected in indifferent attitudes and a lack of commitment to seek remedies for patterns of exclusion and inaccessibility. All of these problems are made more acute by the general problems that all consumers experience, such as child care and transportation costs, lengthy delays and physical distance from agencies (Doyle and Visano, 1987).

Another important finding of recent research is the absence of people of colour at every level in the mainstream human-services delivery system, including boards of directors. In a study of some 1,200 non-profit organizations in Canada, it was found that the boards of directors were predominantly composed of people with British origins—28 percent were at least three-quarters British; an additional 30 percent were at least half British. The next most common group was those of "other Northern European origins" (German, Dutch, Scandinavian), with 47 percent of the boards having at least some representation from this group. French Canadians were well represented, with 47 percent of boards. People of colour, however, were almost entirely absent (Murray et al., 1992). This translates into severe social and economic penalties for visible minority immigrants, and these can result in lingering repercussions. Research on the *Earnings Differentials among Ethnic Groups in Canada* concluded that "despite having Canadian education and socialization, many Canadian-born visible minority ethnic groups (especially among men) face large earnings gaps compared to Canadian-born workers of British origins. A black man born and raised in Canada may still expect to earn sixteen percent less than a British origin man born in Canada" (Pendakur and Pendakur, 1995: ii). Correspondingly, recent task forces and special inquiries on race relations broadly confirm that, while we have a society of immense diversity and a complex proliferation of multicultural and multiracial sensibilities, our major social institutions as well as our criminal justice system are profoundly unprepared for dealing with it (Lewis, 1989; Lewis, 1992; Cole, 1996).

In a wider sense, however, all of the contemporary impediments in the support-services industry emanate from the basic design flaw in immigration bureaucracy's Federal Integration Strategy. Without effective implementation and monitoring of settlement services, there is no effective way to assess the continued performance patterns of immigrants in society or to seek input on how to improve performance. Because the main energy of the immigration system has been put into assessing applicants' chances for successful social adaption, rather than promoting and monitoring that success once immigrants are processed and landed, the immigration bureaucracy is not in a particularly advantageous position when it comes to assessing and preparing for the changing needs of resident immigrants or the changing future of the broader society.

Conclusion

To ensure a full and productive future, a liberal democratic society must mobilize all of its diverse influences and mixed endowments. A broad-based immigration policy that is not grounded in a life-long learning model—where the strategy is to cultivate skills rather than simply import them—will eventually be an impediment to society as once-needed skills become dated. Of course, "the planned delivery of settlement and integration services, setting new directions for language training, and increase funding to make a more flexible range of options accessible to a greater number of immigrants" are all significant steps taken by the Federal Integration Plan in terms of helping newcomers from all parts of the world fit into Canadian society—but the only practical way to propel the country forward, and to ensure continued prosperity, is to incorporate newcomers into an action plan for the future.

Unfortunately, the life-long learning model has failed to take hold or even inspire the immigration policy makers. Ultimately, the skilled immigrant and the refugee, the businessman and displaced person, the entrepreneur and the family member, the nanny and the computer scientist—"the Slav, the Italian, the Frenchman, the Anglo-Saxon" or other—all need to be conceived not only as people we want to integrate into our society but also as potential long-term assets in a forward-looking nation.

References

Abella, Irving, and Harold Troper
1982   *None Is Too Many: Canada and the Jews of Europe, 1933–1948.* Toronto: Lester & Orpen Dennys.

Adelman, Howard
1982   *Canada and the Indochinese Refugees.* Regina: A. Weigle Educational Associates Ltd.

_____ **Allan Borowski, Meyer Burstein and Lois Foster**
1995   *Immigration and Refugee Policy: Australia and Canada Compared.* (Eds.) Toronto: University of Toronto Press.

Agard, R.
1987   "Access to the Social Assistance Delivery System by Various Ethnocultrual Groups." In *Social Assistance Review Committee Report.* Ontario Ministry of Community and Social Services.

Akbari, Ather S.
1989   "The Benefits of Immigrants to Canada: Evidence on Tax and Public Services." *Canadian Public Policy.* XV (4): 424–35.

Allodi, F.
1983   "The Utilization of Mental Health Services by Immigrant Canadians." *Canada's Mental Health*, 3 (March): 9–12.

Appleyard, R.
1991   *International Migration: The Challenge of the Nineties.* Geneva: International Organization for Migration.

Avery, Donald
1979   *Dangerous Foreigners.* Toronto: McClelland & Stewart.

Bambrough, J., W. Bowden and F. Wien
1992   *Preliminary Results from the Survey of Graduates from the Maritime School of Social Work.* Halifax: Maritime School of Social Work, Dalhousie University.

Basavarajappa, K.G., and Ravi B.P. Verma
1990   "Occupational Composition of Immigrant Women." In *Ethnic Demography.* (Ed.) S.S. Halli, F. Trovato and L. Driedger. Ottawa: Carleton University Press.
1988   *Immigration and the Population of Canada.* Report prepared for Strategic Planning and Research, Immigration Policy Group, Employment and Immigration Canada.

Bean, F.D., B. Edmonston and J.S. Passel
1990   *Undocumented Migration to the United States: The IRCA and the Experience of the 1980s.* Washington: Rand Corporation and the Urban Institute.

Beaujot, Roderic P.
1992   "The Socio-Demographic Impact of Immigration." In *The Immigration Dilemma.* (Ed.) Steven Globerman. Vancouver: The Fraser Institute.
1991   *Population Change in Canada: The Challenges of Policy Adaption.* Toronto: McClelland & Stewart.
1989   *Immigration and the Population of Canada.* Report prepared for Strategic Planning and Research, Immigration Policy Group, Employment and Immigration Canada.

Becker, Howard
1963 *Outsiders: Studies in the Sociology of Deviance.* New York: The Free Press.

Belfiore, Mary Ellen, Jill Bell, Marjatta Holt and Barbara Burnaby
1985 "A Framework for Assessing Immigrant Integration to Canada, Phase II: Final Report." Study prepared for the Department of the Secretary of State.

Benthall, Jonathan
1976 *The Body Electric: Patterns of Western Industrial Culture.* London: Thames and Hudson.

Bergin, B.
1988 *Equality Is the Issue: A Study of Minority Ethnic Group Access to Health and Social Services in Ottawa-Carleton.* Ottawa: Social Planning Council of Ottawa-Carleton.

Bernier, B.
1979 "Immigration et utilisation de la main-d' oeuvre ethnique au Canada." *Perspectives Anthropologiques.* Montréal: Editions du Renouveau Pédagogique.

Berry, Ronald R., and Ronald Soligo
1969 "Some Welfare Aspects of International Migration." *Journal of Political Economy.* September/October.

Billingsley, Brenda, and Leon Muszynski
1985 *No Discrimination Here?* Toronto: The Urban Alliance on Race Relations and the Social Planning Council of Metropolitan Toronto.

Blackburn, Jean-Pierre
1990 *Interim Report on Demography and Immigration Levels.* Report of the Standing Committee on Labour Employment and Immigration. Issue No. 40.

Blum, Alan, and Peter McHugh
1984 *Self-Reflection in the Arts And Sciences.* Atlantic Highlands, N.J.: Humanities Press.

Blau, Peter, and Richard Scott
1962 *Formal Organizations.* San Francisco: Chandler.

Bodkin, R.G., and K. Marwah
1987 "Some Observations on Demography in Select Macroeconometric Models of Canada." Discussion Paper 87.A.1, The Institute for Research on Public Policy.

Borowski, Allan, and Derek Thomas
1994 "Immigration and Crime." In *Immigration and Refugee Policy: Australia and Canada Compared.* Vol. II. (Eds.) H. Adelman, A. Borowski, M. Burstein and L. Foster. Toronto: University of Toronto Press.

Borrie, W.D.B.
1975 *Population and Australia: First Report of the National Population Inquiry.* Canberra: Australian Government Publishing Service.

Borts, George H., and Jerome Stein
1966 *Economics in a Free Market.* New York: Columbia University Press.

Boyd, Monica
1987 *Migrant Women in Canada: Profiles and Policies.* Employment and Immigration Canada and The Status of Women, Canada.

Brigeman, G.
1993 *The Place of Mainstream and Ethno-Racial Agencies in the Delivery of Family Services to Ethno-Racial Canadians.* Masters of Social Work thesis submitted to the Faculty of Graduate Studies, Graduate Program in Social Work, York University.

Brimelow, Peter
1986 *The Patriot Game.* Toronto: Key Porter.

Bryce, P.H.

1928 *The Value to Canada of the Continental Immigrant.* Ottawa: Department of Immigration.

Burnet, J.

1983 "Multiculturalism 10 Years Later." In *Two Nations Many Cultures.* (Ed.) J.L. Elliott. Toronto: Prentice-Hall.

Campbell, Charles M.

1989 "A Time Bomb Ticking: Canadian Immigration in Crisis." The Mackenzie Institute for the Study of Terrorism, Revolution and Propaganda. Toronto.

Campbell, Colin, and George J. Szablowski

1979 *The Superbureaucrats: Structure and Behaviour in Central Agencies.* Toronto: Macmillan.

Campbell, Joesph

1973 *The Hero with a Thousand Faces.* Princeton, N.J.: Princeton University Press.

Carere, Sharon

1987 "Life World of Restrictive Behaviour in an Elementary School Setting." In *Social Studies of Child Development.* (Eds.) Patricia A. Adler and Peter Adler. Greenwich, Conn.: JAI Press.

Chan, K.

1987 "Ethnic Minorities and Accessibility to Services in a Two-Tiered, Social Services System: The Case of Chinese in Montreal." *Currents: Readings in Race Relations,* 4 (3) (Summer): 6–7.

Chimbos, Peter D.

1980 *The Canadian Odyssey: The Greek Experience in Canada.* Toronto: McClelland & Stewart.

Clement, Wallace

1975 *The Canadian Corporate Elite.* Toronto: McClelland & Stewart.

Collins, Doug

1979 *Immigration: The Destruction of English Canada.* Richmond Hill, Ontario: BMG Publishing Company.

Collins, Randall, and Michael Makowsky

1984 *The Discovery of Society.* New York: Random House.

Cook, Ramsay, and Kenneth W. McNaught

1963 *Canada and the United States: A Modern Study.* Toronto: Clarke, Irwin & Company Limited.

Dafoe, John W.

1931 *Clifford Sifton in Relation to His Times.* Toronto: Macmillan Canada.

Denton, Frank T., and Byron G. Spencer

1987 "Changes in the Canadian Population and Labour Force: Prospects and Implications." *Canadian Studies in Population,* 14: 187–208.

de Silva, Arnold

1992 *Earnings of Immigrants: A Comparative Analysis.* A study prepared for the Economic Council of Canada.

Dominelli, L.

1989 "An Uncaring Profession? An Examination of Racism in Social Work." *New Community,* 15 (3): 391–403.

Dorais, Louis-Jacques, Lois Foster, and David Stockley

1994 "Multiculturalism and Integration." In *Immigration and Refugee Policy: Australia and Canada Compared.* (Eds.) H. Adelman, A. Borowski, M. Burstein and L. Foster. Toronto: University of Toronto Press.

Doyle, R., and L. Visano
1987 *Access to Health and Social Services for Members of Diverse Cultural and Racial Groups.* Reports 1 and 2. Toronto: Social Planning Council of Metropolitan Toronto.

DeVoretz, Don J.
1995 *Diminished Returns.* (Ed.) Don J. DeVoretz. Toronto: C.D. Howe Institute.
1992 "Immigration and the Canadian Labour Market." In *The Immigration Dilemma.* (Ed.) Steven Globerman. Vancouver: The Fraser Institute.

Durkheim, Emile
1964 *The Rules of Sociological Method.* New York: The Free Press.
1947 *The Division of Labour in Society.* New York: The Free Press.

England, Robert
1929 *The Central European Immigrant in Canada.* Toronto: Macmillan Canada.

Erikson, Kai T.
1966 *Wayward Puritans.* New York: John Wiley & Sons.

Fanon, Franz
1968 *The Wretched of the Earth.* New York: Grove Press Inc.
1967 *Black Skin White Masks.* New York: Grove Press Inc.

Fernando, T.
1991 "'Mosaic Madness' or Sensible Public Policy? Some Reflections on Canadian Multiculturalism." In *Sociological Insights.* (Eds.) N. Guppy and K. Stoddart. Vancouver: Department of Anthropology and Sociology, University of British Columbia.

Fleras, A., and J.L. Elliott
1992 *Multiculturalism in Canada: The Challenge of Diversity.* Scarborough: Nelson Canada.

Frankl, Viktor E.
1978 *The Unheard Cry for Meaning.* New York: Simon & Schuster.

Fukuyama, F.
1991 "New World Order." *Guardian Studies.* April: 29–32.

Galbraith, John Kenneth
1991 "The New World Order." *Guardian Studies.* April: 13–18.
1985 *Anatomy of Power.* London: Corgi.
1958 *The Affluent Society.* New York: New American Library.

Gibbs, J.P., and W.T. Martin
1964 *Status Integration and Suicide: A Sociological Study.* Eugene, Oregon: University of Oregon Press.

Giddens, Anthony
1987 *Social Theory and Modern Sociology.* Cambridge: Polity Press.
1985 *The Nation-State and Violence,* Vol. 2 of *Contemporary Historical Materialism.* Cambridge: Polity Press.

Globerman, Steven
1992 "Background to Immigration Policy in Canada." In *The Immigration Dilemma.* (Ed.) Steven Globerman. Vancouver: The Fraser Institute.

Goffman, Erving
1959 *The Presentation of Self in Everyday Life.* Garden City, New York: Doubleday.

Habermas, Jurgen
1973 *Theory and Practice.* Boston: Beacon Press.

Henry, Frances, and Effie Ginzberg
1985 *Who Gets the Work?* Toronto: The Urban Alliance on Race Relations and the Social Planning Council of Metropolitan Toronto.

Henry, Francis, Carol Tator, Winston Mattis and Tim Rees

1995 *The Colour Of Democracy: Racism in Canadian Society.* Toronto: Harcourt Brace & Co.

Herberg, E.N.

1989 *Ethnic Groups in Canada: Adaptions and Transitions.* Toronto: Nelson Canada.

Hersak, Gene, and Derrick Thomas

1988 "Recent Canadian Developments Arising from International Migration." Working Papers, Policy Analysis Directorate, Immigration Policy Branch, Employment and Immigration Canada.

Innis, Harold

1971 *The Bias of Communication.* Toronto: University of Toronto Press.

Ishwaran, K.

1980 *Canadian Families: Ethnic Variations.* Toronto: McGraw-Hill Ryerson Ltd.

James, C., and H. Muhammad

1992 *Children in Childcare Programs: Perception of Race and Race Related Issues.* Toronto: Multicultural and Race Relations Division and Children's Services of the Municipality of Metropolitan Toronto.

Joe D., and N. Robinson

1980 "Chinatown's Immigrant Gangs: The New Yong Warrior Class." *Criminology,* 18 (3) (November): 115–27.

Kalbach, Warren E., and Wayne McVey

1979 *The Demographic Bases of Canadian Society.* Toronto: McGraw-Hill Ryerson.

Kelly, J., and I. McAllister

1984 "Immigrants Socioeconomic Attainment and Politics in Australia." *British Journal of Sociology,* 35 (3): 387–405.

Krauter, Joseph, and Morris Davis

1978 *Minority Canadians: Ethnic Groups.* Toronto: Methuen.

Lanphier, Michael, and Oleh Lukomskyj

1994 "Settlement Policy in Australia and Canada." In *Immigration and Refugee Policy: Australia and Canada Compared.* (Eds.) H. Adelman, A. Borowski, M. Burstein and L. Foster. Toronto: University of Toronto Press.

Lawrence, Peter J., and Raymond Hull

1969 *The Peter Principle.* New York: Bantam Books.

Lewis, C.

1989 *Report of the Task Force on Race Relations and Policing.* Toronto: Government of Ontario.

Lewis, S.

1992 *Report to the Premier on Race Relations.* Toronto: Government of Ontario.

Li, Peter S.

1990 *Race and Ethnic Relations in Canada.* Toronto: Oxford University Press.

1988 *Ethnic Inequality in a Class Society.* Toronto: Thompson Educational.

1988 *Racial Oppression in Canada.* Toronto: Garamond Press.

_____ and Singh Bolaria

1985 *Racial Oppression in Canada.* Toronto: Garamond Press.

Lipset, Seymour M.

1965 "Value Differences, Absolute or Relative: The English-Speaking Democracies." In *Canadian Society.* (Eds.) Bernard R. Blishen, F.E. Jones, K.D. Naegele and J. Porter. Toronto: Macmillian.

1963 *The First New Nation.* New York: Basic Books.

1989 *Continental Divide: The Values and Institutions of the United States and Canada.* Toronto & Washington, D.C.: Canadian-American Committee.

Lynd, Robert S.
1957 "Power in American Society." In *Problems of Power in American Democracy.* (Ed.) A. Kornhuser. Detroit: University of Michigan Press.

Lysenko, Vera
1947 *Men In Sheepskin Coats.* Toronto: Ryerson.

Malarek, Victor
1987 *Haven's Gate: Canada's Immigration Fiasco.* Toronto: Macmillan of Canada.

Mannheim, Karl
1936 *Ideology and Utopia.* New York: Harcourt Brace & Company Ltd.

Marocco, Frank N., and Henry M. Goslett
1995 *The Annotated 1995 Immigration Act Of Canada.* Scarborough, Ontario: Carswell.

Marr, W.L.
1992 "Post-War Canadian Immigration Patterns." In *The Immigration Dilemma.* (Ed.) Steven Globerman. Vancouver: The Fraser Institute.
1975 "Canadian Immigration Policies Since 1962." *Canadian Public Policy,* (1) (Spring 1975): 196–203.

McLeod, K.
1983 "Multicultural Education: A Decade of Development." In *Two Nations Many Cultures.* (Ed.) J.L. Elliott. Toronto: Prentice-Hall.

McLuhan, Marshall
1966 *Understanding Media: The Extensions of Man.* New York: McGraw-Hill Book Co.
1962 *The Gutenberg Galaxy.* Toronto: University of Toronto Press.

Matas, D.
1989 *Closing the Doors: The Failure of Refugee Protection.* Toronto: Summerhill Press.

Medeiros, J.
1991 *Family Services for All.* Toronto: Multiculturalism. Coalition for Access to Family Services.

Mills, C. Wright
1959 *The Sociological Imagination.* London: Oxford University Press.
1956 *The Power Elite.* New York: Oxford University Press.

Mitges, G.
1987 *Multiculturalism: Building the Canadian Mosaic.* Report of the Standing Committee on Multiculturalism. House of Commons, Ottawa.

Murray, V., P. Bradshaw, and J. Wolpin
1992 "Power in and around Non-Profit Boards: A Neglected Dimension of Governance." *Non-Profit Management and Leadership,* 3 (2): 165–82.

Naegele, Kaspar
1965 "Canadian Society: Further Reflections." In *Canadian Society.* (Eds.) B.R. Blishen, F.E. Jones, K.D. Naegele and J. Porter. Toronto: Macmillan.

Nash, Manning
1989 *The Cauldron of Ethnicity in the Modern World.* Chicago: The University of Chicago Press.

Nelles, H.V.
1974 *The Politics of Development: Forests, Mines and Hydro-Electric Power in Ontario.* Toronto: Macmillan.

Neuwith, Gertrud
1987 "Immigration Settlement Indicators: A Conceptual Framework." Employment and Immigration Canada, March.

Olson, Mancur

1965   *The Logic of Collective Action.* Cambridge, Mass.: Harvard University Press.

O'Neill, John

1988   "Techno-culture and the Specular Functions of Ethnicity: With a Methodological Note." In *Ethnicity in a Technological Age.* (Ed.) I.H. Angus. Edmonton: University of Alberta Press.

1972   *Sociology as a Skin Trade: Towards a Reflexive Sociology.* New York: Harper Torchbooks.

Ornstein, M., and R.D. Sharma

1983   *Adjustments and Economic Experience of Immigrants in Canada: An Analysis of the 1976 Longitudinal Survey of Immigrants.* Toronto: Institute for Behavioural Research, York University.

Parsons, Talcott

1957   *The Social System.* New York: The Free Press.

Peter, Laurence J., and Raymond Hull

1969   *The Peter Principle.* New York: Bantam Books.

Pentland, H.C.

1959   "The Development of a Capitalistic Labour Market in Canada." *Canadian Journal of Economics and Political Science,* XXV (4).

Pendakur, Ravi

1995   *The Changing Role of Post-War Immigrants in Canada's Labour Force: An Examination across Four Census Periods.* Social Research Group, Strategic Research and Analysis, Corporate and Intergovernmental Affairs. Department of Canadian Heritage.

_____ **and Krishna Pendakur**

1995   *Earning Differentials among Ethnic Groups in Canada.* Strategic Research and Analysis. Hull, Quebec: Department of Canadian Heritage.

Petersen, William

1965   "The Ideological Background to Canada's Immigration." In *Canadian Society.* (Eds.) (Eds.) B.R. Blishen, F.E. Jones, K.D. Naegele and J. Porter. Toronto: Macmillian.

1958   "A General Typology of Migration." *American Sociological Review,* 23 (3): 256–65.

Petras, E.

1981   "The Global Labour Market in the Modern World Economy." In *Global Trends in Migration: Theory and Research on International Population Movements.* (Eds.) M.M. Kritz, C.B. Keely, and S.M. Tomasi. New York: Center for Migration Studies.

Plaut, W.G.

1985   *Refugee Determination in Canada.* Ottawa: Supply and Services Canada.

Porter, John

1965   *The Vertical Mosaic: An Analysis of Social Class and Power in Canada.* Toronto: University of Toronto Press.

Radford, B.

1989   "Mainstream and Ethno-Specific Social Assistance Delivery Systems." *Currents: Readings in Race Relations,* 5 (3): 34–35.

Ramcharan, Subhas

1982   *Racism: Nonwhites in Canada.* Toronto: Butterworths Canada Ltd.

Rao, G. Lakshmana, Anthony H. Richmond, and Jerzy Zubrzychi

1984   *Immigrants in Canada and Australia.* Volume One. *Demographic Aspects and Education.* Downsview, Ontario: Institute for Behavioural Research, York University.

Reitz, Jeffrey G.

1993 "Statistics on Racial Discrimination in Canada." *Policy Options*, 15 (2): 7–9.

1987 "Less Racial Discrimination in Canada or Simply Less Racial Conflict?: Implications of Comparisons with Britain." (Centre for Industrial Relations and Department of Sociology, University of Toronto). *Immigrants in Canada and Australia*. Volume One. *Demographic Aspects and Education*. Downsview, Ontario: Institute for Behavioural Research, York University.

1980 "Immigration and Inter-ethnic Relationships in Canada." In *Cultural Boundaries and the Cohesion of Canada*. (Eds.) R. Breton, J.G. Reitz and V.Valentine. Montreal Institute for Research on Public Policy.

_____ **and Raymond Breton**

1994 *The Illusion of Difference: Realities of Ethnicity in Canada and the United States.* Toronto: C.D. Howe Institute.

Rhyne, Darla

1982 *Generational Differences between the Canadian Born and Immigrants in Metropolitan Toronto.* Downsview, Ontario: Institute for Behavioural Research, York University.

Ribordy, F.

1980 "Culture Conflict and Crime among Italian Immigrants." In *Crime and Canadian Society.* (Ed.) R.S. Bryce-Laporte. New Brunswick, N.J.: Transaction Books.

Richmond, Anthony H.

1994 *Global Apartheid: Refugees, Racism & New World Order.* Don Mills: Oxford University Press Canada.

1990 "Race Relations and Immigration: A Comparative Perspective." *International Journal of Comparative Sociology*, 21 (3–4): 156–76.

1988 *Immigration and Ethnic Conflict.* New York: St. Martin's Press.

1981 *Comparative Studies in the Economic Adaption of Immigrants in Canada.* Downsview, Ontario: Institute of Behavioural Research, York University.

Robertson, R.

1990 "Mapping the Global Condition: Globalization as the Central Concept." In *Global Culture: Nationalism, Globalization and Modernity.* (Ed.) B.S. Turner. London: Sage Publications.

Roy, P.E.

1974 "The Oriental 'Menace' in British Columbia." In *Studies in Canadian Social History.* (Eds.) M. Horn and R. Saburin. Toronto: McCelland & Stewart.

Samuel, John T.

1989 "Immigration Issues: A National Perspective." In *Policy Forum on the Role of Immigration in Canada's Future.* (Eds.) C.M. Beach and A.G. Green. Kingston: John Deutsch Institute.

1988 "Family Class Immigrants to Canada, 1981–1984: Labour Force Activity Aspects." *Population Working Paper No. 5.* Employment and Immigration Canada.

1987 "Immigration, Visible Minorities and the Labour Force in Canada: Vision 2000." Ottawa: Centre for Immigration and Ethnocultural Studies.

_____ **and T. Conyers**

1986 *The Employment Effects of Immigration: A Balance Sheet Approach.* Policy and Program Development, Employment and Immigration Canada.

_____ **and R. Faustino-Santos**

1971 "Canadian Immigrants and Criminality." *International Migration*, XXIX (1) (March): 51–76.

Sanga, D.

1987 "A Systematic Approach to Discrimination in the Provision of Social Services: South Vancouver." *Currents: Readings in Race Relations*, 4 (3): 8–9.

Schachter, Linda
1884 "Defining the Minority Population." *Currents: Studies in Race Relations.* (1): 28–31.

Seward, S.B., and M. Tremblay
1990 "Immigrant Women in the Clothing Industry." In *Ethnic Demography.* (Eds.) S.S. Halli, F. Trovato and L. Driedger. Ottawa: Carleton University Press.
1989 "Immigrants in the Canadian Labour Force: Their Role in Structural Change." Discussion Paper 89. B.2. The Institute for Research on Public Policy.

Siegfried, Andre
1978 *The Race Question in Canada.* Toronto: MacMillan.

Simmel, Georg
1978 *The Philosophy of Money.* Tom Bottomore and David Frisby (trans.). London: Routledge & Kegan Paul.
1971 *Georg Simmel: On Individuality and Social Forms.* (Ed.) Donald N. Levine. Chicago: University of Chicago Press.
1950 "The Metropolis and Mental Life." In *The Sociology of Georg Simmel.* New York: The Free Press.

Simmons, A.B.
1988 "How Social and Economic Trends in Other Countries Affect the Composition of New Immigrants to Canada." *Report for the Review of Demography and Its Implications for Economic and Social Policy.* Ottawa.

Simon, Julian L.
1989 *The Economic Consequences of Immigration.* Oxford: Basil Blackwell Ltd.

Speigleberg H.
1972 *Phenomenology in Psychology and Psychiatry.* Evanstan: Northwestern University Press.

Spencer, Herbert
1898 *The Principles of Sociology.* New York: Appleton.

Spencer, Metta
1976 *Foundations of Modern Sociology.* Englewood Cliffs, N.J.: Prentice-Hall Inc.

Stoffman, Daniel
1993 *Towards a More Realistic Immigration Policy for Canada.* Toronto: C.D. Howe Institute.

Swan, N., L. Auer, D. Chenard, A. dePlaa, A. de Silva, D. Palmer, and J. Serjack
1991 *Economic and Social Impacts of Immigration.* Ottawa: Economic Council of Canada.

Tawney, R.
1969 *Religion and the Rise of Capitalism.* Harmondsworth: Penguin.

Tepper, E.
1988 *Changing Canada: The Institutional Response to Polyethnicity.* Ottawa: The Department of Political Science, Carlton University.

Theodorson, George A., and Achilles G. Theodorson
1969 *A Modern Dictionary of Sociology.* New York: Thomas Y. Crowell Company.

Thomas, B.
1987 *Multiculturalism at Work.* Toronto: YWCA.

Thomas, Derrick
1992 "The Social Integration of Immigrants in Canada." In *The Immigration Dilemma.* (Ed.) Steven Globerman. Vancouver: The Fraser Institute.

Thomas, William I.
1980 "The Definition of the Situation." In *The Pleasures of Sociology.* (Ed.) Lewis A. Coser. New York: New American Library.

Thorburn, H.
1989 "The Political Foundations of Canada's Pluralist Society." In *Canada 2000: Race Relations and Public Policy.* (Eds.) O. Dwivedi et al. Guelph: Department of Political Studies, University of Guelph.

Turner, Ralph H.
1960 "Sponsored and Contest Mobility and the School System." *American Sociological Review,* 25 (6): 855–867.

Underhill, Frank H.
1960 *In Search of Canadian Liberalism.* Toronto: Macmillan.

Weber, Max
1964 *The Theory of Social and Economic Organization.* (Ed.) Talcott Parsons. New York: The Free Press.
1978 *From Max Weber: Essays in Sociology.* H.H. Gerth and C. Wright Mills (trans.). New York: Oxford University Press.
1958 *Protestant Ethic and the Spirit of Capitalism.* New York: The Free Press.

Wattenberg, Ben J., and Karl Zinsmeister
1990 "The Case for More Immigration," *Commentary.*

White, P., and Samuel T.
1991 "Immigration and Ethnic Diversity in Urban Canada." *International Journal of Canadian Studies,* 1 (3): 69–85.

Winks, Robin W.
1971 *The Blacks in Canada.* New Haven: Yale University Press.
1977 "The Black Tile in the Mosaic." In *Modernization and the Canadian State.* (Eds.) D. Glenday, H. Gwindon and A. Turowetz. Toronto: Macmillan.

Wolfe, Tom
1970 *Radical Chic & Mau-Mauing the Flak Catchers.* New York: Bantam Books.

Woodsworth, J.S.
1972 *Strangers within Our Gates.* (Reprint; Original, 1909). Toronto: University of Toronto Press.

Young, Margaret
1994 *Canada's Immigration Program.* Law and Government Division, The Research Branch of the Library of Parliament.
1993 *Canada's Immigration Program.* Law and Government Division, The Research Branch of the Library of Parliament.
1992 *Immigration: Constitutional Issues.* Law and Government Division, The Research Branch of the Library of Parliament.
1992 *Refugee Protection: The International Context.* Law and Government Division, The Research Branch of the Library of Parliament.

Zolberg, A.
1989 "The Next Waves: Migration Theory for a Changing World." *International Migration Review,* 23 (3): 403–430.

Additional References

Agenda Jobs and Growth: Improving Social Security in Canada. HRDC, 1994.

Amnesty International Report. Amnesty International Publications, 1988.

Citizenship and Immigration Canada. *Annual Report to Parliament: Staying the Course.* Minister of Supply and Services Canada, October 1996.

Canada's Immigration Law. Minister of Supply and Services Canada, 1989.

Canadian Employment and Immigration Advisory Council *Perspectives on Immigration in Canada.* Final Report to the Minister of Employment and Immigration, August 1988.

Canadian Task Force on Mental Health Issues Affecting Immigrants and Refugees in Canada. Ottawa: Ministries of Multiculturalism and Citizenship and Health and Welfare, 1988.

Economic Council of Canada. *New Faces in the Crowd: Economic and Social Impacts of Immigration.* Ministry of Supply and Services Canada, 1991.

Employment and Immigration Canada. *Annual Report to Parliament: Immigration Plan for 1991–1995.* Minister of Supply and Services Canada, October 1990.

Employment and Immigration Canada. *Annual Report to Parliament: Staying The Course.* Minister of Supply and Services Canada, October 1996.

Employment and Immigration Canada. *Future Immigration Levels: 1988 consultation issues,* by T. J. Samuel and T. Conyers. Policy Development, Policy and Program Development Immigration, March 1988.

Employment and Immigration Canada. *"The Green Paper on Immigration: The Canadian Immigration and Population Study."* Vol. I., Ottawa, 1975.

Employment and Immigration Canada. *The Employment Effects of Immigration: A balance Sheet Approach.* Policy Development, Policy and Program Development Immigration, 1986.

Employment and Immigration Canada with Government of British Columbia. *Job Futures,* 1989.

Government of Canada. "Statement by the Prime Minister (Response to the Report of the Royal Commission on Bilingualism and Biculturalism, Book 4, House of Commons)." Ottawa: *Press Release,* October 1971.

Harbanjanir Singh v. The Minister of Employment and Immigration. [1985] 1 C.C.R. 178.

Manpower and Immigration Canada. *Canadian Immigration Policy: The White Paper on Immigration,* October 1969.

Report of the Royal Commission on Bilingualism and Biculturalism. Vol. 4, Ottawa, October 23, 1969.

"Into the 21st Century—A Strategy for Immigration and Citizenship." *Immigration Consultation Report.* Citizenship and Immigration Canada, 1994.

Immigration Intelligence Division Bulletin. Intelligence Division, National Headquarters, Bulletin No. 89–02.

Improved Program Delivery, Citizenship, Labour and Immigration. Task Force on Program Review. (Neilsen Task Force) 1985.

Improving the Selection System for Skilled Workers. Citizenship and Immigration Canada, November 1995.

United States Congress. *Report of the Commission on Population Growth and the American Future.* Washington, 1972.

"Reinventing the Civil Servant." *York University Profiles,* 3 (5): 8–11, 1993.

Multiculturalism and Citizenship Canada. *Attitudes about Multiculturalism and Citizenship.* Multiculturalism and Citizenship Canada. Ottawa, 1991(a).

Multiculturalism and Citizenship Canada. *Multiculturalism: What Is It Really About?* Minister of Supply and Services Canada. Ottawa, 1991(b).

Office of the United Nations High Commissioner for Refugees. *Handbook on Procedures and Criteria for Determining Refugee Status.* Geneva, 1988.

Report of the Commission on Systemic Racism in the Ontario Criminal Justice System. Government of Ontario. January, 1996.

Statistics Canada. "Projections of Visible Minority Population Groups: Canada, Provinces and Regions 1991–2016." Catalogue 1-54XPE, Feb 27, 1996.

Statistics Canada. "Population Projections for Canada, Provinces and Territories, 1993–2016." Catalogue 19152, 1996.

Index